THE PATCHWORK GIRL

Content Warning: This book contains graphic depictions of sexual assault, violence, suicide and drug use.

THE PATCHWORK GIRL

KATE ELYSIA

MIRROR BOOKS

MIRROR BOOKS

All of the events in this story are true, but some names and details have been changed to protect the identities of some individuals where appropriate.

1

Written with John McDonald

Published in Great Britain and Ireland in 2026 by Mirror Books, a Reach PLC business.

www.mirrorbooks.co.uk
@TheMirrorBooks

Print ISBN 9781917439619
eBook ISBN 9781917439626

Editing and Production: Christine Costello, Nick Webster
Cover Design: Adam Ward

Printed and bound in Great Britain by
CPI Group (UK) Ltd, Croydon, CR0 4YY

FSC www.fsc.org MIX Paper | Supporting responsible forestry FSC® C013604

To the girl I looked after for one night. I never knew your name, but I've never forgotten you.

Contents

Author's Note

Most people will have heard of the Telford grooming scandal. But for those who haven't, it involved a gang of Asian men who sexually exploited young girls. It was reported that Telford had the highest number of cases in the UK, most of which were ignored when they were reported – the ones that were reported, that is.

An enquiry conclusion, released in 2022, revealed that over 1,000 girls had been abused and, of those reported, most weren't investigated because the authorities were afraid of being branded racist.

Victims were trafficked with drugs and alcohol, rape, beatings, threats and intimidation and were blamed and accused of willingly prostituting themselves. Of course, I didn't know all that at the time – when I was one of those girls. When I found out, I became part of Operation Chalice, the police investigation into mass child abuse in Telford, and gave evidence in court which put several of the perpetrators behind bars.

It took a long time but when I finally emerged from the nightmarish events of those experiences, I trained to be a nurse and that's where I am now. I've been a registered nurse (RN) for 14 years and have worked my way up to Senior Mental Health Nurse (Band 7).

It's a career which has saved me and restored my love and passion for human beings. Something which I thought was gone forever when I was way down in the darkness.

In primary care, I've tended to people in the same streets where I was once a ghost, wandering in the limbo that was my life back then. Those people didn't know my history, nor did they need to. I was there for them, especially the young people in Sheltered Accommodation

Units (SAUs) with undiagnosed trauma or neurodivergence, the same flats where I once lived – and died, more than once.

The crisis line was probably the most challenging for me after what I'd been through. But it sharpened my senses, my auditory presence. I learned how to assess risk inherent in silence, in tone. It developed the voice inside me that told me to be careful, the voice I wished I'd had when I was being broken into pieces.

My profession gave me the opportunity to return to Telford – the town where I was abused, used, bruised, accused. Some will ask why I wanted to go back there, after all the traumas. But avoidance was keeping me trapped. Exposing myself to those demons lessened their power over me and I was able to defeat them. I didn't want to spend my whole life avoiding my hometown. So, after 15 years away, I came back.

At one point in my career I retrained as an autism assessor, which I loved. In a way, I could identify with people on the autism spectrum, who are often severely bullied. Because grooming is an extreme form of bullying, enforced with sexual violence, that role was deeply meaningful to me. I also had trauma-informed care training and ran emotional stabilisation workshops.

Helping people matters to me and, even if some of my methods might be seen as unconventional, if they help, they help. How I wish I had access to that kind of support when I was drowning in self-disgust.

I've been involved in 'lived experience' work for many years, which involves using personal experience to inform and shape services. I've supported a London Trust to build a sexual safety policy for their wards. I've appeared in Channel 4's *Rape: The Hunt for Britain's Sex Gangs*, which was BAFTA nominated. I attended NSPCC meetings in Sheffield where the #ItsNotOkay emerged from a line I'd repeatedly written in my diary, to keep me sane when I was being dehumanised. I gave evidence to the

Independent Inquiry in Telford and was part of Operation Chalice, as a result of which, many sexual predators were sent to prison.

I'm not one for standing still. I like to keep moving forward, into new roles, new versions of myself. Not because I'm particularly restless, but because I'm continuously healing and lessening the impact my trauma has had on me. That's why I'm now doing an MSc in Psychological Trauma – because psychological trauma destroys your identity and there's no therapy model that truly addresses what grooming does to a person's psyche.

You see, apart from the physical trauma, I was emotionally and psychologically broken down and, after I survived, I had to put myself back together. A new version of myself had to emerge. I was deconstructed down to the most fundamental level and the only way to keep going was reconstruction. What came back wasn't what went in. The same ingredients, but a different girl. A patchwork girl.

My PTSD first presented itself in dissociative flashbacks. I didn't realise that's what they were until I found myself shouting the names of my abusers. At the time I thought it was normal. I had hypervigilance, avoidance, intrusive thoughts. I studied my own symptoms because I didn't trust a system which hadn't been there for me when I needed it. It was a process of exorcism – of expelling the demons I believed were inside me. And a new phoenix rose from the ashes.

I never imagined that my abuse, and the abuse of others, would become a national scandal, or that politics would weaponise it. Now there's a national inquiry – and I'm a panel member.

I only hope I can make a difference. I hope we all can, for the women and girls who come after us.

For the heartbroken.

Kate Elysia, 2026

Prologue

When I was a practicing Muslim, I learned that an important part of the religion was *sabr*, which means patience. I think understanding and exercising patience is probably the most difficult thing a human being has to do when they're experiencing trauma in their lives.

This is because our minds are limited when it comes to understanding things we've never experienced before. When I was really struggling, I found it difficult to see a future that would be any better than the present I was living in. When I felt I wanted to die and there was a grey fog consuming my soul and I hated myself, it was as if that feeling had always been there and would never go away and I'd always feel like that. Forever. When I think back to those times now, I wonder how I hung on to any hope – why I didn't try more often to end my life.

I used to think, *If I'm patient, I'll eventually get too old for this shit – I'll be 50. Or dead.* It was a time when my enemies were my only friends, if you can understand that paradox, and I had to learn how to survive in those surroundings.

But it was no use just hanging around feeling guilty for my sins; I had to focus on how to stop sinning.

At the height of the abuse and the lowest points in my life, I hated myself. I felt like a worthless slut which is exactly what my rapists wanted me to think. I was spiralling out of control, sinking down into something horrible. I was being swallowed up by a disgusting sea of black slime.

My soul was being taken over by an evil demon inside me that had been put there by them the first time they raped me. The more I was abused, the bigger and more evil the demon was becoming. I could never get away from it now. If I went to the police it'd kill me from the inside. It'd eat me from the inside out. I could hear it laughing inside my head.

'No one will believe you.'

What is a sin? What person or book could tell me what 'sin' was? My sins were crimes against myself that damaged me, physically and mentally. I had a problem no one could understand, a problem people reading this book will find difficult to understand. Even now, although I know what caused it, I find it difficult to understand myself. But some things are impossible to comprehend, until you find the human being underneath it all.

I expect some people to judge me after reading this book, for being a slut, for taking illegal drugs, for putting myself in dangerous situations.

But I'm not a victim anymore – I'm a survivor now. I'm strong enough within myself to deal with anything that comes my way. Abusers took away my individuality and made me an object, but I've rediscovered my personality that was hidden underneath the hate. The truth will set you free, I guess.

I no longer consider myself to be worthless, or a bad person. I know who I am. A new person has emerged from all the chaos and trauma of my life – a person I'm proud to be!

1

Before The Darkness

Complex trauma can alter a person's instinctive responses to risk and danger. Survivors often don't recognise hazards, or just stop caring about their safety because trauma has eroded their sense of self-worth and agency. Chronic abuse shapes, and often distorts, the development of identity, trust, relationships and values. Profound paradoxes face those who experience abusive environments, particularly in cases of repeated sexual abuse.

But, to really understand how the grooming gangs got control of me, we have to go back to the beginning. To understand the events of my life, I have to explain who I am – or who I used to be, before I became a patchwork version of my former self.

My parents, while probably not typically average, were good people. Dad was an eccentric man who wore his hair long and liked to dress extravagantly, while Mum was quite beautiful, in an understated way. They loved me in their own way, as most parents do. I liked my mother and father – they were nice and the only ones I had experience of.

My mother was a midwife and a nurse who had all three of her children at home. She reckoned no patriarchal doctor was going to have her lying on her back with her legs spread wide when she knew the best way to give birth was on her hands and knees. I remember she was constantly doing Open University courses on the dining table in the living room. My father described it as an addiction to learning.

I was born in Birmingham on 2 January 1988. My sister Amanda was born in the summer of 1989 and my brother Richard came along early in 1992. And that was us – our little family. Quite normal, really, for the time and place, nothing there to indicate what was to come – how it would all be disrupted and blown apart.

My father was part of an organisation that worked the raves across the Midlands and on boats and at fairgrounds – selling whistles and lighters and neon necklaces and horns and party poppers. He and Mum were both part of the fading hippie scene – that didn't mean they were into counterculture in a big way, but they had their harmless eccentricities. Both were highly intelligent, but in an alternative way. I don't remember much about my very early life and, even after that, it was really quite uneventful.

We moved to Shirlett when I was still a small child, a remote little place about seven miles from Telford where we lived on the outskirts and I was really just an average kid from an average family. Nothing special. Nothing anyone could point to and say, *"That girl's going to turn out bad. She'll be a right whore when she gets older."* I started off slowly at school, but my parents worked hard to help me. They bought all the book sets and sat and read with me – my mother loved Enid Blyton, and she'd read one of her books to me and my sister every night.

'Are you sitting comfortably? Then I'll begin,' she would say to us.

My primary school was a half-hour walk each way and there were no buses. My mother took me to begin with, but eventually I had to walk on my own. My sister and I went to breakfast club in the morning and after-school club in the afternoon, while my mother worked as a health visitor in Market Drayton.

We had a black pot-bellied pig that lived in the back garden, but I'd let her into the house and she'd lie on a mat in front of the fire like a dog. All very normal, eh?

I suppose you could say I was a bit of a tomboy: I preferred Mighty Max to Barbie or Polly Pocket and I was into K'Nex, which was a kids' mechanical building set that could make dinosaurs and cars with motors that moved. My best friend was called Joe and he lived on a farm. We'd go off into the woods and climb trees, and his dad made us a treehouse with a rope swing. We made clay pots out of mud from the banks of a stream and Joe's dad baked them in the oven for us. We roamed all over the farm and I have a scar on my leg from the time I rescued a sheep that was caught in barbed wire.

So, life went on in a normal way – until my parents decided to get divorced. I could hear them arguing when I was in bed at night, mostly about money. My father didn't work after he stopped being a raver-trader. My mother was working full-time and she was always exhausted. So my father decided to leave home. For good.

He told my sister and me in the car: 'I'm not going to be living with you anymore.'

We burst into tears there and then, on the back seat.

I missed my father a lot when he left. I developed anxiety about using the phone – I couldn't cope with not being able to talk to the real Dad, only a disembodied voice that wasn't him as far as I was concerned. It made me afraid of telephones for many years. Even as a teenager I couldn't call the emergency services I needed to because I was too scared. My subconscious told me the sound at the other end wasn't a real person – the real person's voice had been stolen from them to fool me. What was there at the end of the phone line was something dark and cynical – something that made promises it would never keep.

At first, my father moved into a trailer at the bottom of someone's garden. It was a huge garden with lots of trees and the caravan seemed so little and lost in it. My sister and I took it in turns visiting him in the small, cramped trailer. It was so small we had to sleep on a pull-out sofa. This lasted until he moved to a room over a launderette. He had bunk beds for us there and enough space for both of us to stay. I was visiting with my sister once when I decided to play a joke. I was sitting on the window ledge when my father and sister left the room to get something.

While they were gone, I ran downstairs and lay on the ground below the window and screamed, as if I'd fallen out. My sister saw me through the window and she screamed and started crying. My father ran downstairs with her in his arms and found me standing up and all right. He was angry at first and I thought his face was going to explode. Then anger turned to relief and he just said, 'Don't *ever* do anything like that again, Kate!'

I had a weird sense of humour.

I don't know why I started getting picked on at school, but that might've had something to do with it, my sense of humour that is – aside from having red hair and dyslexia.

Some of the kids thought I was uncool, which I didn't understand as I didn't go out of my way to be different. My dyslexia was undiagnosed and I didn't know I had it at the time. It wouldn't be diagnosed until I was 16 and had started at college. Later, when I was 20 and at university, I had an extensive assessment by an educational psychologist and I was told I had a very 'dyslexic personality'.

Anyway, people didn't get my sense of humour, or the way my mind worked. If I was in a group conversation, I'd find myself thinking differently to everyone else. I'd come out with some comment that made perfect sense to me, but no sense to anyone else – or I'd change the subject just out of the blue. The kids would tell me to shut up because what I was saying was weird to them. It made me feel a bit stupid.

I know now I wasn't stupid, I just saw things differently and from a different perspective. The dyslexia also manifested in my concentration. If I was walking and talking, I wouldn't hear what was said to me, as if I couldn't concentrate on two things at the same time. My mother even sent me for a hearing test when I was about seven because she noticed I sometimes didn't respond when she was speaking to me, especially if we were some distance away from each other.

The test showed that there were no problems with my hearing. But, generally speaking, school was okay, my dyslexia made me think outside the box and, in a way, I was more intelligent than the people who thought I was stupid.

My mother didn't have a lot of money after the divorce and couldn't really afford fancy holidays – in fact, she couldn't afford any kind of holiday. But we started going to Rainbow 2000 Super Camp with her. Rainbow 2000 was a 10-day festival at the end of August each year. It was run by peace and land rights campaigner, Sid Rawle, near the Forest of Dean in Gloucestershire.

It was held in a big field where people would pitch their tents in circles. Different groups would have their own circles and there'd be campfires in the middle.

People came from all over the UK and even from abroad. It started off in just one field but, over the years, it spread out over several more. The Village was the centre of everything with a giant tepee where people meditated to the sound of gongs and went on 'power journeys', which was a kind of hypnosis.

There was also a big marquee where they held the opening ceremony and the closing ceremony, along with morning meetings where all the people held hands and chanted a mantra. There was a vegetarian café called the Lettuce Inn, and two domes for holding workshops. There were drumming and humming workshops and everybody liked the chanting workshop because it was led by a blond hippie guy called Oak who all the women were in love with.

Children were born at the camps and people got married there too and, for us kids, it was 10 days of total freedom. We lived in tepees and slept on sheep's-wool rugs. During the day, we explored and made ornaments, gem-trees and fed the sheep. There was 'story time' at 7pm every night in the big lodge for the younger children and everyone got hot chocolate. For me, it was a colourful escape from the grey routine of life outside the camp. And I loved it all.

Although I missed my father badly, I never felt disadvantaged by not having him at home. I wasn't a tearaway and I didn't hang around with a bad crowd, or want to do bad things, or disobey my mother. What I'm saying is, despite being dyslexic and having a weird sense of humour, I was just an ordinary girl. My life wasn't any worse than anyone else's. In fact, it was better than a lot of girls'. It wasn't as if I was 'conditioned' in some way to be groomed by the gangs I'd eventually fall in with, so the reasons have to be rooted elsewhere. It proves, for me at least, that anyone can be manipulated by these people – it's not one kind of girl or another kind of girl. We don't go around with a sign on our foreheads saying: VICTIM.

All I'm saying here is that this was me.

Before I became the other me.

As I got older, people my own age seemed a bit primitive to me, if that's the right word – they were so predictable, while I saw myself as more emotionally 'intelligent'. It's not like I thought I was smarter than the other kids, it's just that I wasn't interested in the things they were interested in. I was diagnosed with polycystic ovary syndrome (PCOS) at 13, which caused me to gain weight and, along with my red hair, made me a target for school bullies at secondary school. It damaged my sense of self-esteem and made me more anxious.

My mother helped me as much as she could. I wanted to dye my hair, but she advised me not to, saying my red hair was beautiful and the other kids were just jealous because their hair was mousy and dull. I was a bright kid and intelligent, despite the dyslexia, and I developed my wicked sense of humour as a defence mechanism to the bullying. I realised I could make people laugh by acting dumb; I was saying dumb things anyway, so it was easy to act the part. It worked as a kind of manipulation, as if I was manipulating how people treated me. They'd like me if I was a joker and funny to be with.

'Knock, knock.'

'Who's there?'

'Dora Belle.'

'Dora Belle who?'

'Dora Belle broken, that why I'm knocking.'

The downside was, some people misunderstood what I was doing, they didn't get the joke and believed I was crazy, like when my father thought I fell out the window. That made them hostile.

Around this time, my relationship with my sister began to deteriorate. When we were younger, she and I got along but, as she got older, she spent a lot of time in her room and became territorial.

'Get out of my room!'

Only it wasn't totally her room, as we shared it. I'd get out just to keep the peace and not give my mother hassle she didn't need. I don't really know why her attitude towards me changed, but we went from being close as young kids to being at odds with each other all the time.

Secondary school was almost exclusively white and English, so I never got much enlightenment regarding other cultures. Black people were seen as criminals and Muslims prayed five times a day – that was about it. I tried to read up about other religions whenever I could, because it was a subject which interested me, particularly different communities and different people in the world. The other thing that was lacking at secondary school was sex education. They taught us about 'safe sex' and using a condom, but nothing about protecting ourselves from sexual predators and how girls could be groomed.

I met my first boyfriend when I was 15. His name was Alan and he was less than a year older than me. He lived in Walsall, which was close to where my maternal grandmother had her house. He was a nice enough boy and we were going out together for 10 months. He came over to my house a lot and I went to his on weekends. I didn't actually stay at his house; we travelled back and forth on the train between Walsall and Telford, maybe four or five times a day. We didn't have sex until we'd been seeing each other for four months. It was our first time for both of us.

I look at 16-year-olds now and I think that's far too young to be having sex, but I didn't feel young at the time. I was over the legal age and most of the other girls I knew had already experimented. I was still an 'outsider' in many ways and I didn't want to be an outsider in that respect too. I started taking the pill, so there was no chance of me getting pregnant. I can see now that I was very young and naive, but

Alan was young and naive too, and having sex with each other was just part of growing up as far as we were concerned.

By the time I started at college in Telford, life was better than it had ever been. My sense of humour was even more outrageous: I once bought a dildo in an Ann Summers shop and brought it into class for 'Show and Tell'. I considered myself to be open-minded about sex and I espoused feminist thinking on sexual freedom, which is ironic, considering what was to happen to me later. But, behind the facade, I reckon I was still insecure and guileless.

By now my father had moved down to Kent, which was a long way from Shirlett and it meant we didn't see very much of him anymore. He still telephoned but, like I said before, the voice on the end of the line wasn't really my father to me. My mother had always been my role model and I looked up to her even more and admired her strength, helping her as much as I could. But then, when I was 17, she went and found herself a boyfriend. I mean, what did she need a boyfriend for? She was the one who always said women didn't need men, that they could do everything for themselves!

He moved into our three-bedroom semi and she stopped doing all the stuff she used to do with us kids and did everything with him instead. I didn't want to be a typical, resentful step-daughter, so I tried to like him at first. But he was rarely civil to us and it seemed like we were an inconvenience he had to put up with to be with my mother. He had two kids of his own, from a previous marriage, who came and stayed every other weekend. They slept in my brother's bedroom and he had to use the sofa.

My mother's boyfriend had trouble sleeping – maybe back problems from his work as a gardener, I don't remember. So when he moved into our house, he imposed a curfew of 10.30pm. We all had to be in bed by then and not make any noise for the rest of the night. Even texting on our phones was too loud. Watching television, which he called 'the idiot box', was out of the question, and listening to music with earphones was also banned. We couldn't sneeze or cough or fart. Even if we went to the toilet during the night and flushed it afterwards, he'd start an argument with my mother and she'd relay his threats down to us. Life was hell after he moved in. I felt that my family had been destroyed. The general atmosphere in the house increased the tension between me and my sister, who I still shared a bedroom with.

The fighting became unmanageable for me. What was I supposed to do if, every time I stepped into our bedroom, I was faced with fits of horrible nasty screaming? My mother was too preoccupied with the boyfriend and he wasn't interested in us kids, as long as we kept out of his way and stayed quiet at night. I had to cope with it on my own and it made me angry. This caused friction between me and my mother, who believed that, because I was the eldest, I should be able to cope better.

It reached a boiling point one day when I came upstairs from the living room because my phone had died and I needed my charger. My sister started screaming at me as soon as I opened the bedroom door. I lost my temper and slapped her on the back of the head. That started her screeching as loud as she could:

'Don't hit me! Don't hit me!'

She lunged at me and, as I pushed her away, she slipped on the laminate flooring and slid across to the wall. Just then, my mother came into the room and saw me standing over her, lying on the floor, crying. She ran to my mother and hugged her like she was afraid and accused me of trying to rip one of her ear piercings out. My mother fell for the act. I guess it looked worse than it actually was and my sister was able to turn on the waterworks at will when she wanted to.

'I've had enough of this, Kate!'

'I didn't …'

'You're older! You should know better!'

I always thought my mother was smarter than me; she knew more than I did and I looked up to her and believed she could never be wrong about anything. Now it seemed to me that she was wrong about everything. How could a strong woman like her allow the man who'd moved into our house to manipulate her the way he did? How could she believe my sister, just because she was younger than I was? How could she treat me this way? Like I meant nothing to her, after all we'd been through together. I left the bedroom and slammed the door behind me.

Something ended for me that day – something precious.

Later, my mother came to me and said she thought it was time I moved out of the house. After all, I was 18 now. I wasn't a kid anymore, I was a woman. She said it in front of my brother and sister and they agreed with her. It was like they were ganging up on me, to get rid of me.

'You can finish college, Kate, but I'd like you to leave at the end of term.'

I saw my mother's request for me to leave as a complete betrayal of the closeness we'd had before the man moved in and upset everything.

I was in my second year of college when this happened, and it affected me. I wanted to go on to university to study psychology and become a relationship therapist, but the tension in the house was affecting my results. I had to resit some of the exams to get the grades I needed. I also found it easier to study at college than at home. Every day when I finished, I didn't want to go home, I didn't want to get on the bus. It was intolerable, and I stayed at the library until it closed rather than head back to face the 'family'. So I thought that leaving would be the best thing for everyone.

The way I saw it back then was, I didn't want to stay in a place where I wasn't wanted. I'm sure, in hindsight, it wasn't like that: I'm sure my mother was trying to cope with a new relationship, her work, and two teenage girls. Things just get on top of people at times and they say stuff they don't mean. But, at that age, I was pretty defiant and hurting from what I saw as my mother's rejection. There was a Sheltered Accommodation Unit near my college offering supported housing for homeless teenagers. So I went along to the office and told them my mother was kicking me out and I had nowhere to go. They helped me fill in an application form and took my number.

I was surprised when they called after about four weeks. I hadn't expected to get in – my situation wasn't as bad as for other girls who were applying. But I was glad when they did, as I had to get away from the intolerable situation at home.

I got the tenancy of the flat at the SAU on Monday 7 May 2007 and I moved in on Friday 11 May. I was raped for the first time by Shahmeel on Sunday 17 June 2007 and was orally raped three days later by Ali Sultan and his mate, Bazam.

I had my six final A level exams that same week.

2

The Sheltered Accommodation Unit

Trauma and recovery study tells us that a victim must develop a capacity for self-regulation in an environment in which her body is at the disposal of other people's needs – that she must develop an identity out of an environment which sees her as a whore and a slave. Of course, I knew none of that when I moved into the Sheltered Accommodation Unit.

I'd been told about the SAU by a kid at college who lived there. He pierced my tongue without anaesthetic for a giggle when we were with a bunch of mates, and he explained the procedure for getting in.

Once I was there, I filled out some more forms and they gave me a flat, like a little studio-bedsit. It had a tiny kitchenette with a doorway into the living room-cum-bedroom and a hallway that led to the front door and bathroom. It was furnished and the kitchen had a little electric oven the size of a microwave, with two little hob rings, and a mini fridge. It was small, but it was like a palace to me at the time.

My mother was sorry for asking me to leave and she wanted to talk about it. She sat me down in the bathroom when I was a day away from moving out.

'Are you sure you want to do this, Kate?'

'You gave me no choice.'

'I didn't mean it like that, you know that …'

'I don't want to stay where I'm not welcome.'

'Kate, please …!'

'Anyway, it's too late now.'

She'd hurt me, betrayed me with her boyfriend, taken away the closeness we'd had for all those years I was growing up. Okay, it wasn't as if now it was my turn to hurt her or anything, it was just that the hurt I felt tasted bitter.

I moved into the flat at the SAU the next day. I was really excited to have my own space at last, my own bathroom and my own kitchen.

I had a bit of money saved from my part-time job at Primark and I was able to buy a few things – a pink television stand, a matching pair of curtains and bed covers. There was no TV, so I brought the crappy old one me and Amanda had in our bedroom. The buttons were broken on it and I had to change the channels with the handle of a spoon. I stocked the kitchen with emergency food, like pasta and rice and 5p noodles from Asda, and frozen peas that I kept in the ice-cube maker in my mini-fridge, in case of starvation. I was allocated a key worker who came around once a week to see how I was. The SAU staff worked 9am to 5pm during the week, and 9am to noon on Saturdays.

The first week was fun – I invited all my friends from college and we had a pizza party. That weekend, a girl moved into the flat next to me. She used different names, like Danielle Rizzo or Dani Diamond, whatever took her fancy on the day. I invited her round for dinner and I made a pasta bake with tinned tomatoes and vegetables and herbs and cheese. She loved it and we got on really well and chatted for ages, late into the night.

She said her father's girlfriend didn't like her and she'd had to leave home, but I got the feeling from her that she'd been abused, even though she never actually said so. Dani was 18, just like me, and she moved to the SAU from B&Bs, where they used to house homeless people if there was nowhere else for them to go. She pretended to be American and faked an accent, and said she had an illness called 'sepsis', where she had to go and have blood transfusions every four weeks – but I don't know if that was true or not.

Then I met William, who lived in a nearby flat on the same floor as mine. William was a lovely boy – he'd been hurt a lot and was very vulnerable. He was 18 as well and had been to a young offender's institution. His family moved to Australia without him, I don't know why – maybe he couldn't go because he had a criminal record. He never told me. I liked William and we started spending a lot of time in each other's flats. His was in a terrible mess and his toilet was the worst I'd ever seen, even worse than the holes at Super Spirit, part of the Rainbow 2000 experience. An Asian gang had taken over William's flat and were using it as a drug den and doss house.

My key worker at the SAU told me that William kept company with some bad people, but I didn't know what she meant. When I asked William about it, he said his best friend was a man called Imran, who was 21. He'd known Imran before he moved to the SAU, and he was a really good guy. Imran was mixed race – half Asian and half white, which gave him a tanned appearance, and he was really good looking. He talked about God a lot and seemed placid and spiritual.

Imran and the rest of the Asian gang lived very close to the SAU flats. Ali and Imran's extended families lived on the other side of the street. They saw me leave to go to college, they saw me on the way to work, they saw me when I went shopping. They didn't seem to have regular jobs or do anything and it was impossible to avoid them. They just hung around on the street and watched me and other girls coming and going. It was very intimidating. Ali Sultan was about 20.

William told me Ali was bullying him and was taking his key off him to have sex with girls in his flat. When that happened, William had nowhere to go and had to walk the streets for hours, sometimes all night. I was horrified. I liked William a lot and wanted to try to protect him, because he seemed so vulnerable.

'Give me your key, William.'

'Why?'

'If this Ali guy wants it, he'll have to come to me, and I won't give it to him.'

It wasn't that I thought I was big and hard or anything like that, it was just that William needed someone to stand up for him, because he couldn't do it for himself.

One evening, William, Dani and I were round my flat when Ali and two of his friends knocked on my door. They were looking for William, so I let them in. One of them started smoking and I asked him to put the cigarette out. He refused. This took me by surprise. I'd expected him to apologise and either put it out or go outside. Ali asked William for his key. I stood up.

'You can't have it.'

'What?'

'It's his flat, you can't just take his key.'

'Don't play games with me, bitch!'

I was angry. I wanted to tell them to get out of my flat, but I was scared. William had told me these people were violent criminals. My heart was racing and adrenaline was pumping through me. They spoke in their own language to each other, then they left.

On his way out of the door, Ali turned around to me and held out his hand.

'We shouldn't leave on an argument.'

He wanted me to shake his hand.

'Friends?'

This intimidated me even more than his harsh words had earlier. If I didn't shake his hand, he'd be insulted and we'd be enemies. He knew what he was doing – it wasn't a friendly gesture, it was dark and a threat in itself. I shook his hand.

He'd made me do something I didn't want to do, that let him think he had some kind of control over me. I didn't realise it at the time, but the gang saw the SAU as an easy source of young girls for grooming purposes, as most of the residents had social issues and were vulnerable prey. They saw me, a new arrival, as potential for sexual exploitation.

Very soon, Ali Sultan was knocking on my door on a regular basis, asking if William was around.

'He's not here.'

'Who's in there, then?'

'No one's in here.'

'Just you, eh, Kate? Can I come in?'

'No, I don't think so.'

He'd make blowjob gestures at me, like sticking his tongue into the side of his cheek. I'd close the door. These gestures were part of the grooming techniques these guys had been using since they were too young to know what a blowjob was.

Looking back now, the first time I was raped at the SAU wasn't as physically brutal as what was to come. However, it was the sheer underlying menace, the psychological terror of being abused by a dangerous psychopath, that traumatised me.

After about three weeks in the SAU, William told me about this guy called Shahmeel who'd just got out of prison – he'd been sent down for breaking a complete stranger's jaw in the street. Shahmeel wasn't right in the head. He'd get involved in random street fights and just attack people for the sake of it, William explained. He was Imran and Ali Sultan's friend. Ali treated him like his pet pitbull – he'd tell him who to attack, and Shahmeel would go and do it.

* * * *

It's Sunday June 17, and William's round my flat and we're just chatting like we always do. There's a knock on the door and I look through the spyhole, but I see no-one.

'I can't see anyone, William.'

'Just open the door, Kate.'

As soon as I do, this Shahmeel guy appears in front of me. He has a weird look on his face. Really weird, like with protruding eyes and a grin that's more of a grimace.

He wedges his foot in the door before I can close it and tries to force his way in. I'm pushing against him with all my might and I'm shouting to William for help. William comes and sees who it is. He's frightened.

'It's Shahmeel. You'd better let him in.'

I don't want to, but I let go of the door and Shahmeel pushes past me and puts his face up very close to William's.

'Imran's looking for you, William.'

'Where?'

'Over in your flat.'

William doesn't want to leave, but he's scared not to. He gives me an apologetic look and kind of half-shrugs his shoulders, like there's nothing he can do.

When William's gone, Shahmeel starts to circle around me. He's saying crazy, weird things that make no sense. Random stuff that I can't understand. It's like he's raving or something. Then he grabs me and holds me close to him. I can smell his breath, feel his heart beating very fast. I try to pull away, but he just holds me tighter. He's trying to kiss me and I'm turning my face away. He kisses my chest, all the time saying weird things.

'I'll buy you a house and a car,' he says.

I'm really scared. He tries to get my clothes off. I tell him I have a boyfriend who'll be here any minute, but he just laughs hysterically and shakes his head. He says he wants to see me naked and I tell him I don't want him to. He's strong, a lot stronger than me.

He manages to pull my dress off and I'm standing there in my girl boxers and bra – not very sexy. He starts to take off his own clothes and I freeze like a frightened rabbit. I know I should try to get past him – get to the door and get out. But I don't; it's like I'm paralysed and I can't move.

He grabs me again and I try to pull away, to back away, but he pushes me towards the bed. I want to fight him but I can't because I'm scared he'll hurt me badly if I do. I'm physically powerless and all I can do is say 'no' repeatedly and try to bargain with him.

'Please don't take my underwear off.'

I fall backwards onto the bed and he's on top of me. He pulls my boxers to one side.

'Please don't put it inside me.'

He sticks his penis into me. He doesn't use a condom and he keeps going until he comes.

When he's finished, he stands up and faces me, still lying on the bed with my hand over my mouth. I feel sick.

'You think I got a big dick?'

He says this as if he's talking to his girlfriend or a prostitute and like it's a natural thing to say – as if there's nothing wrong and he hasn't just raped me. I don't reply.

'Don't worry, I'll tell William you just gave me a blowjob.'

This is just so surreal to me. Nothing makes sense. I just want him to go so I can get to the bathroom and throw up and wash his filthy sperm out of me. But the ordeal hasn't finished. On his way out, Shahmeel turns and shows me a knife he's carrying in the side of his boot. He doesn't say anything, just holds his head slightly to one side and pouts his lips and smiles in an insane way.

Then he's gone.

* * * *

Why didn't I run to the nearest police station and report the rape? Why didn't I get on the phone and dial 999? Good questions. What I did was ring my friend, Andria, from school. When she answered the phone, I just started crying. I cried and cried uncontrollably for ages while my friend tried to find out what was wrong with me. I cried so much I couldn't speak. Eventually the words came out.

'I've been raped.'

Andria started crying too. We cried together on the phone until she told me I had to go to the police.

'You have to report this, Kate.'

But I was confused and in shock; I didn't know what to do. I thought at first I could just pretend it didn't happen – or pretend it was just sex and when it's just sex you don't have to keep remembering it or feeling bad about it. Maybe I'd led him on without realising it? Maybe he had a learning disability and didn't realise what he was doing?

Monday was a complete blur. I'd been preparing for my exams that started on Tuesday with English and psychology – but I just couldn't study. I think I went to the college and hung out there, just to be away from the flat. I got school dinner tokens, went to the canteen and sat on my own and ate chocolate chip cookies. I was still in a daze when I walked back home.

I turned the corner and there was Shahmeel and Ali Sultan, sitting on a wall. Seeing him again startled me; it was like my blood had turned to ice and was clogging up my veins. I backtracked quickly and went another way.

Tuesday came and I had one of my English exams first, at 9am. I still felt depressed and numb. I didn't care about my future anymore, not because I didn't want one, but I just couldn't see it. It was lost in the confusion inside my head. I just wrote stuff down, I don't know what – just went through the motions. The psychology exam came next and I coped with that the same way, like a robot, or a person hypnotised.

On my way home, I saw Ali sitting on the wall outside his house. He started to follow me. I quickened my step, but he caught up with me and walked alongside.

'I hear you had sex with Shahmeel.'

'Against my will.'

'He said you loved it.'

I wanted to scream out that he raped me, but I was afraid to. These people were dangerous and, if they found out I was thinking about going to the police, I'd be in big trouble.

On Wednesday I had another psychology exam and a biology exam. I felt even worse than I did on Tuesday. The man who raped me had just got out of prison – what if he had HIV? I felt physically sick. This time I didn't write anything; I just sat there through the whole exam like someone who'd been petrified and turned into a pillar of inertia.

The biology exam seemed like a foreign language to me. By then I'd stopped caring about anything, even the possibility I had AIDS. I'd die and that'd be the end of me. Thoughts kept flashing through my mind again, images, questions. Did Shahmeel know what he'd been doing? Had I tried hard enough to get him off me? Why had I let him into the flat?

I started doubting myself. Was it really rape? Did I encourage him? Then I thought, *maybe I love him* – I don't know why I thought that. I was lost. The examiner noticed and asked if there was anything wrong. I just got up and left the room and went to see the college counsellor.

After explaining what happened, she told me I had to go to the police.

* * * *

There's a knock on the door of my flat. It's later that Wednesday evening. It's Ali Sultan and a chubby Asian guy, who I haven't seen before.

'Can we come in?'

'No.'

'Why not?'

'Because I'm busy, I have to study.'

'You can study later.'

'I have a boyfriend.'

'So what?'

'I don't want you in here!'

It doesn't matter what I say. What I say is irrelevant to them. It's worthless, just like me. I'm scared. I have my foot against the inside of the door, but Ali's able to push it open and the two of them step inside. The chubby one – Ali calls him Bazam – sits on my sofa.

'Give me a blowjob, Kate,' Ali says.

I start to laugh, kind of in disbelief. This isn't really happening. It's a nightmare and I'll wake up in a minute. Ali grabs me and drags me into the bathroom and makes me sit on the toilet with the seat down. The curtains are beige and they create a golden glow from the sunlight outside.

'Isn't this light romantic, Kate?'

I don't answer, the situation's too surreal. I just sit there as he drops his pants and sticks his erect penis into my mouth. I have no choice but to comply. I do the work. The faster I work, the faster it'll be over. It makes me gag every time it touches my throat and I want to bite it off, but I don't. I keep on working. He holds the back of my head until he comes, which is very quickly and I spit onto the floor. He pulls up his jeans and leaves the bathroom quickly. When I look up, Bazam is standing in front of me.

'Oh, no!'

'Oh, yes!'

When they leave, I sit on the toilet seat for a long time, with the golden light streaming in through the curtains, until it fades from the sky and darkness falls.

* * * *

I had another English exam on Thursday followed by another biology exam on Friday. On Saturday I went to the police. Two officers took me into an interview room – one male and one female. I told them what happened with Shahmeel and the policewoman was sympathetic; more so than the man, I thought.

'We'll need to come to your flat, Kate.'

'Oh, no, please don't do that!'

'Why not?'

I was really scared of what Shahmeel might do if he found out I'd reported him. I couldn't tell anybody, not William or Dani or anybody at the SAU, in case it got back to him. If the police came to my flat, he'd find out and hurt me – maybe even kill me.

'We'll have to arrest the man… question him.'

'Oh, no, please don't! I don't want him to be arrested.'

I hadn't really thought this through. The police were patient. The policewoman wanted to know if I was reporting a rape or not?

'If you say it's rape, we'll have to arrest him.'

What if I had to go to court and tell my mother, my family? What if he got off? There were no witnesses – it was my word against his. I wasn't underage or anything. What if he didn't get off and the others came for me? I'd have to go home and live in the same house with my mother's boyfriend again, share a room with my sister again – it'd be intolerable!

'You can just report it as intelligence if you like, Kate.'

'What does that mean?'

'We take a statement from you and if this man does anything again, either with you or another girl, then we'll have your evidence on file.'

She said they wouldn't have to arrest him and I wouldn't have to do anything else, like go to court or anything.

'But you'll have to say it was consensual, Kate.'

Looking back, I guess it was the way they dealt with rape at that time. The way they dealt with rape victims then was shit from the top down. It was an organisational failing. I gave my statement and the policewoman wrote down that it was consensual, but I felt pushed into it. I didn't want to say it was consensual – that was a lie! But I was feeling paranoid. The room had a window and the blinds were open. Anyone could see me through that window. I imagined Shahmeel outside, watching me, with a knife in his boot. So, when they asked me to sign the statement, I did – with the word 'consensual' in it. I just wanted to get out of there. I didn't tell them about being orally raped by Ali and Bazam. What was the point? Don't forget, my understanding of 'consent' was very poor and I suppose I wasn't fully convinced they'd raped me. Part of me thought it was my own fault.

The local police Station was within walking distance of my flat. I knew any one of the Asian men could've seen me going in or coming back out. I half expected Shahmeel to walk up behind me any second and plunge his knife into my back. I kept looking round, shaking with fear, seeing dark shadows everywhere.

But the nightmare was only just beginning.

3

Deeper And Deeper

Soldiers are taught that one of the keys to survival is to constantly scan their environment, assessing risks and anticipating enemy movement. They learn how to make split-second calls under intense pressure, deciding when to move, when to hide, and how to escape. They know how to suppress panic to stay functional and think clearly, even when adrenaline is racing through the body. But my brain was not trauma-trained and I couldn't properly evaluate the danger around me.

Looking back, I should have never been in the SAU. What I should've done was have a conversation with my mother and tried to resolve the problems in our house. But, when you're young, difficult conversations are uncomfortable. It's something you learn to do as you get older. Leaving home was my way of avoiding confrontation.

On the other hand, I found my new independence exciting. I had my own space at last; able to eat when I wanted, sleep when I wanted, live how I wanted. So I thought my life had improved when I moved to the SAU. What I didn't realise was that I was already traumatised to some extent from being kicked out of my home and rejected by my mother.

Nobody told me moving to the SAU wasn't going to be good for me. I didn't understand that looking after myself also meant keeping myself safe. And I didn't get enough time to learn how to do that, I didn't know how vulnerable I was, living so close to a gang of rapists. The staff at the SAU must have known what was going on, maybe not the full extent of it, but they knew bad stuff was happening.

Once my exams were over, I had a lot of time on my hands. It would be two months before I got the results and found out if I'd got into uni or not. To be honest, I didn't expect to because of the state I was in when I was sitting the exams.

I took on as much overtime as I could at Primark, doing split shifts on Saturdays with two hours off in between. During the break, I'd hang around in Telford Shopping Centre. I'd go to the bagel shop and get a smoked salmon and cream cheese bagel with a cup of tea and sit there. The tea reminded me of my mother – she loved tea. And it was somewhere to go. I figured the more time I spent away from the flat, the less chance I'd have of getting raped again.

When you're 18 you're supposed to be an adult. But if I was a real adult, I'd have known what to do. I loved my mother so much and looked up to her, I tried to think what she'd do if this happened to her. But I couldn't imagine it, because I knew she wouldn't have let it happen to her in the first place. She was a real adult and they wouldn't have tried to do it to her. They were doing this to me because I was young and white and they had no respect for white girls who were vulnerable and living at the SAU with nobody to defend them.

In hindsight, I believe that, to them, being parentless was a reason to be disrespected. Asian parents would never let their children go to the wall like that because it would bring shame on the family. You're white and alone, therefore you're a slut and worthless. In my case I was weak and dyslexic and red-haired and stupid and bullied. Even though nobody told them, they knew that – they could see it as soon as they looked at me. They knew I was alone inside myself and I wouldn't do anything about it, no matter what they did to me. So they could do whatever they liked. They knew it. They could see it. It was who I was.

Once, when I came home from work, Ali Sultan and four other men were outside my door. Ali demanded I let them in. I said no.

'Let us in or we'll kick the door in.'

'Kick it in, the police will come.'

'Let us in or we'll kick *you* in!'

So I had to let them in. I knew they would've hurt me if I didn't. Ali Sultan began coming to me regularly for blowjobs after that, and he'd bring other men with him. He spread my name to interested locals, and random men would turn up at my door or pester me in the street.

One evening, when I was on the way to Londis to get electricity on my card, a car pulled up next to me. There were four Pakistani men in it. I started walking quickly away. They kerb-crawled beside me.

'We've heard about you… you give good blowjobs.'

I walked faster, but the car kept up with me. I was really scared that they were going to jump out and drag me into it and gang rape me. But they didn't. After a few minutes, they drove off laughing. This continued to happen to me randomly, wherever I went – men followed me in cars and spoke in an abusive way to me. It scared and upset me.

A couple of weeks after the exams I was home from work and there was a knock on my door. I didn't want to answer it in case it was Shahmeel back again – or Ali, or Bazam. It wasn't; it was Imran and an elderly man who he said was his uncle, Nabi. They'd heard about what Shahmeel did and they'd come to apologise; he'd just come out of prison and he wasn't right in the head. They hoped I was okay and there was no need to take the matter any further, because Shahmeel would just be sent straight back to prison.

'Can we come in?'

I didn't want to fall out with Imran. I saw him as a friend at that particular time. I now see he'd conditioned me to think of him as a friend. If I didn't let him in I'd make an enemy of him and I knew he was connected to the rest of the gang. It was best to have him on my side.

That's how they tricked you, with friendship in one hand and the threat of violence in the other. But this was all new to me and I wasn't clued up.

It was a mistake to open the door. Once inside, their attitude changed and they seemed to become surer of themselves and more threatening. Imran looked the place over, while Uncle Nabi just stood leering at me.

'You're Kate, right?'

'Right.'

'Do you have any tea, Kate?'

'In the kitchen… I'll make some.'

'No, I'll do it. You stay here with Uncle Nabi.'

****

Uncle Nabi is old and bald and he has a gold tooth that glistens as he leers at me. I move away from him, but he follows; the room is small and it's difficult to keep my distance. Imran doesn't go to make tea. He leaves the flat. I call out after him.

'Imran… come back!'

He ignores me. Uncle Nabi starts to speak, his voice shaky and sort of excited.

'I hear you're a bit of an exhibitionist.'

I don't know what an exhibitionist is – that's because I'm an idiot, a dumb redhead. A dyslexic dumb ginger. Is that a reasonable excuse? I don't seem to know anything, 24/7. I can't even control what's happening to me. I can't do anything about it. Because I'm stupid. It'd be funny if it wasn't so sad. Uncle Nabi grabs my hand. I try to pull away from him, but his grip is strong for an old man. I'm scared, but I don't want to show it because I think that'll get him even more excited. It's dawning on me that this visit was planned. I pull away and try to get to the front door. Uncle Nabi is in the way and I can't get past him. I try to scream, but my mouth opens and nothing comes out. No sound.

Uncle Nabi grabs me and pulls me close to him and rubs his body up against mine. I know I'll have to have sex with him, there's nothing I can do about it. He pulls me to the bed and pushes me down. I don't struggle as he undresses me, because I know it's futile. He spits on my vagina to lubricate it and this makes me heave. I feel sick. He doesn't care. I don't like what he's doing to me so I decide to go somewhere else in my mind.

I go back to when I was a young girl, watching television with my family and I fall into a trance.

When I come to, Uncle Nabi is gone.

* * * *

I never saw him again. I hated myself. I felt like a worthless slut which is exactly what they wanted me to think. I was spiralling out of control, sinking down into something horrible. I was being swallowed up by a disgusting sea of black slime.

'No one will believe you now.'

And it was right; how could I tell anyone what a worthless slut I was? I was over 18. It wasn't a crime to have sex with a woman my age. I tried to tell the voice that rape was a crime. But it came right back at me.

'You said it was consensual.'

And I had – I'd signed the police report.

Was it even rape in the first place? Why was I allowing myself to be treated like this? The only answer I could give myself was because that was who I was – a worthless slut! They wouldn't believe someone like me – a girl who was living in a Sheltered Accommodation Unit. They'd assume a bad background, a history of drugs or alcohol, someone who'd lost the right to be believed. They'd check the statement I made and see the word 'consensual', even though it was a lie.

Was it a lie?

I tried to tell myself that that wasn't me. It wasn't the 'me' before – the 'me' my mother knew.

But it was the 'me' now.

I felt like an open wound – like my whole body was bleeding, like I was just a rag that had wiped up a floor covered with vomit and urine and excrement.

After Nabi's attack, I was physically sick in the toilet. I then lay in a bath full of cold water for hours and hours, hoping I could soak off the smell of the sin that had infected me. Afterwards, I just sat on the floor, as if in a trance. I found comfort in the floor. The floor was my friend. It helped me hide from the windows, so nobody could see I was in. My mind was completely blank and I deliberately kept it that way, so I didn't have to think about what was happening to me.

The extended shock manifested itself as disassociation. The feeling was like being in a trance or daze – not being able to concentrate. It was my brain trying to cope, taking me out of reality and putting me somewhere else. It was the first time I'd experienced disassociation and I didn't know what it was. I couldn't make sense of reality, so I couldn't understand what was happening to my mental state either. People might say I should have protected myself. Sure, I could've stayed in bed and covered my head. I could've run somewhere. I could've killed myself. Then I'd have been safe. But no young girl experiencing that level of trauma would be thinking clearly. There were adults around me who could have, and should have, seen the state I was in – that I was in trouble, mentally. But they didn't.

One night there was a knock on my door – I was already in bed and I didn't want to get up and answer it. But they kept on knocking and I was afraid they'd wake up other people in the flats. I looked through the spyhole in my door and it was Imran with a young girl. The girl looked scared, so I opened up. Imran said it was his cousin and she'd run away and couldn't go back home to her parents. He wanted her to stay at my flat for the night until he could 'arrange' something for her. I didn't believe him.

When he left, I tried to make her feel at ease. I gave her a pair of my pyjamas that were too big for her and made her a hot chocolate with marshmallows.

'What's your name?'

She didn't answer or, if she did, I didn't hear as she spoke so softly.

'How old are you?'

Again, I didn't catch her answer, but she looked about 14 or 15.

'Is Imran having sex with you?'

She just nodded and I could tell she felt ashamed, just like me. Neither of us mentioned the word 'rape' – neither of us wanted to admit to the other that we'd been raped. It would've made both of us feel even more ashamed than we already were. I kind of felt on the same level as her, even though she was 14 or 15 and I was 18 – it was like we were sisters in strife.

'For how long?'

'Since I was 12.'

Imran was a man who was always talking about God and all his friends looked up to him as a man of dignity and respect and were always nodding in agreement with everything he said. Yet he'd been raping this girl since she was young.

She was small and had black hair. I felt so sad for her. I tried to cheer her up by making silly jokes. She was so sweet and polite and a pleasure to have for company.

Now that all the grooming stories have broken, I know what was going on. But I didn't know then. I realise I should've asked her more questions, like where she lived, and maybe taken her home to her parents, but I didn't. There was no point calling the police – they wouldn't have helped, just got angry if they'd found her with me and reckoned she was just having a sleepover or something. Imran would've denied everything and then taken it out on me. I feel guilty now for not doing more to help her. When I woke in the morning she was gone.

During my time at the SAU, I began to suffer from PTSD, even though I didn't recognise it then. It first manifested itself as panic attacks. I mistook strangers in the street for the perpetrators, as if I had recognition problems. I kept thinking I could see them, even when it wasn't them. I was obsessing over whether they knew I was in and were trying to get to me. I was taking different routes home, trying not to walk the same way all the time so they wouldn't be waiting for me. After a bit, these feelings became strange, compulsive urges to give in to the abuse and become part of it, to let it swallow me up and devour me. I think this is why so many abuse victims end up either being trapped by their abusers, or going back to them after they've made their escape.

It's hard to explain; it's like your mind is stuck in a loop and your behaviour follows, going round and round in circles. I've learned since that behaviour is an expression of what's in your mind, and what was in my mind back then was the abuse – playing over and over and over.

These predators were able to 'read' their victims – they could find our vulnerabilities and prey on them. What chance did I have, even if I was 18, against men with years of grooming experience? It was my first time living away from my mother and I missed her. I wanted to call her, wanted to run home and grab hold of her and never let her go. But I couldn't. These men lived close by and they were desperate and hardened criminals. They'd hurt my family, my mother, wouldn't they? As well as killing me.

In August that year I went to Super Spirit and saw my family, but only from a distance. It was like they weren't my family anymore; they belonged to him – the boyfriend. Some Asian kids found out I wasn't in the flat and they broke in and covered all the windows with baked beans and sand and leaves and condoms – I think Dani and other teenagers from the SAU joined in. They assumed for some reason that I thought I was better than them, even though I'd never think I was better than anyone. So they were making some kind of deluded statement – that I was untouchable or something. Scummy.

I felt as if I'd been shattered again.

Gang rape became a way of life at the SAU and it got so bad I believed I'd kill myself if they didn't kill me first.

One day I was walking past some of the terraced houses near the

SAU when Shahmeel grabbed my arm and pulled me inside. The place was a doss house. It was in desperate need of repairs and was full of junk.

He dragged me up a flight of stairs and into a kind of living room. There were other people in the room, including a mixed-race woman, but no one I knew, and they just ignored me. After a while, Shahmeel caught me by the wrist and pulled me out of the room and up another flight of stairs.

'I don't want to go up there.'

I was pulling hard against his grip, but I couldn't get free.

****

Shahmeel takes me into a room at the top of the stairs. It's a small room with a bare mattress on a bed frame. The frame's broken so the mattress has fallen down into the base on one side. I try to leave, but he shuts the door and stands against it. I ask him to please move. Why am I saying 'please'? He does that thing with his head, holding it slightly to one side and pouting his lips in an insane smile.

'You want me to smash your face into the pavement outside?'

I know he'll do it if I resist.

People talk about the 'fight or flight' response to danger. But it should be 'fight or flight or freeze'. Sometimes people can't fight or escape, so they freeze. I freeze like a statue while he undresses me. He wants to film me naked, but I try to cover myself and take the phone off him because I don't know who he'll show the images to. While this is happening, the mixed-race woman from downstairs sticks her head round the door, but withdraws quickly when she sees what's going on. Shahmeel pushes me down onto the scabby mattress. I'm kind of upside down, because my head's on the side that's fallen through into the base. He digs his shoulder into my face and his chin into my collarbone, so hard it bruises me. I freeze again while he rapes me. I just want to get through it. If I try to fight he could kill me – if I try to escape he could kill me.

By not resisting I survive. I stay alive.

He comes inside me quickly and it's over.

I put my clothes back on and we go downstairs. I want to leave, but he makes me go back into the living room. There's a screwdriver on the table and I want to pick it up and stab him in the neck. I wonder if I have enough strength to pierce the skin. What if it doesn't work? What if he doesn't die and they all jump on me and kill me? I don't care if they kill me, but I want him dead first, and I can't be sure that'll happen. The mixed-race woman is laughing and talking about my 'fat white ass'. It's mortifying.

After a while, I can't take it anymore and I run out of the room and into the hallway. Shahmeel comes after me and corners me against the wall, with both arms either side of me.

'Don't go, Kate. Come back in.'

'I don't want to.'

'But I love you. You can be my girlfriend and I'll buy you a house.'

I can't tell if he's serious or not. All I know is, he's a crazy, fucked-in-the-head, control freak. He forces his tongue down my throat and then he lets me go.

* * * *

Tina was 18 and lived in the flat upstairs. William told me that Tina was a 'p***-shagger'. She had a friend called Maria who was 16, but everybody called her Jay-Boy. Tina and Jay-Boy always hung out together. Jay-Boy was a kind of tomboy, I suppose that's why they called her Jay-Boy, and Tina was really skinny, like a stick. I locked myself out of my flat one time and Tina was the only person thin enough to get through the bathroom window to open the door for me. We became sort of friends after that.

One day, Tina and Jay-Boy came round my flat and brought three Asian guys I didn't know with them. Jay-Boy had some ecstasy pills called love hearts and she offered me one. I don't know why I took it, probably because I was so traumatised from being raped all the time. What experience could be worse than that?

It was a really stupid mistake.

The effect was like being possessed – I wasn't me anymore. I began to run around the flat saying ridiculous things. I lost all control and I wasn't even aware of what I was doing.

'This is great! Give me another one!' I said.

Jay-Boy gave me another and she and Tina sat on my bed, laughing. I took all my clothes off and ran around naked while two of the Asian men filmed me on their phones. They got me to put the neck of a vodka bottle into my vagina and masturbate. They smeared bananas all over my body and completely defiled me. I didn't feel a thing, only the effect of the drug in my system.

It's like when you get out of hospital after a serious operation, you're not supposed to be left on your own for fear of what you might do in that drugged state.

I was experiencing huge trauma and I needed support, being completely disassociated, vulnerable and naïve as I was. People might say I just had to tell somebody, but I wasn't able to make even simple decisions like that because I was in turmoil, spinning round, not knowing how to stop the spiralling. I mean, disassociation isn't something you can just switch on and off, like a light. Psychologically, I was a total mess. I had no control over myself or my actions. At times I felt like I'd lost my mind completely.

I'd always been a bit curious about Islam and now, in my drugged state, I asked one of the men a question about it.

'What are the Five Pillars?'

The whole room went immediately silent, like all the sound in the world had been muted. Their faces became filled with hate and I'm sure, if they'd been carrying knives, they'd have stabbed me to death. It felt as if it would've been their moral duty to honour-kill me, and I was very lucky they didn't. Why? Because of who I was. I was less than an animal to them and I'd just insulted them deeply by mentioning their religion. They looked at me with such disdain and disgust, they obviously had a deep hatred towards me and my behaviour – even though they'd manipulated and encouraged me into that state.

Look at who I was: a white slut – a *guri* – who'd dared mention Islam. I was worthless on a moral level no human beings ever reach. They'd moulded and shaped me into something they could justify abusing for their own amusement, so that I was no longer a human being to them; they'd dehumanised me, and now the thing they made had unwittingly insulted them.

I'm not singling out Islam for criticism here; I think all religions are just as bad as each other – and self-righteousness is one of the greatest evils in the world. It has been since religion was invented. There's an inherent darkness in believing there's a supreme deity and that you're favoured in some way by that deity. That's sectarianism, which is really a form of sanctimony.

Personally I think it's dangerous for religion, any religion, to be the foundation of morals and what's right or wrong. I'm not saying there should be ethical anarchy, but the very fact of the existence of dogma, theological law even, creates its own twisted notion of what's good and bad.

I mean, mental illness is culture-dependent, isn't it? Crime itself is culture-dependent – different cultures have different crimes, not that crime only occurs in some cultures. What I'm saying is, the notion of good creates the notion of bad. Without 'good', there would be no 'bad'.

Back when I was being abused, a lot of people, both inside and outside the Asian communities, knew what was going on, but did nothing about it. Asian community leaders did nothing because they lived in a patriarchal culture that saw women as second-class citizens, even their own Muslim women.

White girls like me were just trash and deserved everything they got – asked for it, even. People outside the Asian communities who were in a position to do something were afraid of being called racist, or being accused of having a racist motive, and the abusers used that to their advantage.

An abuser is an abuser, whether Muslim, Christian, Jewish, Buddhist, white, black, brown or any other colour or creed.

The abuse of white girls by Asian men was, and still is, a racist phenomenon in itself. It was born out of cultural racism and nurtured in hatred and gender elitism. Racism affects a person's self-esteem and I hope I can demonstrate how evil and dangerous it is in any culture.

Towards the end of the night, I began to come back to my senses, enough to realise what was going on. I realised I was naked and I began to cry. I cried and cried and cried. I cried so much I could hardly breathe. I cried because I believed I'd insulted them – that I'd insulted their religion. I actually apologised for being unworthy of any religion. Jay-Boy laughed.

'I don't know how you can cry on those pills. They're supposed to make you happy.'

But I couldn't stop. I realised they'd been filming me and I begged them to delete the images. I begged and begged. I tried to appeal to whatever goodness there might be inside them. But it was useless. The next day they told everyone. The kids in the street threw stones at me and tried to hit me with sticks. I had to run a gauntlet of abuse and, when I got back to my flat, I sat on the floor and cried.

****

A few days later, the same three men come back. They threaten to put the stuff they'd filmed on YouTube or Facebook or some other social media site unless I give them a blowjob, so I do – one after the other. When I'm finished, I notice my Xbox is gone.

'Where's my Xbox?'

'What Xbox?'

I deadlock the door and tell them if they don't give it back, I won't let them out and I'll call the police. They laugh, so I dial 999. That freaks them out and they start running around the flat, waving their hands in the air. They throw the Xbox at me and beg me to let them out, which I do.

****

What they didn't know was, when I dialled 999, the policewoman I spoke to said I was wasting her time and she got angry with me. The police weren't coming. But what messed with my mind was this: I got angry when they stole my Xbox and did something about it, yet I'd just meekly allowed them to rape me a few minutes before. That's how conditioned I was becoming to the constant abuse. Everybody started to shun me after that, even William, who'd been my friend since I moved into the SAU.

'Why're you treating me like this, William?'

'Because you're a p***-shagger, like Tina.'

'You brought them to my flat in the first place.'

'But you let them in, Kate.'

I couldn't believe it. All I'd tried to do was protect William from Ali Sultan's bullying, and now he was calling me names and sneering at me. The worst thing about it was, I believed he was right. I *was* a 'p***-shagger'. I was a slut and a tramp and a ho.

I decided to do something about it.

I made a sign saying DON'T LET THEM IN and I hung it on the back of the door. I put Blu Tack over the keyhole so they couldn't spy in. I wedged the living room door open so I could get to the spyhole without making any noise. I put the deadlock on and put the key in a drawer – that way, I'd have time to think before opening the door. I turned my buzzer off so they wouldn't hear it. The gates to the flats made a squeaking noise and, as soon as I heard it, I'd know someone was coming and I'd rush to the spyhole in the door to see if they were coming for me.

Ali came and banged on the door. I didn't answer. He banged and banged.

'I know you're in there!'

But I still didn't open up for him. In the end he left. I'd done it!

I started getting up early in the mornings and trying to get everything done before 10am, which was the time they started to surface. I'd get what I needed from the shops and go to the library or the post office or whatever else I had to do outside. Then I'd rush back to the flat and sit on the floor. I started crawling everywhere – to the bedroom, to the cupboards for food and to the kitchenette to make a cup of tea. I watched TV with headphones on, sitting on the floor with the lights off. I listened to music with headphones too and if anyone banged on the door, I'd turn the music up. If I couldn't hear them, they weren't there.

I was living like a prisoner under house arrest for something I didn't do, feeling guilty for a crime I didn't commit. I'd have massive panic attacks, which came on like a black cloud in my head that I couldn't think through. I'd cry and find it hard to breathe and I'd get dizzy and couldn't calm myself down. I was distressed and needed help, but I didn't know who to ask or where to get it. I thought about going to the office and asking for help from the SAU staff, but I couldn't let them see me in such a state – and what would I say to them? They'd tell me to go to the police. I'd say I already had. They'd find out about that word 'consensual' and they'd know I was a slut and a tramp and a ho.

I eventually decided to call my mother. It was the first time I felt I could actually tell her what was happening to me. It was as if I'd been hiding behind a wall the whole time and now, suddenly, it had burst with the weight of it all. Everything came crashing down and the floodgates opened. I called her mobile and it rang. She didn't answer. My mother was a community nurse and I knew she was often in patients' houses and couldn't take a call – but she'd ring me back. I knew she'd ring me back.

I called my grandmother, who always answered the phone. But when I heard her voice, I realised how ridiculous it was to try to tell this elderly woman that I was being serially raped. She couldn't do anything about it and it'd distress her so much. She knew by my stuttering voice that something wasn't right.

'What's wrong, Kate?'

'Nothing.'

'Are you sure?'

'Well… is it normal for men to knock on your door looking for sex?'

She didn't know what I was talking about. I don't know why I asked that stupid question, but I didn't know what else to say. I didn't know what I was doing wrong, only that everyone here was blaming me for something that wasn't my fault. I was so confused. Someone started banging my door while I was on the phone to my grandmother, so I hung up and stayed quiet, until they went away.

My mother phoned back later. By then I'd calmed down and the wall was back up again, and we just talked about normal stuff, like how I was getting on or the weather, and I lied and said everything was okay. I didn't have the words anymore – they were gone. I felt defeated. I was so close to telling her everything, but now I couldn't.

She didn't know how much I needed her right then. I loved and missed her so much, but I just couldn't tell her. It made me feel so sad and I cried again. I cried into the cushions on the sofa and the pillows on the bed. I cried until I fell asleep.

4

To Die Or Not To Die?

I was trying to cope on my own, with no support, while an organised crime gang raped and trafficked me. I thought it couldn't get worse. It was veering towards kill yourself territory. I felt I had no other option. The clock was ticking and I had neither the time nor the capacity to safeguard myself against what was coming. My mind was out of control. Trauma after trauma with no time to process it. My brain couldn't keep up.

At the same time, I was beginning to internalise how they viewed me and adopt their point of view that I was worthless. Dark thoughts came and negative emotions shattered my self-image. I was suffering from complex PTSD, over and over. It's called disturbance of self-organisation, but I didn't know that back then. I didn't see the abnormal mood regulation and self-conceptualising for what it was.

After the panic attacks, I began to go a bit strange. I became suicidal. I started to feel like I was going to explode, that at some point soon I was going to crack and kill them all, along with myself. I was trying to think of a way to do it, while also feeling guilty because I'd let them make me like that. I really wanted to die, and things were only getting worse.

Every time something horrible happened, I regretted that I hadn't already done it. I regretted every day that I woke in the morning, every extra day I was alive. I didn't care about situations that people would've considered dangerous and I didn't have any regard for my safety.

One day this scary Turkish man was threatening William outside my flat – I think it was something to do with drugs. This man looked really dangerous. It seemed to me that William was going to get badly hurt and, even though he and Dani and the others at the SAU weren't really my friends anymore, I didn't want that to happen. I went out.

'What's up?'

I could see the panic in William's eyes.

'I owe some money.'

'Can I help?'

The man put his face up close to mine and his mouth twisted into a threat: 'You got the money he owes?'

'No.'

'I hear about you… maybe you got something else?'

He pushed me back inside my flat and made me give him a blowjob. I thought, at least it gave William the opportunity to get lost. He still wanted his money, but it bought William some time.

I guess that's when the transition from innocent to not-so-innocent started. Or maybe it was when the real grooming began. I was damaged from everything that had happened and I considered myself worthless. I blamed myself for everything. I'd let these men abuse me and now I'd become exactly what they treated me as – a whore. It's like breaking a wild animal and they eventually comply and are comfortable with complying. It comes when it's called, when it could easily run away. I gave up crawling around the floor and hiding and just let it happen. I had no feelings about it one way or the other – no emotions at all. I grew cold inside.

My life was what it was and it would end soon, either by one of them or by my own doing.

I continued to have premonitions of impending doom, convinced I wouldn't make it to Christmas because something fatal was going to happen. I wanted to kill myself, but I didn't want to do it without taking some of them with me. Any day now I was going on a murderous rampage culminating in my own death.

I thought about God a lot; I'd never really been religious but, if there wasn't a god, then I was completely alone and no one would ever know that I didn't mean for all this to happen – that it was all an accident. I needed there to be a god and I asked him to help me put an end to it. I couldn't imagine spending Christmas with my family after all this. I couldn't imagine any future at all.

The me I used to be was gone. Dead.

Suicide was framed not as an escape from danger, but as self-erasure. I was already dead and there was nothing left worth protecting. But I knew the demon inside me would try to stop me killing myself – the demon Shahmeel put in me when he raped me for the first time. The demon that grew and grew every time I was raped after that. It wouldn't want me to die, because it'd die with me.

I bought sage and incense and burned it in my flat to get rid of the evil. But it didn't work. I needed the Qur'an to do real damage. I needed to recite some *surahs* to really upset it. I needed an exorcism, but not a Christian exorcism – a Muslim exorcism. The demon was evil and the Qur'an was good. If I could read the Qur'an to the demon it would turn to ashes and blow away – like throwing holy water on an incubus. The purity of the Qur'an would make it burn like a vampire in the sunlight. But I had no Qur'an and, of course, I knew nothing about Islam.

I was walking around like a zombie – not dead, but not really alive either. Someone threw a bunch of condoms on the street and, as I was passing, the dangerous-looking Turkish man came up to me and started shouting. It was probably some teenagers from the college, since everyone there was entitled to 24 free condoms a month, and the street the SAU was on was a shortcut from the college to the high street. But the man blamed me and now he was screeching.

'I will kill you! I have a young sister, what if she sees this filth?'

I didn't try to say it wasn't me. I didn't care what he thought.

'I will kill you!'

'Kill me, then.'

I stood and looked straight into his threatening eyes. I mean, the hypocrisy of this man. He came into my flat to force me into giving him a blowjob, and now he was being so sanctimonious and afraid a few condoms would corrupt his sister.

'Kill me, then!'

He stared hard at me and I saw his hand move inside his *jubba,* a kind of robe. I waited to feel the knife penetrate my ribs. I wanted it. But he just turned and stormed off, shouting back at me in Turkish.

In the middle of all this I went out with a few college friends to a pub called the Black Dog, just to get away from the flat for a while. We were joined by a guy called Mike Nolan, who the others called 'Mickey'. He said he was in the army, and he seemed all right, fitting in with our little group.

As the night wore on, it was decided that we'd all go back to my flat for a bit of a party. Mickey said he'd pay for some booze and the rest of us chipped in for pizzas. I didn't normally drink but, that night, because of the way my mind was, I got drunk on vodka. All of a sudden I burst into tears and sat on the floor in a stupor of depression and wailed on about how Shahmeel raped me and how all the Pakistani men wouldn't leave me alone and how I hated myself and didn't want to live any more. Some of the girls tried to comfort me until I fell asleep or passed out, but I don't remember much after that, until I woke up in the early hours and found that everyone had left.

Late the next night Mickey called me. I didn't remember giving him my number, but he said I did. He said he'd been clubbing nearby and couldn't get home and could he stay at my flat for the night. I agreed and went to get out the spare mattress for him.

I was wearing my favourite Snoopy pyjamas, a long- sleeved top and three-quarter-length trouser bottoms when he knocked on the door. I checked the spy-hole – it was him. As soon as I opened the door, he lunged at me, grabbing me and pushing me against the wall. I was totally startled. It was the last thing I expected from a white guy who was in the army and who'd seemed so nice the night before.

****

He's trying to kiss me and I'm shouting at him to stop. I can see there's something wrong with his eyes. His eyes look so weird, as if he's on drugs or something. He's grabbing at my breasts aggressively and I'm desperately trying to get him off me. He goes for my pyjama bottoms and I hold them up, but the force he's using rips them with a loud tear. This seems to unnerve him and he backs off.

'I just want to talk to you for a minute, Kate. I just want to talk to you. I just want to talk. I want to talk!'

'I want you to get out of my flat!'

He sits down and I know I should run – but to where? I don't want to be running on the streets in ripped pyjamas.

'I want to talk to you, but can you get all these other people out of the room!'

I'm terrified. The flat's empty. Everything goes eerily silent. We're like motionless ghosts in the gloom, him sitting and me standing, ready to run.

He jumps up and attacks me again. I scream and run, but he grabs me by both arms and forces me towards the bed.

'I want to tie you up, Kate.'

'Leave me alone!'

There's nothing for him to use, so he forces me down and uses his body weight to hold me there. I struggle and try to get my arms free, but I can't. He's strong, maybe from his army training. When he's down to his boxers and I can see his erect penis, I finally lose hope and realise this is going to happen. As he's about to insert it into me, I shout: 'Condom! Please use a condom!'

He pauses for a second and decides it's a good idea. He searches his pockets and now that my arms are free, I try to run again. But he's quick and catches me and starts to rape me. He's aggressive and biting me all over my body. He bites me on the face really hard and I scream again. The neighbour upstairs is banging the floor with a broom or something to tell me to keep the noise down.

****

When he finished and rolled off me, I was totally exhausted. He got dressed and stumbled over the spare mattress on the floor. On the way out of the door, he turned to me and his voice was a mumble.

'Did we just have sex?'

I was quiet when he left. I didn't wash, like I normally did. I just curled up in a ball, facing the wall. Then I started crying. Not because he raped me, but because he'd ripped my favourite pyjamas. Why did he do it? Because I was worthless. He'd raped me because he knew I was already a rape victim, and that made it more acceptable. Now that I was a worthless slut it was all right for everyone to use me for sex.

The next day I went to college. I had bruises all over my breasts and a massive bruise on my face where he bit me. One of my friends, Josie, asked me what had happened.

'Nothing.'

I just felt numb – nothing else.

By now, Imran and Shahmeel were regularly bringing men around to my flat for sex and I just acquiesced. I was broken and came when I was called. One of those men was Tamjeed. He was big and muscular and he had a gold tooth. I was sitting on the edge of my bed and he stood in front of me without saying anything and began to unzip his trousers. Normally, I would have gone through the motions and rinsed my mouth out afterwards but this time, for some reason, I jumped up and ran behind the TV to create a barrier between us.

'I don't want to do it!'

He stared at me like he'd been hit in the face.

'I'm sorry… Shahmeel said…'

'That I liked it?'

'Yes.'

'I don't.'

He turned and left, but called me the next day from a mobile number. He was Shahmeel's cousin and was actually doing five years in the Category D section of HMP Redwood for dealing drugs. Once a month he got overnight leave to stay with his family and that's when Shahmeel brought him round to me for a blowjob. He was apologetic on the phone.

'I'm sorry, I thought you were…'

'A prostitute?'

'No. I mean, Shahmeel said…'

'I know what he said.'

It was clear to me that Tamjeed thought sex with me would be consensual and not rape. Maybe it was because he didn't want to risk another stretch in prison, but he seemed okay and not like the others.

'Is Shahmeel raping you?'

'Yes.'

'That isn't right. I'll speak to him next month. I'll make him leave you alone.'

He never did. Or, if he did, it was only to warn Shahmeel for his own sake, because I was telling people he raped me. Tamjeed called me several times from prison and, when he got his next overnight leave, he came round to my flat. It wasn't a matter of me *wanting* to have sex with him. I just did it because he wanted to do it. I didn't have sex with men because I wanted to, that concept was beyond my imagination by then. I think, in the end, Tamjeed genuinely didn't want to rape me, but he realised he needed to groom me a bit more before I'd agree to have sex with him of my own free will – and all he had to do was be nice to me.

I don't know if you could call the sex with Tamjeed consensual or if it was rape. By then I didn't really know the difference. It was just like – a job, I guess. It was easier to do than fight it. I remember him telling me what to do, like giving me orders: do this, now do that, now let's try this. He even used a dildo on me. It hurt and I didn't want him to do it, but he did it anyway. It was like he was experimenting, without really knowing what he was doing. I was glad when it was over.

Cemal and his brother, Hafeez, were others who were 'nice' to me too. One day I got a call from Tamjeed's mobile, but it wasn't him. The man who called said his name was Cemal and he was a friend of Tamjeed's from prison. Tamjeed had been moved to a Category C jail for some reason – I don't know why – and he'd passed his phone on to this Cemal. Cemal was nice to me over the phone. He sounded sympathetic and told me things were never as bad as they seemed. He said I was young and had my life ahead of me and I shouldn't be thinking or talking about ending it. He said all this in a way that made me feel a bit better about my situation.

After a few weeks of talking to me on the phone every night, he convinced me to meet him when he got his next overnight release. I didn't know at the time that he was serving 11 years for kidnapping and chopping a man with a machete. He'd been in prison for about six years and was coming up to being eligible for release on license; that's how he was in a Category D jail, to help reintegrate him back into the community.

I don't know why I agreed to meet him, but after our phone calls and the smallest show of sympathy, I had warmed towards him. It became quickly apparent that this was another grooming tactic. After the really nasty rapists at the SAU, men like Tamjeed and Cemal seemed nice. It was nice to talk to men who were being nice to me, even though, as I realised later, it was still grooming. These men were evil and raped me in a hateful way. They raped me because they considered me to be a slut and as a punishment for being a dirty white girl. In their eyes, I was born a slut because I went around uncovered and was shameless and deserved to be abused.

They raped me to intentionally cause mental and physical pain. These 'nice' men still wanted sex, and that was their ultimate goal. They were only being nice because they wanted sex, but they did it in a much less hateful way or, at least, that's how it felt at the time. I associated sex with rape and I really didn't know the difference – I didn't understand that some guy giving me bullshit on the phone was almost as bad as the people who were banging on the door of my flat.

I agreed to meet Cemal in Birmingham when he got his next overnight release. I wasn't aware of how dangerous he was, although I did know it was a risk. But I didn't care about my own safety. When you lose the will to live, you lose your sense of fear along with it. You lose your sense of self-preservation. What was I preserving anyway? Everyone hated me. Everyone thought I was a bad person, so I *must* be a bad person. I was just a slut and a p***-shagger and there was nothing I could do about it.

I got the train to Birmingham and I met him in the station, by Burger King. He was short, with a big nose. His brother, Hafeez, was with him and he was going to drive us somewhere in his car. Hafeez was showing off as he drove like a maniac down residential streets. They were puzzled because I didn't put my seatbelt on.

'Aren't you scared?'

'No.'

We stopped at a house in Billesley, on the outskirts of Birmingham. Hafeez drove off and left us alone. Inside, Cemal took off his T-shirt and asked me to give him a massage. He was really muscular, like he'd been working out a lot in prison. We went upstairs and, just as with Tamjeed, the distinction between consensual sex and rape was blurred beyond recognition. I remember pleading with him to use a condom, but he said he didn't have one. He was sorry later because I'd caught chlamydia off Ali Sultan, but I didn't know it at the time.

Back in prison, Cemal called me and asked if he could give my number to his brother. For some reason I said okay. I should've known better, but of course I wasn't thinking straight at the time. Hafeez called me the same day, asking me to meet him in Birmingham. I didn't want to, so he came to my flat in the SAU. During my studies in later years, I learned that the area of the brain responsible for the fight-or-flight response is called the amygdala. When someone's going through prolonged trauma, the synapses in the amygdala can become burnt out from sending surges of adrenaline through the body. That's what accounts for the numbness people experience. They become desensitised and the amygdala no longer responds to danger as it should.

I'd given up by now and I was too weak to say no anymore, so I just gave in. It was easier to let them do it because they'd end up doing it in the end, one way or another. Hafeez was one of the very few men who used a condom. As he was putting it on, I noticed he had little black lumps on his penis.

'Are they genital warts?'

'No, they're birthmarks.'

'They look like warts.'

'They're fucking birthmarks! All right?'

Afterwards, he told me he wanted a steady girlfriend and he thought I'd be perfect for him. He said he had a son with a white girl, but they weren't together anymore. He also had a wife, but they were separated and he lived with his parents. Arranged relationships are common in Pakistani culture so, even when they want a 'bit on the side', they think long term.

Hafeez didn't think it was worth considering how I felt about this: my future, or what I had planned for my life. He expected me to move into a house that he'd arrange and have kids for him and bring them up. This man didn't even know me, but that didn't matter; all that mattered was how good I was at sex.

He saw me as a piece of white meat who was desperate and would be grateful to him. He wouldn't have to share me with anyone if I was in his house and he was in full control of me. Or maybe he had a more sinister motive. Maybe he was going to pimp me out to his friends once he had me where he wanted.

But, even though I didn't think much of myself at the time, I knew I was worth more than that – to be someone's sex slave and to have children who wouldn't know their grandparents, who their grandparents wouldn't even know existed. He thought I'd see his offer as a better alternative to my life in the SAU, but it wasn't. I told him the house thing wouldn't work, but he believed he knew more than me, was cleverer than me. He talked down to me like I was intellectually inferior to him, whereas he was really the idiot. But if I tried to argue with him, he'd shout at me and I'd shut up. What was the point? I let him think I'd do it, even though I knew I'd kill myself first.

A few days later, Imran and Shahmeel came banging on my door. I didn't want to open it, but they kept banging and shouting and I knew it was only a matter of time before they attracted the attention of the SAU staff, who were already looking crooked at me because of all the rumours and name-calling. I was afraid I'd get kicked out and have nowhere to go. So I let them in. They both looked agitated and panicky. I asked them what was up.

'The police…'

'They're raiding the houses, looking for Shahmeel.'

Now I was panicking too.

'He can't stay here!'

Imran grabbed me by the throat and shoved me against the wall.

'You want to go out there and tell them where he is?'

'No…'

'Then shut the fuck up!'

They paced up and down, talking urgently to each other in Urdu. I guess it was decided it'd be better for Shahmeel if he gave himself up. The police were at the front of the SAU by now and Imran went out to talk to them. While he was gone, Shahmeel swallowed a bag of ecstasy pills. I don't know why he did that, instead of trying to hide them somewhere. But, like I said before, Shahmeel wasn't right in the head.

The police came and took him away and I noticed that he'd dropped his asthma inhaler, so I ran after them with it. Why did I do that? He'd raped me, abused me – why would I care about his inhaler? It was because I was already past the process of being conditioned, broken – like an animal broken by its master and accepting of its fate.

Some time afterwards, I heard he'd been arrested for threatening people at ATMs and forcing them to hand over money. He got an indeterminate life sentence – a minimum tariff of nine years, with 99 years on licence. I also heard he had to spend months recovering in a prison hospital because of the pills he swallowed. The police never asked me what he was doing in my flat. I didn't see Shahmeel again until I picked him out at a police line-up and gave evidence against him in court, five years later, in November 2011.

At the end of August, my key worker at the SAU told me there was chlamydia going around with some of the girls and I should go and get checked out. I wasn't worried because I had no symptoms – I didn't know then it could be symptomless – but I still went to the clinic as a precaution.

'How many sexual partners have you had in the last six months, Kate?'

'Six.'

I lied. It was more like 20, but the doctor still thought six was a lot. The results came back a week later and they were positive. They put me on antibiotics and told me I should inform the people I'd slept with. They said I could do this anonymously by giving the clinic phone numbers, and they'd call the people and tell them they needed to go get checked.

'I'll tell them myself, thanks.'

I didn't want them to know the extent of the sexual activity in my life.

I'd passed it on to Cemal, who was able to get treatment through the prison health service. I probably passed it to Tamjeed too, but I wasn't able to contact him. Hafeez used a condom, so he didn't catch it. Shahmeel was already back in prison; and I gave someone else a leaflet and told him to pass it around and go to the doctor for a test. I don't know whether he did or not. Ali Sultan was too scary to tell, so I didn't.

When they tested me for chlamydia, they tested me for everything else too, including HIV. I'd thought about going for a HIV test earlier, after Shahmeel first raped me. But, back in 2007, they didn't have the rapid test they have now – there was a three-month incubation period – and then all the other stuff happened to me, so I thought it was pointless. If I got AIDS it would kill me and I didn't care – maybe I'd take a few of those fuckers with me.

The HIV test they did at the end of August was clear.

5

Escape?

There's a condition called anhedonia – the inability to feel pleasure in activities that are usually considered to be pleasurable. There was no enjoyment in my life. I was fatigued all the time and my appetite was all over the place. Things I used to love no longer gave me pleasure, like listening to music, or watching TV. Everything felt numb. I know now it was psychotic depression. I was delusional and the demon had taken over. I wasn't exactly hallucinating, but I did have a physical sensation in my stomach which I associated with the demon.

Moral injury describes the psychological harm that occurs when someone is exposed to, forced into, or survives events that violate their own moral compass or sense of who they are – particularly when they're made to act in ways that are wrong, degrading, or fundamentally against their values – leaving lasting shame, confusion and damage to self-identity. The idea of a demon inside me emerged as a way of externalising that damage – a symbolic representation of feeling contaminated and no longer recognisable to myself. My mind was expressing the idea that something had been put into me that didn't belong there and it had taken over my choices and my identity.

When sex is non-consensual, there's still sensation. But that sensation becomes a negative experience. What I felt every time I was raped gave me physical sensations that were interpreted negatively in my mind and that's what manifested the feeling in my stomach. I started to view this feeling as a demon inside me. I came to feel complicit in the harm and considered myself to be contaminated and my distress became organised around shame rather than fear. It manifested in the repeated internalisation of worthlessness, the belief that responsibility for the abuse lay with me and the shift from understanding the harm as something being done to me towards experiencing it as something which defined who I was.

It was May, towards the end of the summer term, when I first moved to the SAU. I was in my second year of A levels then and I had aspirations to study psychology at university. During that horrific summer of 2007, I lost all sense of reality. I wasn't thinking straight and I didn't know what my options were. At the end of the summer holidays, everyone was going back to college and I was stuck in the clutches of the gang.

My A level results came through and I couldn't believe it. I'd expected to fail everything because of the first rape and the state I was in after it. Overall, I got a C in English and a B in the first psychology exam. I got an E in biology and I had a D in sociology from the year before. Better than I expected. I reckoned I could go back to college for another year and do health and social care and retake the second psychology exam, which I'd failed. It'd give me something to live for and get me away from the SAU and the abuse for as long as possible every day.

Although I was suffering from constant trauma and self-hate, somewhere at the back of my mind was the desire to escape. I was constantly thinking about solutions, apart from suicide, even if most of those solutions weren't realistic. It showed that there was still a glimmer of hope – I hadn't completely descended into my own private inferno. Hope was still possible, the suffering might not be endless.

Escaping and getting to university turned out to be a fluke. I attended an open day at college and they told me that, as I had A levels, they wouldn't be able to fund me for another year. They passed me on to a student advisor and I told her I wanted to do psychology as a first choice, or mental health nursing as a second choice.

'Do you want to go to university this year or next year?'

I gave her a blank stare. Did she say *this* year? I laughed nervously.

'Well, this year, if I can.'

She looked at the universities where I could apply through clearing. Psychology was a popular subject and there were no places available. She looked at mental health nursing and there were loads of places. This gave me hope – a light began to shine at the end of the dark tunnel. I felt something I thought I'd never feel again – a sense of worth. But it was tenuous, fragile, and it'd have to be protected or it'd be devoured by the demon inside me. I didn't want to go to Birmingham or Wolverhampton universities, as I would be too close to my abusers. Plymouth and Aberdeen were too far away.

'What about Anglia Ruskin University, Kate?'

'Where is it?'

'It's in Essex.'

About 170 miles from Telford. Perfect!

The student advisor arranged an interview for me and got me a loan of £70 from the college to make the round trip to Chelmsford. It was nice to have somebody care about me, somebody who thought I was worth caring for. I grasped at every morsel of kindness and devoured it like a dog. It seemed, at that moment, like escaping to university would be the best thing that ever happened to me. I filled out the application form overnight, but I didn't know what to put in the personal statement. I wrote it on the way to the interview, about my work ethic and how I had a paper round and my job at Primark. I mentioned my GCSEs and my A levels and that my mother was a nurse and that I'd always been interested in psychology. I didn't know if I was saying the right things and I was worried that they'd see through me, that I was really a p***-shagger and not a proper university student. I couldn't think of anything I was proud of about myself. It's hard when you hate yourself; you don't believe that anyone could possibly see any good in you.

What I didn't realise was that PTSD doesn't fully develop until you're removed from the situation – that's why it's called "post"-traumatic stress disorder. The safety of uni would turn out to be a collapse rather than resolution. I was experiencing "imposter syndrome" and a constant fear of being found out.

At the time, universities were over-recruiting nursing students on purpose as so many dropped out. Since they intentionally over-recruited, maybe they didn't care who I was and just gave me the interview to make sure I wasn't an axe murderer or something.

I booked into a cheap hotel when I got down to Chelmsford and went to see where the university was, so I'd know where to go the next morning. I got lost and wandered about for two hours and, when I finally found the campus, the reality of it broke over me like a wave. It was a big place. The library was on the right of the main entrance – it was four storeys high and stuck out, as if checking to see who I was. The other buildings were huge too. I actually said 'wow!' to myself. I was scared and elated at the same time – optimistic and pessimistic. Could I do this? Could I turn my life around completely and start again?

On the day of the interview, I wore appropriate clothes and low heels. I felt nervous. I was so insecure and still carried those feelings of worthlessness. I told myself I didn't deserve this chance and I'd mess it up. There was a man and a woman in the interview room and I answered the questions as best I could.

'What do you know about current mental health nursing?'

My mother had a lot of nursing experience and I'd spoken to her on the phone about what I was doing. She'd told me that a lot of mental health nursing was based in the community with teams, but I mentioned hospitals first, meaning to go on to the topic of community. The man started shaking his head and this made me stutter and lose my concentration.

'I'm sorry, I meant to say that mental health is often treated in the community now.'

'What would you do if a patient was threatening and trying to get something that's not allowed?'

I wondered if this was some kind of trick question, because it was exactly what was happening with the gang in Telford. My mother always said that interviewers like it when you can use an example to demonstrate a point.

'I don't know if you can tell from my address, but I actually live in supported housing.'

The man shook his head to indicate that he couldn't tell from my address, but he seemed intrigued.

'Well, sometimes it can be difficult there. I have to stand up for myself in situations like that, and say that no means no.'

I could feel my nose growing longer. On the way back on the train, I got a call from the university saying they'd like to offer me a place. I can't explain how happy I was. If I could go back in time, I think I would have requested to do an access course to get into psychology. I still wish I'd studied psychology to a degree level. But, at the time, I was desperate, and getting the mental health nursing place was a lifeline. There was only one problem: I'd need somewhere to live.

'Could I get a room in university halls?'

'Did you not arrange accommodation before you applied?'

'I applied through clearing. It was, kind of... an emergency.'

'We'll see what we can do.'

They were able to offer me a room, but not until after the first week of term. They could arrange temporary accommodation for that week, but I'd have to pay a deposit of £200, which I didn't have. I'd applied for a student bursary, but I wouldn't get that until I actually moved to the university. It was time to talk to my mother again.

I was surprised when she agreed to help me. I don't know why I was surprised. After all, she was still my mother, still the woman she always was, still the one thing that sustained me and kept me sane. Not only did she pay the deposit, but she also paid off the £70 loan from the college. She helped me to escape.

Thanks, Mum!

I'd gone for the interview and got my place. There was a choice of levels – I could either take the Diploma course or the Degree course. I had enough qualifications for the Degree course, but I wouldn't get the non-means-tested bursary, just a student loan. In any case, the Diploma and Degree students were all in the same classes until the third year and you could transfer to the BSc (Hons) Nursing Mental Health course after two years.

But I wasn't due to start at uni until 26 September.

I still had 20 days to endure at the SAU.

I met Hakim on 11 September 2007. I'd made many mistakes, with really bad consequences, but Hakim was probably the most dangerous mistake of my life up until then. I was walking down the street when a big 4x4 car pulled up next to me. The guy inside was well groomed with a perfectly shaped beard stubble along his jaw line. He said his name was Hakim and he wanted my number. I told him I didn't give my number to strangers.

'I can help you out, Kate.'

'How d'you know my name?'

'Everyone knows your name around here. Look, I'm not like the other Pakistani guys. I'm more cosmopolitan. I have white friends and I have influence. They respect me around here.'

I don't know why I believed him. I have no explanation and I know you'll say, *'she should have known better after everything that happened to her'*. And you're right, I should have, of course. But I didn't. These days, people are more clued-up about this sort of thing, because of reports in the press and programmes on television and books like this. But, back in 2007, I was surrounded by a huge gang of experienced sex offenders and I was only 18. Nobody was doing anything about it, even though a lot of people knew what was going on. I didn't know the extent of the grooming. I thought it was just me.

I was thinking I only had a few more weeks to go here and, if this Hakim could keep the others away from me until I left, what was the harm?

Everyone has moments where they look back and say, 'Why did I do that?' or 'I should've known better'. But these people were planning my mistakes for me before I even made them. I was naïve and stupid and being set up at every turn.

Later that same day, Hakim called me and said there was a party that night and I should come to it. I asked him why.

'Because there'll be people there you should meet.'

'What kind of people?'

'White people.'

I agreed to go. I thought if I didn't, he might rescind his offer to protect me.

Hakim picked me up at 8pm and we headed out on the Telford ring road dual carriageway. I wondered where we were going and, when we got into a more residential area, I realised we were back where we started. I thought this was bizarre and it rang alarm bells. Why had we driven all that way, just to come back? I was getting a bit scared by then, but I kept reassuring myself in my mind. This man was different – he wasn't like the others. Was he?

We stopped outside a flat and I knew exactly where we were. He'd driven me all 'round the Wrekin' in an attempt to disorientate me and make me feel I was too far away to get home. But it didn't work. I was going to make a run for it, but decided against it. After all, he knew where I lived and I'd begun to realise how much danger I was in.

It was a two-bedroom, ground-floor flat and, when we got inside, I saw half a dozen other guys and a couple of women. The men were a mixture of white, black and Asian, which was unusual, but they were all connected in some way to the rapists at the SAU. I later came to realise that it was a town full of rapists, and full of rape survivors – full of victims, because the powers-that-be did nothing about the treatment of young women and the problem just grew and grew. And it still hasn't been fully addressed.

The women in the room were older than me and already very drunk – the men weren't drinking at all. Hakim poured a very strong vodka and gave it to me. I remembered the night in my flat, before Mike Nolan raped me – I hadn't drunk alcohol since. I pretended to take a sip, then made my way to the kitchen, where I leaned against the sink. Every time I got the opportunity, I poured a bit away so it looked like I was drinking. I realised by now that Hakim's plan was to get me drunk.

I almost wish he'd succeeded: what happened that night might have been less traumatic and painful if I had been.

* * * *

As the night wears on, Hakim gets me to sit on his lap and pours me another strong vodka. He knows I'm scared from the way I'm asking him questions and answering them myself.

'Why did you drive me all around the houses?' *To disorientate me?*

'Is this your flat?' *I don't think it is.*

Then he takes me into one of the bedrooms that has a bed with just a bare mattress on it. He looks at me with a sadistic leer on his face.

'Take off your clothes.'

'I don't want to.'

'Take them off, or I'll take them off for you.'

I don't really know this man – I don't know what he's capable of – so I undress. He takes his clothes off and pushes me onto the mattress. Suddenly, all the men from the living room burst in. I try to cover myself – I'm so ashamed of my nakedness. I want them to go away, but they won't.

Hakim puts on a condom and turns me over, so I'm lying on my stomach. He slips his arm under me and raises my bum up, then he violently forces himself into my anus. I scream in pain and try to crawl away, but he follows my body movement and continues to force himself into me. My head smacks against the wooden headboard and he pins me there, forcing my face down into the mattress until I'm trapped in that position and can't move. I'm screaming for him to stop because he's hurting me so much, but he won't. When he finishes, he pulls out and leaves the room.

I lie there in a state of shock, in a daze, not fully understanding where I am or what's happened. Then I realise I'm not alone in the room – the men are still there. Some of them have their penises out and are stroking themselves, ready to go next.

I search frantically for my clothes and start to get dressed. One of them comes and sits on the bed beside me and puts on a condom.

'Why are you putting your clothes back on?'

'No! No! Please, no!'

I tell him I need to go to the toilet. As soon as I get outside the bedroom, I make a run for the front door. Hakim sees me and grabs me by the arm. He pulls me back into the living room and sits me down. I'm shaking with fear and pain, trying desperately to hold myself together – trying to stay focused, because I know I'm in a very dangerous situation.

The guys from the bedroom begin to sit close to me, one by one. I'm still dopey from shock. They're taking it in turns to tell me how sexy I am and leering at me. They think I'm drunk and are trying to lure me back into the bedroom.

This white guy comes over to me. He says his name is Gazi Amir – he's half-English and half-Iranian.

'Just call me Gaz. You're from Shirlett, aren't you?'

'Yes… yes, I am.'

'I knew Alan… Alan Thomas.'

'He was my first boyfriend, when I was 16.'

'I know. You're Kate. What are you doing here?'

'I was brought here.'

'This is a sex party – didn't you know that?'

He tells me Hakim and his friend, Farzin, pick up girls from the street – he points to the two drunken women who've been off into the bedrooms several times with different men. I tell him I'm scared and want to go home.

'Don't worry, Kate, I'll get you out of here.'

But he doesn't. He leads me into the hall and then into another room.

'Listen, Kate, I had to pay Hakim to get into this party. You have to make it worth my while.'

I don't want to have sex with him, but I have to get out of here – and I've been raped by so many men, one more won't matter. I lie down and let him have straight sex, hoping it'll be over quick and I can get out of this place. But he has some kind of dysfunction and can't ejaculate. It goes on and on for ages and I just want it to end. The condom's dried out and the friction is unbearable, I can feel every dry thrust cutting at me. Every second I think he'll come and that'll be the end and it'll be over. But he doesn't and it isn't, not until it gets light outside. He finally gives up and goes back into the living room. I'm horrified. He said he'd get me out.

I try the front door, but it's locked. My flat's only a 15-minute walk away, but there's no way out. I shuffle back into the living room and sit beside Gazi Amir. I need to get out of this place and I swear at myself for believing Hakim and for putting myself in this situation.

'I thought you were going to get me out of here?'

'I will. Stick with me and no one else can touch you.'

It turns out that the flat belongs to a friend of Gazi Amir's called Leon who's there too, and he wants to have sex with me as well before I can leave. I say no way.

'Just sit on his knee for a bit.'

'No!'

Leon comes over.

'I want to fuck her.'

'I'm not doing it… I want to go home.'

Gazi and Leon are both rapists and I find out later they employed a technique called 'cockblocking', which means they trick girls into sticking with them so they can't be pushed into sex by other men. It makes them look like heroes because the girls will be desperate to be rescued. That's exactly how I feel.

Hakim is bragging about all the women and girls he's slept with. It makes me feel sick listening to him.

'Hakim means "wise king". I want every woman I've slept with to get a tattoo of my name on their breast… that way, I can mark my territory.'

I can't stand it any longer.

'I'll get a tattoo of your name on the bottom of my foot!' *So I can walk on you every day.*

Hakim is highly offended by this and jumps to his feet. To show someone the sole of your foot is an insult in Pakistani culture. He's really angry, but I don't care anymore. I know it's an insult and that's why I say it. He looks like he could kill me right there and then.

Hakim drags me into the bathroom and forces my jaws open, then he urinates into my mouth, shouting at me to swallow, taunting me and telling me how much my screams of pain turn him on when he rapes me again. Then he drags me back to the living room and flings me across the floor. I cower there, spitting and spluttering and trying to wipe the urine from my face.

* * * *

After a while, when everyone had forgotten about me, Gazi Amir stood up and came across. His voice was quiet but urgent.

'Follow me.'

He unlocked the front door and took me home. I was so grateful.

Gazi Amir was a pizza delivery man and, a few days before I was due to go to university, he was at my door with a large takeaway box. What could I do? He'd got me out of that horrible place and, back then, I knew nothing about his 'cockblocking' scam. As the evening went on, he started getting closer and I knew what he was after. I didn't want a repeat of the last time, when it took him all night, but he said that was because he'd been drinking a lot. So I gave in.

When we were on the bed, however, he flipped me over and started trying to stick his penis into my anus, just like Hakim. I screamed and pulled away. He apologised and tried to stick it into my vagina. I said no. I tried to stop him, but he was stronger and, in the end, I just gave up and lay there. It took him ages, like before, and I don't know whether he came. I was completely zoned out, not even in the room anymore. That night I felt a pain in my kidneys – an infection, a direct result of what Gazi Amir did to me. The next day I went to the emergency doctor and got antibiotics.

Like I said before, the lines between consent and dissent were blurred. Sex was something I had to do – a chore to be performed mechanically, without feeling. It was done to manage danger, reduce the threat of harm, to appease and survive.

The concept of consent became functionally meaningless because there was no choice. Even when force wasn't overt, the internal conditions required for consent were absent.

It was my grandmother's 70th birthday that weekend and I was invited to a party at her house. Everyone was there, all the family: aunts and uncles and cousins, all asking me about my flat. How could I tell them how horrible it was living there? What would they have thought of me? I got quite ill at the party and had to leave early. The next day I had a fever and was vomiting and had to spend the day in bed. I kept drinking water to flush out the infection and took the antibiotics and paracetamol. But I wanted to die. What was the point of living? So I stopped drinking the water.

I hadn't drunk anything for a day and a half and I was really dehydrated – they say once you get over being thirsty, the rest is easy – when I heard a knock on my door. I didn't want to answer it.

'Kate.'

It was my mother's voice. She'd come to see how I was and to help me pack, as I was going to uni the next day. I was light-headed and dizzy and it was a miracle I could even get to the door. My mother was a nurse and she immediately saw how dehydrated I was and made me drink – she sabotaged my plan to kill myself.

Once she'd packed my stuff and made sure I was okay, she left, saying she'd be back the next day to drive me down to Chelmsford.

* * * *

Later that night, Shahmeel's half-brother, Tajammul, comes banging on my door, looking for sex. He's been in a mental hospital because he heard voices when he stabbed a man.

'Let me in!'

'Go away. I'm sick.'

'Let me in or I'll break the window.'

'Please… I'm ill.'

He won't go away, so I have to let him in. He can see I'm sick, but that doesn't matter to him.

'What's wrong with you?'

'I have a virus. You'll catch it if you have sex with me.'

'Give me a blowjob then.'

'No…'

He forces me down to my knees. I'm too weak to stop him. He unzips his jeans and sticks his penis into my mouth. He smells foul and I'm gagging. He comes quickly and then leaves. I throw up.

****

I could still smell him years later, as if he was inside my olfactory nerves – a sensory hallucination that wouldn't go away. It made me feel sick. I'd wake up in the morning and that smell would be there, not coming from anywhere in particular, just in my nose, and I'd have to spray stuff to get rid of it. That was the last time I was abused at the SAU. It had continued right up to the night before I left for university.

My mother came for me the next day and we made the journey down to Chelmsford in Essex. I was sick several times on the way. When we got there, they gave me the keys for the temporary accommodation where I'd live for the first week. It was a small room that I shared with a nice woman in her 30s called Gloria.

Gloria was new to the area, like me, and she liked to play hockey. It was a six-bedroom, purpose-built flat, but there was only me and her staying there at that time, so we had the run of the place and a big kitchen all to ourselves. Gloria and my mother helped me unpack, then I got into bed. My mother didn't want to leave me because I was so sick, but she had to. Gloria told her she'd look after me, and she did – she helped me as much as she could on that first day. I'm so grateful to her.

My mother told me later that she cried all the way back home.

The next morning was the first day of induction and I should've taken it off sick. I tried my best to keep the fever under control with co-codamol and, despite how ill I was, I went along so I'd know everything I needed to know. This was a little bit of me, the real me, resurfacing – my work ethic – who I was before the darkness and who I am now.

There were hundreds of students and we had to walk from one lecture hall to the other and back again. I managed to keep my fever down through the first half of the day, even though I felt weak and dizzy. I was determined this would be the beginning of my new life. But when we were in our separate classes, we had to sit in a circle to introduce ourselves and that's when the world started to spin. It felt like me and the chair I was sitting on were the only things not moving and if I dared to stand up, I was sure I'd collapse.

I started to cry because I thought I was dying. One of the other students offered to take me to the campus doctor. I was already on antibiotics and there was nothing else they could do, so they told me to go back to my room and rest. It was all so surreal.

As well as the infection, I was still experiencing symptoms of acute traumatic shock. I'd been exposed to multiple traumas which were left untreated, with no intervention, no support, no protection from the aftermath. Despite being at university and having "escaped", I was experiencing feelings of hopelessness, fluctuations of mood and panic attacks. I couldn't see a future, even though I tried. Suicidal thoughts intruded and the risk to my life was increasing because my decision-making capacity had been completely eroded.

6

Metamorphosis

After a week of being ill at Chelmsford, I finally recovered from the kidney infection. It felt amazing to be away from the SAU and out of danger, after more than four months of absolute hell. There was a parade of shops right by the university: a Spar convenience store, a book shop, a pharmacy, a bank and a pizza parlour. I took a walk through the area and everything seemed to be brand new.

Chelmsford town centre was only a 15-minute walk away – it was a nice walk, past the police station, the courthouse and the cathedral. So reassuring. There was a New Look and M&S on the high street, along with Debenhams, H&M and McDonald's – even an Odeon cinema. To have all those nice places within walking distance of where I lived made me so happy! Maybe now I could become a real person again.

Little things made me smile, like the automatic light sensors in the university toilets and the blow-dryers on the wall. I'd told myself I wouldn't see Christmas and, in a way, I wouldn't. In a way, it felt like my life ended when I left Telford and now I had a new life. I'd been reincarnated. I felt as though God had helped me – I'd prayed to him, and he could see I wasn't a bad person like everyone thought I was, including myself. He'd sent me an angel in the form of the student advisor who got me into university.

Uni was great. I met all my housemates when I moved into the flat in halls after the first week – all young people like me. I immediately started to apply for jobs in town and I got a couple of interviews – one at a student bar called Edwards, which I didn't get, and one at a fast food place called Big-Burger, which I did get. I started working in mid-October, for £4.62 an hour. It was less than I'd been getting at Primark in Telford, but I didn't mind. It was all part of my new life.

I made friends in my class and I made friends with the people living in halls. We'd go to the university student bar and they had fancy dress parties there: I went as Catwoman once, and as a pirate another time – I just loved it: I loved the lectures; I loved learning; I loved the huge library; I loved setting up with my different stationery and taking notes in pretty colours. It might not sound like much to some people, but these things were massively uplifting to me. I loved the canteen, where I could have a nice lunch, and the campus coffee shop, where I could get cheap cups of tea. I loved the cherry smell of the soap they used in the dispensers in the female toilets. I met lots of people my own age – boys and girls – all studying different subjects. It was so good to hang out with nice people – it'd sometimes bring me to the brink of tears.

I loved putting my opinion across in class and asking questions in lectures. When I got my first assignments, I realised they were very similar to the ones I'd written in college for psychology. I was in my element. I even found myself helping other student nurses. It was like studying my biology and psychology A levels all over again, and I was streets ahead of everyone else. It made me realise that I wasn't stupid and worthless after all – I was bright and valuable as a human being.

Little did I know that the disciplines I was studying would soon apply to my own circumstances and would eventually help me recover from the appalling lifestyle I was about to succumb to again.

My flatmates were really nice. One of them was West African and her name was Kathleen – I guess there must've been some Irish in her as well. She taught me how to cook, so I could make more than pasta bake and spag bol. She took me to a little delicatessen where they sold stuff you couldn't get anywhere else, like spices, plantain, scotch bonnet chillies and red pepper paste that came in a jar. My skin reacted to the scotch bonnets and my fingers looked like I'd spilled boiling water over them. I wore gloves after that. The other flatmates were white girls, third-year students, and were nice too. I don't remember much about them because they finished their courses and left.

I also met some Jordanian Muslims who were doing PhDs – they used to sit out on the grass in front of the campus halls and smoke a shisha pipe. It was strange meeting Muslim men who didn't want to rape me and I was wary of them at first. But when I got to know them, they explained things about Islam to me and I realised not every Muslim was like the rapists that lived in Telford.

I loved going out on student nights with a group of mixed people my own age, even though I didn't drink. It was uncool not to drink, so I'd have lemonade or cola with ice and lemon and lime, and pretend it was alcoholic.

At Christmas, at the end of term, all the students went home for the holiday. I couldn't go home. I could, but it'd just be awkward with the noise ban and the curfew and all the other rules my mother's partner had brought with him. And I'd probably just ruin Christmas for everyone. At least, that's what I thought, but it wasn't really a problem as nursing students stayed on. Our courses were funded by the NHS and they taught us the responsibilities of being a nurse and how, when we qualified, we'd only get five weeks' leave a year. It helped prepare us for registration when we'd be fully qualified and working.

But even though there were other student nurses about, the university was strangely quiet over the Christmas holidays. It made me feel alone and vulnerable for the first time since I'd arrived in Chelmsford. I didn't know it at the time, but I was beginning to experience the more serious symptoms of PTSD. I felt like all these lovely people I met would turn against me if they knew the truth about me. How could I explain to them what happened if they ever found out? They'd behave in the same way as the people in the SAU and call me a p***-shagger. They'd point fingers and laugh at me and I'd be disgraced, maybe even expelled. I began to believe I had to be careful what I said to people – not tell them too much about my past. Things spread like wildfire on social media. I couldn't isolate myself either, as that'd look suspicious. No, I had to keep hanging out with everyone, just like I'd been doing, but I couldn't really trust anyone. No one!

When everyone came back after Christmas and the New Year, it wasn't the same as when I first came on campus. I'd changed over that holiday period and things began to get worse and worse – signs that the full PTSD was coming, as my mental state deteriorated.

I tried not to think about the abuse, but it began to play on my mind every day. Every time I walked into the reception area of the main building, which was circular and very wide, I imagined the ground was going to open up and I was going to fall into a hell below. My stomach would churn and I wanted to edge my way around the walls, my back pressed against them, and not cross the floor. But I couldn't do that. I tried to ignore it, tried to tell myself there was no big hole and I wouldn't fall in, and I'd force myself to walk across the chasm.

I was starting to feel disconnected from the other students and experiencing emotional distress. Everything was becoming surreal and I felt more and more like an imposter, undeserving of the chance that had been given to me. I would come home from lectures and be sitting on the floor in my room, watching TV or something, and I'd end up getting hysterically upset and suddenly realise I was shouting out loud at Ali Sultan to leave me alone. It would ruin the rest of the evening. I wouldn't be able to leave the room after being so upset because my eyes would be all red and puffy. I was an absolute wreck after one of those flashbacks.

The thing is, there was no routine screening when I entered university – no GP contact, no mental health assessment, no crisis pathway. So my symptoms could easily be misread as homesickness, student stress or even immaturity.

I started having nightmares where I was being chased by men. It wasn't something that had already happened; I realised later that they were anxiety dreams about it happening again. The men would be strangers I'd never seen and I'd be running away from them, through doors that I locked as I went. But the locks never worked and the men would come through the doors after me. I'd wake up in a state of shock, just as they got close enough to grab me. I'd rear up in bed, hyperventilating, my heart racing uncontrollably. I would have to fight to try to calm myself and get my breathing under control so my heart rate would slow down.

In the beginning, I didn't see these symptoms of PTSD as anything serious – they only came when I was alone. I still loved being in class and the lectures were interesting and university was my favourite place to be in the world. I also loved the company of the other students, although sometimes I felt strange, like nobody really knew me and I was some kind of fraud.

I also liked my job at Big-Burger, even though it didn't pay very well. I was on the tills and I enjoyed serving the customers; it was hard work but I was kept going because I tended to work during the busy periods. I could be dealing with 10 separate orders at a time, running around getting fries for this one and burgers for that one, milkshakes and drinks, coffee and ketchup. I loved being smiley on the tills and I always found the customers interesting. Sometimes I thought I served more people with mental illnesses in Big-Burger than I ever learned about on my university course.

I always tried to be helpful. One time there was a man with learning difficulties in the queue being picked on by a bunch of schoolgirls. The man was getting more and more distressed and started shouting at the girls, which made them laugh at him even more – until he stood on one of the tables, shouting at them to leave him alone. I went to the office and told the manager, but the idiot just threw the man out. I was horrified. He should have thrown the girls out and I told him so.

'Just serve the customers, Kate!'

Another time I served a guy who clearly had dementia. He was confused and unsteady, and I helped him carry his meal to a table where he wouldn't be bothered. I felt proud of myself for going out of my way to help him at a busy time – I saw myself as a student nurse, not just a Big-Burger crew member.

Late at night I'd get drunks and homeless people coming in. The homeless would ask for food for their dogs. We'd have cheeseburgers that were already made and, after a certain length of time, if they hadn't sold, they had to be thrown out. We weren't allowed to give them away, but I did, when the supervisor wasn't looking. It was just plain criminal to throw good food away when people were hungry. The drunks were a pain, because they'd drop their money on the floor or all over the counter. One time, this very drunk guy took out a huge wad of notes. I told him he should be careful, because someone might try to rob him. He just shrugged and threw me a £20 tip. I knew I shouldn't take it because he was clearly too drunk to be thinking straight, but I was a poor student and I needed the cash. Ethically, it played on my mind really badly and I vowed never to do it again. Later, I'd come to see it as a test from God, which I'd failed miserably – and I'd come to regret ever taking that cash.

Despite the lectures and the job, the strange feelings I was experiencing grew worse and more frequent. When I was alone, I found myself thinking about what they'd done to me in Telford and I would cry. I would be crying for a while before I even realised I was crying, because I was so lost in the memory. By the time I realised, I'd be hyperventilating and barely able to breathe. I wasn't fully aware of what I was doing. Even worse, every now and then I'd find myself talking out loud to no one and repeating the same words I'd said during the abuse and attacks I'd suffered in the SAU. I was so worked up, I'd lie on the floor or under the desk in my room and wouldn't be able to calm myself down until I fell asleep through sheer exhaustion. It was debilitating. Whatever I had to do on days like that had to be cancelled.

I started writing a diary during these episodes, to try to make sense of what was going on. I didn't know what was happening to me and it was getting more and more bizarre. Here's an entry:

'I thought the darkness was gone – the thing that was inside me, but it's not. It's still there. Every time I think it's getting better, it gets worse. It's never going to go away. I don't want to exist like this. I don't want to die, to go through the process of dying, I just want to stop existing. I don't want to be inside my mind anymore, or to be alone with my thoughts. I don't know what else to do, I've tried to be better, but I'm just as much nothing as I was

> *before. Why didn't they just hit me? I wish to God they'd just hit me instead of doing what they did. I wish they'd broken every bone in my body and left me paralysed and disfigured, than do what they did to me. They destroyed me. Hit me, please. Just hit me!'*

I started having these strange visual images that just came into my head uninvited. They're called 'intrusive thoughts' and are related to obsessive-compulsive disorder. You have the 'obsession' and then the 'compulsion' – these intrusive thoughts were part of my obsession. My compulsion was to come later, though I didn't know that at the time.

Three specific images reoccurred in my mind. An image of me cutting my own throat with a knife would pop into my head. It was very graphic and I couldn't control it. It would come at random: while I was in a lecture or on the bus. I didn't want to commit suicide anymore and I tried to ignore the images, which wasn't easy, because they were really violent.

I also had flashing images of the floor opening up in front of me and me falling down into hell – like when I was crossing the main reception area at uni. I tried to act normal when this was happening. I would tell myself it was impossible for me to fall through a hole in the floor that wasn't really there. But it still used to make my stomach flip.

The third type of image was pornographic and they made me sick. No faces, just body parts, not of any person in particular, just random images of genitalia having sex. These were the most distressing because they came at such inappropriate times, like during lectures or while I was speaking to people. They'd just appear, out of the blue – a sudden flash and I'd jump in shock.

It might sound funny to some people, to be standing there just having a chat with someone and a penis or a vagina suddenly appearing in front of your eyes, but it was horrifying to me because I didn't know what the trigger was and I had no control over it.

None of it made any sense to my brain, which was slipping into the depths of mental illness. The images made me isolate myself, so I wouldn't seem abnormal. I'd then have the panic attacks and cry and cry. I felt as if I was either on another planet and all the people around me were aliens, or I was the alien and didn't belong on this planet.

My mind was playing tricks on me and I didn't know what was real and what wasn't. One day, an African man approached me in the bank and said he liked me and wanted to take me to dinner. I immediately freaked out: my mind told me he could tell from looking at me that I was easy – that I was a slut and he could see into my soul. Another time I was walking to the library with some girlfriends and a builder wolf-whistled us. It wasn't clear if he was whistling at anyone in particular or just the whole group. My friends all looked at me.

'He must be whistling at you, Kate. He's certainly not whistling at us.'

Why would they say that? What did they know? They probably just said it as a joke, but I was becoming more and more paranoid. I wrote in my diary:

> *It's not just the Pakistanis who're bothering me now, it's everyone – asking me for sex – thinking I'm easy. Men pulling up in their cars as I walk down the street, shouting, 'I've heard about you.' Men at university trying to flirt with me. It's just everywhere, all the time! I'm never going to be able to believe any man respects me ever again.*

In the end, it felt like I had ended up on the other side of a mirror and I could see Telford through the glass, calling to me to come back. I started to believe something was badly wrong, that everything I thought was right was really wrong. Dangerously, I began to believe that I'd have to relearn everything from scratch and, to do that, I'd have to go back to where it all started. So, when I got some days off from classes, I used the £20 tip the drunk guy had given me to take a trip home to Shirlett. It was a huge mistake.

Things were very awkward when I arrived at my mother's house. Her boyfriend was still living there and the curfew was still in force. It's difficult to cope with grumpy people when you're trying to deal with your own mental health issues, and I just couldn't relax. I couldn't sleep either, because I was so close to the SAU and I just lay awake all night, worrying about it. The family dynamics had changed a lot since I'd been gone. No one spent much time downstairs anymore, so that feeling I'd loved of being close to my mother when we watched TV, for instance, wasn't there like I'd expected it to be. I'd hoped it would help me get the images out of my head. Everyone had TVs or computers or game consoles in their rooms and they spent most of the day upstairs while I was downstairs on my own.

My mother was preoccupied and her boyfriend was horrible and I felt miserable. I couldn't sleep. I felt isolated again and didn't recognise my own family. What was the point of being there? Where did I belong? Not in Shirlett, and not in Chelmsford, either. I was floating on a sea of despair, unwelcome, estranged, isolated. I had no real home to go to. I was homeless.

While you're living through the trauma, you don't experience PTSD, only afterwards. If you return to the source of the trauma, the pain of PTSD temporarily goes away. It's like being on heroin, you know it'll eventually kill you, but you need the escape it gives you from whatever psychological pain you're suffering. So I left and went into Birmingham – it was only 40 minutes on the train from Telford.

When I got there, I didn't know what to do. It was like I was in a kind of trance. It was dark and I was just wandering around the streets with no money to spend, I couldn't do anything more than that.

Then I remembered I still had Cemal's number on my phone. I decided to call him, just for someone to talk to. I knew he'd still be in prison, but just to hear a voice I recognised – to do what? I don't know. I still don't know.

'Hello.'

'Cemal?'

'No, this is Bru. Who're you?'

I hung up. Bru called me back.

'Who is this? Where did you get Cemal's number?'

'He gave it to me.'

Bru didn't tell me, but Cemal was a fugitive from prison by then – they'd let him out on overnight release and he'd run away and never went back.

'What's your name?'

'Kate.'

'Where are you, Kate?'

I didn't want to tell him, but I'd wandered into a weird part of the city. The streets were dirty and the people looked dirty, too – dodgy drug-dealer types, prostitutes, drunks, homeless people. There were rats, too, and the smell of sewage. Guys passing me on the street were giving me looks I didn't like.

'Look around you, tell me what you see.'

'There's a football stadium.'

'You're in Coventry Road. Stay there.'

Bru was in his late 20s and he told me I sounded very posh on the phone. I guess it was my rural West Midlands accent as opposed to their stronger Birmingham, inner-city accent. When he saw me, he said I looked posh as well – maybe that's why the guys on the street had been giving me leery looks. Bru took me to a halal shop and bought me chicken and chips and a can of coke. I sat in the passenger seat of his car afterwards and he was really nice to me. He took me back to his house without asking me if I wanted to go there. I didn't know where I wanted to go – somewhere I'd be welcome.

It was a shared house over a chip shop and it was dark with old-fashioned carpets. The bathroom was grimy and old and looked like it never got cleaned. There was black mould everywhere. Bru's room was big with a double bed in one corner. There was a wardrobe with a full-length mirror and a desk with a chair and a small, old-fashioned TV. All the furniture was heavy and old and looked like it'd been in that room forever. Bru told me he was a forklift truck driver, but I didn't believe him. He had three phones, so I guessed he was a drug dealer of some sort.

I should've been frightened, considering what had happened to me in Telford, but I wasn't. I was calm, cold even, as if my heart had stopped beating altogether and there was no blood pumping through my veins. I couldn't feel anything anymore. I wasn't human – I was an alien; the demon had made me this way.

I sat on the bed and he opened a little wooden box on the desk and took out a big white lump of something grainy. I'd never seen cocaine before and I watched as he chopped some off with a bank card and broke it down into a line of powder. He sniffed the line up his nose, then chopped another line and offered it to me.

'What is it?'

'*Yayo*.'

'I don't want it.'

'Why not?'

'I've never done it before.'

'Try it. It'll make you feel better.'

At the time it had no consequence for me – I didn't feel like a nurse. I needed something to make me feel better because I was going crazy. So I tried it.

The first thing I did was blow the line all over the place, because I didn't think about having to breathe in, up my nose, and not breathe out. Bru chopped another line and, this time, I did it right. It sounded kind of dirty, that snorting sound – not very polite – and I didn't realise you had to keep sniffing to get it to go down your throat.

It was stuck in my nose for ages before it all went down in a big lump. It tasted disgusting, like paracetamol – my least favourite taste in the world was paracetamol. My mother had given it to me dissolved in water when I was a child, and the taste stuck in my memory.

The cocaine made me talk a lot. Bru did another line and then lay down and closed his eyes, like he was going to sleep. I kept talking to him, even though his eyes were closed. I couldn't help it, talking and talking and talking.

'Shhhh!'

Why did he give me the cocaine if he didn't want me to talk? I couldn't understand it. I kept thinking of things to say. I talked about everything, my whole life: the SAU and university and my hallucinations. I don't think he understood any of it, and he finally opened his eyes and looked at me.

'Is Cemal fucking you?'

'He was, at one time.'

'Against your will?'

I couldn't answer that question. I couldn't remember if it was against my will or if it had been consensual. He leaned over to me on the bed and put his arm around me.

'Can I fuck you?'

I didn't say yes or no, but I didn't try to stop him either. So he did.

As I said, the cocaine made me talk and talk and talk and talk. As soon as I said the words, I forgot them. So the memory of the trauma was no longer prominent in my head, no longer at the front of my mind. That's why I kept taking the stuff, it helped me to forget – for a while. Bru was really hairy all over. I think I let him have sex with me because he gave me drugs. I knew nothing about cocaine, whether it was good stuff or bad stuff or what quantity I was taking, I just knew it eased my psychological pain.

That night, me and Bru did line after line of cocaine together until morning. Every time he had a line, Bru gave me some too. I felt that my eyes could see more than usual and the walls bent in around me and protected me. You'd think, as I hadn't done cocaine before, taking that much would've made me sick, but it didn't. I learned that my body had a high tolerance for it. The only thing that made me sick was vodka, while ecstasy pills made me suicidal.

And so began my double life – a university student in Essex, and a homeless cocaine addict in Birmingham.

7

Box-Breaking

The good thing about cocaine was, after taking a lot of it, the intrusive thoughts would disappear for days. No thoughts of any kind. I liked that. Bru seemed to have an endless supply of the drug, and he and I did it together many times. Whenever I got time off from uni I'd go up to Birmingham as many times as I could afford. I had a student rail-card, so the train tickets were £35 for an open return, but sometimes I could get advance tickets for as little as £6 each way.

In the beginning, it was always just me and Bru alone and I'd take the drug and talk and talk about the SAU and everything that was troubling me – how the abuse put the demon inside me and started my mutation from a girl into a grotesque thing. It was all that was in my head when I took cocaine, and I was obsessed. I'd forget I'd told Bru the same story the last time and I'd tell him all over again. He never stopped me or told me to shut up, but maybe that's because he wasn't listening.

In the mornings, he used to spend ages in the bathroom coughing up phlegm. I got to learn this is a cultural thing Pakistani men do, but it sounded so violent and I'm sure sniffing cocaine all night had something to do with it. I said this to him and he got very defensive.

'No, it's not the coke! It's not the coke!'

I kind of fell in love with Bru, in a strange way, even though I knew it was absurd and I knew Bru wasn't even his real name – I think he got it from a can of Irn-Bru as he used different names with different people. He sat and listened to me go on and on about my life while I was high. He never said anything about it, one way or another, but having him sit and listen was good enough for me.

Taking cocaine was probably the worst thing I could've done for my mental health at the time. It made my brain go back over the abuse at the SAU when I was high, and it affected my mind's ability to process the memories. It clouded my judgement and reduced my understanding of what happened to me. It made me more depressed and self-deprecating than I already was. After every high, I didn't want to be alive, the lows were almost unbearable – I hoped I would die. I'd sit in the railway station and think about jumping under the next train. It seemed like doing drugs was making me feel just as guilty as being raped, so I felt doubly ashamed.

As time went on, sex with a cocaine addict became even more disgusting than with the others. When Bru got high, he became incredibly aroused, but he couldn't keep it up and it took him ages to come. He thought it made him good in bed because he took longer, but actually it was torture and I just wanted him to stop. I didn't want to have my head plunged into his groin trying to suck his penis in a desperate attempt to get it hard again. But he wouldn't let me stop. I had to keep going until he got what he wanted, in exchange for what I wanted – the mental relief of the drug. He liked to 'go down' on me too, because it was taboo in his culture, but he had no idea of what he was doing and he just used to rub his beard all over me, which was really painful.

I'm not trying to be coy about it – it was a different scenario to the SAU. I was there of my own free will and I could've left at any time, or so I believed. The lure of the drug was so strong, it kept me coming back.

Bru moved out of the room above the chip shop and into a room in another shared house in Hollinswood, an area in south-east Birmingham. It was a cleaner house and there was an Asian girl sharing, Fatimah, who worked as a masseuse in a beauty salon. Fatimah was really cool and self-assured and I got on very well with her – I called her Fats, even though she had a great figure, and she didn't seem to mind. If Bru was out doing his 'drops', I'd hang out with Fats, which was cool because she was bubbly and great to talk to.

I was still only 19 and Fats and I had this crazy night getting high on ecstasy pills, dancing to music in her living room till morning. I took too many pills and felt really ill afterwards but I had arranged to meet my friend Andria, who I went to school with and who I hadn't seen for a long time. I didn't want to let Andria down because she'd been one of the few people at school who didn't think I was stupid because I was dyslexic. So I went along to meet her for a meal, even though I was feeling really bad.

'Are you ill, Kate?'

'No.'

'You look really rough.'

'That's because I took too much ecstasy last night.'

Andria was shocked. She opened her mouth, but no words came for a few seconds.

'Are you an addict?'

'Of course not!'

At least, I didn't consider myself to be one. I was taking drugs to keep my demons at bay, like taking Valium, or diazepam, or something else that might be prescribed by a doctor. Bru was my doctor and he was taking care of me.

Later, I went to a club with Fats and a blonde-haired friend of hers. The club was called Subway and Bru gave me some pills that he said were Mitsubishis, and they'd help me have a good time. I didn't like drinking alcohol, so I took one of the pills before we left and some more on the way.

When we got inside the club, I went exploring on my own and left Fats and her friend dancing. The Subway was underneath a big railway bridge and the ceiling was very high, giving it a vast, surreal feeling – especially to someone who was on drugs. I went up some stairs and through a door into an even bigger dance area, with entirely different music. I spent ages looking at the ceiling, which seemed to me like someone had flicked paint onto it and the paint was moving. I couldn't decide if it was real or not – in actual fact, it was just the silhouettes of the people dancing. I went back downstairs and through another door, into another massive dance area. The whole place felt like a maze of different rooms and it was like each room was soundproofed, with different music playing. I couldn't believe it. At one point, I walked into an area where everyone was black. They all turned to look at me when I came in, like I was an intruder, so I backed away and left.

I sat down on some sofas for a bit, beside a girl wearing a beautifully coloured dress. She accidentally burned my arm with her cigarette, but I didn't feel anything. She apologised and then asked if I wanted to go for a threesome with her and her boyfriend – nonchalantly, like it was the most natural thing in the world.

'No, thank you.'

Everything became hazy after that and I must've passed out or gone into a trance. The next thing I knew I was in a taxi with some guy I'd never seen before. He was trying to rape me on the back seat.

'Who're you?'

He didn't answer, just looked at me like I was crazy.

'Stop the car! Stop the car!'

I was screaming at the top of my voice, so the cab driver pulled over and let me out. The guy in the taxi didn't get out and the driver pulled away and left me standing there. Alone. I was disorientated and I didn't have a clue where I was. I called Bru.

'Where are you?'

'I don't know.'

'Is there a street sign?'

'I think so. It says… Bordesley Green… East.'

'I'll come and get you.'

About 15 minutes later a car pulled up. The man driving wasn't Bru.

'Who're you?'

'Bru couldn't come. He sent me. Get in.'

He said his name was Asif and he was a big man. He had a big nose and his head was either bald or shaven, I couldn't tell which. He was in his 30s and had lightish, tanned skin. His two front teeth were crooked and he had thick wrinkles in between his eyebrows, as if he were frowning all the time. I didn't want to get into his car, but I didn't want to be left on that street either.

Asif took me to a house on Stafford Road, in the Newdale area of Birmingham. It was at the bottom of the street, near a park. There were a couple of small, three-door cars parked outside that looked like they'd been there for years. They were badly vandalised – roofs caved in and windows smashed. Inside the house, there was damage on the ceiling and floor where a wall had been; it'd all been converted into bedrooms. There was a strong smell in the place, not marijuana or anything like that – it smelled of fertiliser or something chemical. The kitchen was run down and everything was dirty and falling apart. There was a microwave with a rusty hole in the top of it, a battered kettle, and there were cigarette burns in the sink, like someone had been flicking their butts into it. There seemed to be electricity, but no heating in the place. There was hardly any furniture in the sitting room, just a few wooden chairs with an old man wearing a blue turban sitting on one of them, in front of a halogen heater that wasn't very warm. I found out later that he was an illegal immigrant and didn't speak English.

Asif took me into one of the bedrooms and sat beside me on the single bed. He nudged me and started to push my shoulders down. I tried to move away.

'Where are you going?'

'I want to see Bru.'

'Bru's not coming. You must stay here tonight.'

'I don't want to.'

'Then you can go back onto the street. But you must give me a blowjob first.'

'No!'

'Bru said you would, for picking you up.'

I doubted if Bru had told him that – but then, he might have. Asif smiled at me, as if what he was asking me to do was as simple as a handshake. No big deal to a white slut like me.

'It won't take long.'

He was right. As soon as my mouth went round his penis, he came – like, immediately. He smiled again and told me he didn't want to have full sex with me, because that would be being unfaithful to his wife. Apparently a blowjob was okay, that wasn't cheating to his fucked-up mind.

Asif left me in the house and drove away. I went to the bathroom and rinsed my mouth. There were cigarette burns in the bath, too, the same as the kitchen sink. I was used to there being no toilet roll – Pakistani people never use toilet roll, they just use water and their hand. I know that might sound gross, but they think we're gross because we only use dry toilet paper, which doesn't clean properly. I guess it's okay to use your base hand, the one you don't eat with, as long as you wash it with soap and water afterwards. There was one of those funny little jug things and a bar of soap by the bath. The curtains were light blue, but they were hanging off the rail like rags.

I felt dirty and wanted to wash myself. I was shivering from the cold and the after-effects of the pills I'd taken earlier. I ran some water into the bath, but it was freezing – I just ran it to ankle height, then climbed in and knelt down. I washed my hair with soap and rinsed it with the little jug. At first I tried to pour it on quickly, to get it over with, but the freezing water hurt my head and I had to stop, get over the pain, and do it a bit at a time. I didn't have a towel, so I wrapped my hair up in my blouse. I splashed the water up over my body – it was very cold, but I could stand it. I crouched lower and washed my armpits and my face and mouth, then I cupped my hands and splashed the water everywhere. It was so cold I could see my breath and it gave me painful, aching kinds of cramps on my skin. But I was clean and it made me feel better. I liked being clean.

Once I got out of the bath and back on the floor, I realised I wasn't cold or shivering any more. I reckoned the bath had lowered my body temperature so much that the house seemed warm in comparison to the water. I was standing there naked, but not cold. I dried myself with one of the blue curtains, then went back to the bedroom. On the way I passed a bigger room and looked in. There were needles on top of a chest of drawers. Not used ones, as they had orange plastic tops, inside a sterile pack – they were obviously from a needle exchange centre. I kept walking, wrapped myself in my coat and fell asleep on the bare mattress of the single bed. Bru came for me a few hours later and took me to his place.

'Sorry about last night, Kate. I had to work.'

'Did you tell that Asif guy I'd give him a blowjob?'

'No.'

I could tell he was lying.

Over the next couple of months, my journeys up to Birmingham to see Bru brought me into contact with Asif more and more. He was a man who cruised the city streets at night in his car, on the lookout for girls who needed help and who he could 'rescue'. He came round to Bru's a lot and he brought his crew with him: Erald, a white heroin addict in his 40s who was very skinny and had no front teeth, and Blaze, a chavvy Asian teenager. It turned out that they both worked for Asif, doing 'box breaking'. I didn't know what box breaking was, but later learned it was buying prepaid phone handsets, unlocking them and selling them on, usually abroad, for a profit. The prepay subsidies reduced the cost of the handsets and the box-breakers could make a good profit, up to 50 per cent, by selling them on. Asif would get a phone call telling him what handsets to buy, then they'd go round the country, buying phones that were on specific deals, to unlock and sell on. One day he asked me to go with them.

The first time I went out with them it wasn't to 'work', Asif just asked if I wanted to come along for the ride. I thought it might be fun and take my mind off things, like a road trip around the country. They searched for Tesco, Woolworths and Argos stores and Asif gave Erald and Blaze wads of money to go and buy phones, while he and I waited in the car. I wanted to get out and have a look around the places we went to, but Asif wouldn't let me.

'This is business, Kate, not a sightseeing tour.'

At first I was happy just to tag along. Then I realised the money might be fake and I didn't want to get involved with doing anything illegal or get caught with fake money, so I was happy to stay in the car. Asif always had a list of the stuff to buy, maybe Nokia or Sony Ericsson or Samsung, but only specific models. New phones would be coming out all the time and every day there'd be a different deal on a different phone. They'd come with 20 per cent off, or with £20 credit, and those were the phones Asif was targeting. But I still couldn't figure out how he could actually make money when they were so expensive anyway – how could he sell them for more than he was paying in the shops?

After going out with them a few times, Asif gave me £200 and a list of the phones he wanted me to buy. I didn't want to do it, but I was afraid not to. I worried that I was now a witness, and they might turn nasty if they thought I was a potential threat. I had a good look at the money and it seemed real enough to me. If the money was real and all I was doing was buying phones, then what could be illegal about that?

When I went into Tesco with the £200 Asif gave me, I was nervous. It felt like I was doing something wrong, even though I didn't know what it was. There was a sign saying ONLY TWO PHONES PER CUSTOMER and Asif had told me to buy three. I asked the salesperson nicely and he let me have the three phones for £60 each.

Asif told me to say, if they asked, that I was buying the phones for my nieces and I wanted to get them all the same model to save arguments as to who'd have which one.

'And don't tell them you're paying cash until they've rung them up on the till.'

They gave me the phones and I gave them the money. Sometimes the £20 credit came as a little voucher and it was vital that I kept all the receipts. I was never sure why we had to do that. I assumed if we got pulled over by the police with hundreds of phones in the boot of the car, Asif could prove that he'd paid for them and the police couldn't confiscate them.

Asif gave me £1 for every phone I bought – on a good day I could make as much as £35. The money paid for an open ticket to Birmingham from Chelmsford with my railcard and left me with pocket money for food and bus fares if I needed it.

Pretty soon I realised I could buy more phones if I had more money: Erald and Blaze were given £500 by Asif and he only gave me £200. I told him if he gave me more money I could get more phones. But it was like he trusted Erald and Blaze more than me because they were men and I was just a girl. Erald and Blaze were both crazy and very unreliable. They were always having massive arguments in the car – Erald was a heroin addict and Blaze was just thick. Yet Asif thought they were more trustworthy than me, the one with an education and a 'posh' accent who was going to university! I told him I wanted to stop doing it and he finally agreed to treat me as equal to the others and give me £500, just like them.

I know this probably sounds like I'd turned criminal, but I honestly didn't know it was illegal. In any case, I'd lost all sense of good and bad – I'd forgotten the moral code I'd lived by when I was young that was taught to me by my mother and father. The cash helped me in the short term and the adrenaline rush took my mind off the sexual abuse for a while. This lifestyle didn't help my uni studies of course, but I somehow managed to keep both going.

I started to come up with new and innovative lies for the shop assistants – like how I was just starting up a mobile hairdressing business with some friends and I'd been given the job of buying the business phones and there were eight of us altogether. When they said it was only two phones per customer, I'd act all shocked and say I had no idea!

'Why?'

'So people don't exploit the offers by buying the phones to unlock and sell abroad.'

'Oh my God… they do that?'

'Yes, they do.'

'How do they make a profit? I'd have thought phones were more expensive in the UK than abroad?'

That's when I first realised there was something dodgy about what I was doing. Box breaking is buying or stealing prepaid phones and illegally unlocking the SIM-lock on a computer so the handsets can be used on any network. This means that they could then be sold for a higher price, even in other countries.

Once I found out it was dodgy, I started to get nervous about what I was doing. One day I asked Asif to give me something to steady my nerves, so he handed me a pill. It was 11am and by midday I was off my rocker. It was a really warm day and I started burning up in the car. I was red in the face and sweating and I felt like I couldn't breathe, cooped up on the back seat on a long journey. I was really thirsty and my head was buzzing, so I took my shoes off to expose my feet, hoping that would cool me down.

When we got to a town centre somewhere, Erald and Blaze got out of the car to go and get the phones, but I stayed inside.

'Off you go, Kate.'

'I can't do it Asif, I'm too ill.'

'You have to do it. Go and do it now!'

It was a big Tesco, like a Tesco Extra or something, with an upstairs and the ceiling was really high and I thought it might collapse down on me any second. The aisles were like a jungle and it seemed like I was on a military patrol to retrieve something that had been taken by the enemy. I got lost and couldn't find the way to where they sold the phones. Then I saw them, and the guy behind the counter looked like Ali Sultan, even though he was white and I'd never seen him before. He was the enemy. I hid in the aisle, behind some boxes and called Asif.

'I can't do this.'

I was whispering into the phone, like it was a walkie- talkie and I was calling back to HQ.

'Yes, you can, Kate. Stop being stupid!'

I put my walkie-talkie back in my pocket and kept my back flat against the side of the aisle. I thought, *okay, I'll grab some phones and make a run for it.* When the Ali Sultan lookalike guy wasn't watching, I grabbed two of those big, protective, see-through security boxes with the phones inside, but they were really hard to hang onto. I should've got a trolley but there was no time. No time! Then I saw this guy walking towards me – he looked like a manager or something and I freaked out. I was a total wreck. I ran to the nearest checkout and paid for the phones. As I was doing so, I felt a hand on my shoulder. When I turned, I saw the manager-looking guy standing behind me.

'Excuse me, Miss…'

'No, I didn't…!'

'Didn't what?'

'I wasn't…'

He looked at me like I was crazy or something. My head was buzzing like a hive of hornets.

'You can't be in here without shoes on.'

I looked down at my bare feet.

'We're not insured. If you have an accident…'

By now I'd paid for the phones, so I said sorry and took my bag and left the shop. Sweat was dripping off me as I stood with my back to the wall outside, trying to calm down and stop myself from totally freaking out. Back in the car, Asif wasn't happy that I'd only managed two phones.

'And they're the wrong ones. You'll have to take them back.'

'No way!'

So he got Erald to do it instead. That was the beginning of the end of my career in box breaking. Some time after, both Erald and Blaze got sent to prison – but not for box breaking. Erald got caught smuggling cannabis in from Jamaica, and Blaze kicked some guy half to death in a fight.

Asif needed some more worker bees so he got hold of two complete idiots called Dean and Stan. They were young white kids and they were really stupid and immature and I hated them. One day Asif gave Dean £1,000 in cash and told him to divide it out – £400 for himself and £300 each for me and Stan. When I counted the money Dean handed to me, it was £20 short.

'Hey, Dean, this money is short 20.'

'Well, it was all there when I gave it to you. You must've dropped it.'

I knew that was a lie, but Asif took his side and said he'd take it out of my wages.

That was the last time I went box breaking.

Inevitably, Bru got into trouble for owing money to the bigger dealers and my free supply of cocaine dried up, but not before I was addicted to it. I'd been going to Birmingham every other week for months to see Bru and do loads of cocaine – well, it was loads to me because I was getting it for free, and Bru kept the supply side away from me. It must've been costing him a lot of money, but I never thought about that. All I knew was, it made me feel good and kept the demon out of my head. I didn't know what deal Bru had with his suppliers, or how he was able to get away with taking so much without the threat of being killed. Maybe he was being paid with cocaine, or maybe the threat of being killed was there and I didn't know about it.

One day, when I was in my room at uni, Bru called me up. He spoke with a quiet, careful voice.

'Hey, Kate, you okay?'

'Yes, I'm okay.'

There was silence on the other end. I knew something was wrong.

'I need money, Kate.'

'How much?'

'500. Can you help me out?'

'£500? Jesus, Bru, I haven't got that kind of money.'

'Okay, sorry for asking.'

He hung up. Bru was a nice guy and I was really sorry I couldn't help him because I knew I'd sniffed more than £500 worth of cocaine up my nose. All right, I paid for it with sex, but I still felt sorry for him.

I don't know what happened to Bru regarding the money. He probably owed a lot more than £500 and was trying to spread the debt out. I met up with him a couple of times after that and he said he couldn't give me any more cocaine for free. I told him it wasn't for free.

'You know what I mean, Kate.'

Since I couldn't get free cocaine from him, I didn't see any reason to hang out with Bru anymore. I saw him briefly once or twice after that and then he just seemed to disappear and I never saw him again. I tried to get the cocaine from other sources, but it was far too dangerous, so I stopped looking.

When I couldn't get cocaine, I turned to amphetamine, which Asif called 'poor man's coke'. Asif was a drug smuggler as well as a box breaker. He gave me his number and told me to call him at any time of the day or night – if I was in trouble, he'd take care of me. After that, he owned me. The amphetamine kept me awake for days on end and made me paranoid and depressed and suicidal again, but I saw Asif as a kind of saviour, who'd rescue me when I hit rock bottom.

8

Setbacks

Once Asif had control over me, I slept in squats and lived in some terrible conditions when I came up to Birmingham. I sometimes stayed in the house on Stafford Road, which I found out used to be a cannabis farm, but was then derelict and condemned. Nobody knew where the pay-as-you-go gas card was, so there was never any hot water.

Sexual abuse was a constant thing now. It didn't even seem like abuse any more, it seemed like normal life. The men I came into contact with made me believe I was nothing more than a slut – a white whore. They treated me like a leper, apart from when they wanted sex. They wouldn't use a glass after me without it being washed first; they wouldn't smoke a joint if it was being passed around and came to me. The worst thing about it was, they wouldn't let me wash. They'd go straight to the bathroom after sex and lock themselves in and leave me on the bed, naked and dirty and gross. I'd always try to cover myself up, because I felt so ashamed. I was like a piece of tissue they'd masturbated into and, once they were finished, I was just thrown away. I was given no respect as a woman whatsoever.

I didn't say anything because I knew there was no point: I was less than human to them. I was rubbish. I used the microwave with the hole in it a lot when I was at Stafford Road. I knew it was dangerous, but I didn't care at the time. I lived in a constant state of self-loathing and didn't care if the microwave killed me. It was what I deserved. As a matter of fact, I probably used it on purpose and hoped something would happen to me. Cancer would've been better than the diseased life I was leading.

Why was I doing this? I wasn't really aware of the strange compulsions I was experiencing as a result of the PTSD – compulsions to relive the abuse, over and over. In fact, I didn't understand anything about my behaviour until I started going to therapy in 2015, several years later. Why did I keep coming back to these people? Why was I taking drugs? I never took drugs before, I never drank, I never even smoked. I hated it. So why was I doing it? Back then I put it down to who I'd become. I wasn't the me before – I was the new me: the slut, the whore, the p***-shagger.

I was a university student down in Essex during the week and a denizen of the night in Birmingham whenever I had the opportunity. I mixed with the wrong people, the homeless, the prostitutes and the rats. I hung out in halal chicken and chips shops – on Coventry Road and Alum Rock Road and Green Lane and Bordesley Green and Ladypool Road – smelling the putrid dustbins as I shuffled past graffitied shutters and fly-tipped old sofas and beds. I got to know the seedy side of Birmingham pretty well, the densely Pakistani and Yemeni areas, where the homeless sat on the filthy ground with a tin and a sign in Arabic in front of them, begging for money. At least they only begged – they didn't do what I did. They had some self-respect left. Sometimes it was like living in a foreign country – and I belonged there. I was an alien in my former country, my old culture, so this was my new country and culture now.

If things got too desperate or dangerous, I'd call Asif and he'd come rescue me. He'd bring me to Stafford Road or to a room over a garage close to Northland Street. It was owned by some friends of his called Akram and Hazma, who were brothers and who had a car repair shop underneath. It was a tiny room, not really fit for people to live in. I think the old guy with the blue turban probably stayed there before they moved him to Stafford Road, because there was a little shrine with pictures of holy people in a circle. I imagined what a sad life it must've been for him there – a halogen-cold, stone-grey, heart-sick life. I was glad he'd moved on.

There was a shabby old sofa that looked like Asif found it in a skip. It was what's called a 'narrow-boat sofa' – very thin, and it could be laid out flat into a bed with storage underneath. It wasn't very comfortable as a bed because of the big lump in the middle where the two sides met, and I had to sleep across it. There was a river behind the garage called the Rea. It ran through the middle of the factories and just had brick walls on either side instead of grassy banks. It didn't look pretty like rivers usually do; it was brown and full of rubbish, and probably rats as well.

The room was like a little dungeon. The one window was old and didn't close properly and let in a polluted breeze from the river. There was no bathroom, but there was a toilet cubicle and shower downstairs for the garage use – there was no towel, just blue-rolls that cleaners use. Asif would find me places like that to stay in when I needed sanctuary – and I'd have to give him a blowjob for it. Then I'd go take a shower and dry myself with the blue-roll.

I was sometimes too messed up from drugs to make the train journey back to Chelmsford. Once, when I met Hafeez, Cemal's brother, we did some drugs – I can't remember what. I was out of it at the station on the way home and Hafeez was worried about me making it back to Essex. Not because he particularly cared about me, but in case something happened to me and he got into trouble.

'You can't do the journey, Kate.'

'Then I need somewhere to stay.'

'You can't stay with me… my wife…'

'You told me you separated.'

'Did I?'

Hafeez made a call and a guy named Suri came to the station and picked me up and he took me to a pizza place. I thought maybe he was going to buy me food or a soft drink to try to bring me round, but he only fed himself and ignored me. Then he took me to a house and tried to have sex with me. I kept moving away from him and he kept moving after me.

'No sex, no place to stay.'

I kept moving away, so he grabbed me and dragged me out and put me back into his car. He drove to Coventry Road where he threw me out onto the street. It was late and I was terrified. I looked like a prostitute and guys were coming up to me – so I called Asif. He came and took me to the room over the garage – for a premature ejaculation blowjob. It was better than the other alternatives.

I was stuck in a loop, replaying the memory of the trauma from the SAU, both consciously and subconsciously, and my behaviour was following that loop. All behaviour is really a form of communication, an expression of what's on your mind, and what was playing in my mind at the time were the rapes – over and over again.

One day I got a call out of the blue. I was in my bedroom at uni and the number calling was withheld. I answered the phone.

'Hello.'

'Hello, is that Kate?'

'Yes.'

'I am Dabir.'

I'd never heard of anyone called Dabir and I was about to hang up.

'You like *yayo*?'

'Who told you that?'

He wouldn't say.

I thought it must've been Bru. Dabir told me he had plenty of cocaine and I reckoned this was Bru's way of making things up to me – he was putting me in touch with another free supply. I didn't agree straight away, but after a few calls and conversations, I arranged to come up to Birmingham to meet Dabir.

I went up on the train a couple of days later and he met me at the station. Dabir was a big man, muscled up like a bodybuilder. He was about 40 and had a bald head and a big nose. He took me to a house in Small Heath and, as he was driving, I noticed a big round scar that took up nearly all of his forearm.

'How did you get that scar?'

'Shotgun.'

'Wow, that must've been scary?'

He didn't answer, just flashed me a look that told me I shouldn't be asking questions about it. The place he took me to was another doss-house, just like Stafford Road. We did a few lines of cocaine, but it wasn't as good as the stuff Bru used to have – it made the back of my throat feel sticky and I kept having to suck my tongue back to unstick it. Not very nice.

* * * *

We go upstairs to the bedroom and its crap – I'm used to this by now

– bare mattresses on the floor; paper peeling from the walls; grimy windows you can't see out of; the smell of mould and stale decay. We get naked – he doesn't have to make me, I know what's expected in return for the cocaine. The sex is rough and perverted. He wants to sniff lines off my vagina and he wants me to sniff lines off him, which I do. His erection keeps going down and he keeps making me get him hard again, but I'm not really getting anywhere. Then he decides it's hard enough, when it clearly isn't, and he tries to put it inside me and fails. He asks me to give him a blowjob to make it hard again. Which I do. It's awful. He takes ages to come and I notice another big scar on his leg, just like the one on his arm. He finally comes and I think, *thank God for that.*

****

When he finished and we were lying there, I asked him about the scar on his leg – was it from the same shotgun? He just stared ahead and didn't answer me. I got a terrible feeling that I was in real danger. From the look on his face, I felt like he could flip at any moment and beat me or even kill me. I stopped talking mid-sentence and shut up completely. I told myself to just stay still and silent, not to move. We lay like that for a while, then he got up and told me to get dressed and we'd go and get some more cocaine. We went back out to his car and he drove me to a house in Billesley. I was really scared now. How had I put myself in this situation? How had my longing for cocaine got me into this? Was I completely crazy?

The guy who owned the house was called Hak. He was a tall, skinny, Asian man and he looked a bit camp in a scruffy way. He looked me up and down as he walked around me.

'Hello, hunny-bunny.'

This annoyed me and, even though I was scared of Dabir, I wasn't going to stand for that.

'I'm not your hunny, nor your bunny.'

Hak gave me a shocked look and I didn't know what was coming next. Then he began to laugh. Dabir laughed too.

Hak was another drug dealer. People were turning up at the house and he was measuring stuff out on a set of scales and selling it to them. He was smoking big spliffs of cannabis all the time while he was doing this. I asked if I could make myself a cup of tea and he pointed to the kitchen. I love tea and my throat felt funny after the stuff I'd sniffed with Dabir.

There was a plastic ice-cream box on the draining board with a spoon in it. I don't know what I thought it was – maybe something sweet to take the taste of Dabir out of my mouth. So I picked up the spoon and took some.

It tasted disgusting and chemical and I realised it was some kind of drug someone had been making in the kitchen. I could tell it wasn't cocaine because it didn't make my lips go numb. Then I started to panic – what had I taken? Maybe it was ketamine or something that would paralyse me. Oh no! I looked round and Hak was standing behind me, smiling.

'Crank.'

Which meant amphetamine. I was relieved.

Hak wasn't parting with any cocaine, even if he had some. I knew I'd been brought here under false pretences and I was annoyed for letting myself be tricked like that. I needed to get out of there and call Asif. It was becoming apparent to me that Dabir was some kind of nutcase. He was suggesting we had a threesome – him, Hak and me.

He had a very aggressive and dominant personality and I could tell Hak was scared of him, just like me.

I didn't want to do this, but what choice did I have? I thought they might be bisexual and might fuck each other and leave me alone – but they weren't, and they didn't. Dabir bent me over and took me from behind, while Hak stood in front of me and expected me to give him a blowjob at the same time. This was really awkward and it didn't work because I was being pushed and thrust from behind and Hak couldn't keep my head steady enough. It took forever and I was feeling sick by the time it ended.

Dabir had the same look on his face after the sex as before. I was still and silent again, and so was Hak. After a while he got up, dressed and left the house. He didn't take me with him. I stayed in Hak's house that night and he let me sleep in his big king-sized bed, which was luxury compared to some of the places I had been left to sleep in. Hak asked me how I came to be with Dabir, and told me I should be very careful around him because he was a woman beater. I'd already guessed that and considered myself lucky to still be in one piece, or even alive. He apologised for the threesome and said he wasn't really comfortable doing that, but Dabir pushed him into it.

In the morning I felt twitchy for cocaine. I'd been promised some but hadn't got it. I asked Hak if he had any. He said he had.

'Can I have some?'

'No. It's only to sell. I can't afford to give it to you.'

I felt ashamed for asking. I shouldn't have asked. What had I become, begging these people for drugs, letting them do the things they did to me? After I went back to Chelmsford, Dabir rang me again a couple of times.

'I have some pukka *yayo*, girl.'

But I stopped myself from believing him – even if he had, it was too dangerous to go anywhere near him. I was polite and put him off every time he rang, saying I had to study or some other excuse. After a while, he stopped ringing and I never saw him again.

But now, when I was going up to Birmingham, I was hanging out with Hak as well as Asif. Hak and Asif didn't know each other, so sometimes I'd hang out with Asif and the next time I'd hang out with Hak. I told Hak to let me know if Dabir was coming round and I'd make myself scarce. Hak always had plenty of friends around, girls as well as men. They'd go upstairs and have sex. I was expected to do that too, and I did. It was normal now – a normal part of what my life had become. It didn't bother me anymore. It was just mechanical. I still felt used and depressed after it, and I still hated myself and believed I was worthless. But I had no other alternative. I couldn't go home: no one wanted me there. University was where I studied, but it had become a lonely place and when I was alone the craziness came back and I had to hide from it under the table. At least in Birmingham I had the company of my own kind – worthless people who probably hated themselves, just like me.

Some of the men were horrible to me in the bedroom and made me do horrible things. If they did too much cocaine, they wouldn't be able to get it up – the girls called this 'coke dick' – but none of the men ever admitted to having it. They'd make me give them blowjobs and they'd take their sexual frustration out on me, grabbing my head and forcing it to go faster and harder to get them aroused. They were all disgusting drug addicts with sexual perversions and dysfunctions. They lived horrifically unhealthy lives and it showed. They rarely used a condom, so I had to keep getting myself checked out because I had no idea if they had infections or not. I had to have anal sex a lot – I used to keep little sachets of lube so it wouldn't hurt as much as it did with Hakim. Sometimes they made me put their penises in my mouth after they'd been in my anus. How defiled can one person be? How utterly degraded and desecrated? And yet I kept going back.

Back.

And back.

Hanging out at Stafford Road with Asif was just the same, only colder and lonelier than at Hak's. Asif would have his friends round and we'd sit in the living room smoking marijuana or taking amphetamine – and, one by one, I'd have to go upstairs with these men. They'd come to the house and I'd give them blowjobs, sometimes 10 or 15 men at a time. They'd wait in a line for it – it was called a 'line-up'.

By this time, I wasn't even doing much cocaine anymore – I'd left Bru and didn't want to go near Dabir. I didn't like how it made me, like I was some kind of beggar, on my hands and knees for a line. I felt sort of safe with Asif and Hak, even though I still had to have sex when I was with them. But, in my distorted brain, I believed they were looking out for me and wouldn't let anything really bad happen to me – even though they did.

Nobody cared about me, I was like a prostitute, but without getting paid. This wasn't what I saw my life becoming, back when I was the 'me' before. And it wouldn't have been that way if I hadn't moved close to a family of rapists in a town where it was totally normal and I was surrounded by people who considered it normal and blamed me – kept blaming me, until I blamed myself.

I began to believe I had a 'role' and a 'place' when I was with these men. I believed that as long as I knew my place, they'd like me and protect me from whatever it was that had attacked me in Chelmsford, back when I had the nightmares and mind-flashes and blackouts and hyperventilating and screaming at the walls. I was being treated appallingly but I was keeping the crazy symptoms at bay – just about.

I didn't worry about my appearance. My skin grew patchy and I started to put on weight from eating chicken and chips all the time. My hair was lank and my throat felt sticky. I was drifting further away.

I'm not proud of this time in my life, but it happened. I can never fully explain why, but it happened. I got passed around between a lot of men, more than I can even count, and I was drawn deeper and deeper into a cycle of abuse and exploitation. How could someone like me, considered to be an adult, be brainwashed and controlled like that? On top of that, while this exploitation was going on, I was still attending university and studying for my BSc in mental health nursing. But it was a struggle. The evil thing inside me was gradually getting the better of the me who wanted to learn and move on and be a different person.

It was a battle of good against bad.

And bad was winning.

9

Marrakesh

It was 100°F in Marrakesh and I was lost in the maze of backstreets off the Jemaa el-Fnaa. I'd ducked down there from the square looking for a loo because the lamb they'd cooked back at the apartment had given me diarrhoea and I needed to go really badly. They wouldn't come with me – just laughed and made fun of me like they'd been doing since we left England two days ago. And now I was trying to keep my bowels from exploding everywhere.

They mostly spoke French in Morocco and I knew a little bit of the language because I'd got a D in French when I'd done my GCSEs three years before. I told Asif this back at the apartment, when the Pakistanis were talking to the Moroccans in English. The Pakistanis didn't know any Arabic and the Moroccans didn't know any Urdu.

'Maybe I can be, like, an interpreter?'

'Don't be fucking stupid!'

'I know I'm not fluent, but…'

'No, you're not fluent.'

Then he gabbed on in Urdu for half a minute to make his point.

'That's being fluent. So shut the fuck up!'

'I didn't say I was fluent, I just…'

'Shut up!'

Asif wasn't the worst of them. He came for me and got me out of trouble when I was strung out in Birmingham, but now he raised the back of his hand, trying to prove he was a man in front of the Moroccans. I shut up and shrank back on the sofa. I'd learned when to talk and when to keep quiet. It could be frustrating at times, because I knew I was cleverer than any of them. But Asif thought I was stupid – they all thought I was stupid. So I kept my mouth shut.

As I listened to them try to communicate, I wondered how I'd got there – to Morocco. If I was that clever, why had I allowed myself to be manipulated like this again? Okay, there was the trauma and the PTSD I didn't know I had, but there was really no easy answer, none that anyone would understand. I had no choice. Well, I did have a physical choice; it wasn't like they kidnapped me and threw me in a sack and didn't let me out till we got to Casablanca. No, the hold over me was psychological. They'd degraded me to the point where I'd become this sex thing – this thing that wasn't human, but just an object, to the point where I believed that's what I was.

I finished the box breaking with Asif a few months back. I was 19 now and sick of the dual life I'd been leading. There had to be more – not like bigger breasts, or a bum like Beyoncé, or a record deal with Big Dada or that kind of superficial expectation. I wanted to see things, to experience things, different things – countries, people. Like when I was in an art gallery once and there was this picture of a man at an old gas station in America and he had such an interesting face. I'd always been fascinated by people and what made them tick, even as a girl at Rainbow 2000 – why they did the things they did.

When we first arrived in Morocco, this Yusuf guy met us off the plane at Menara Airport. It was empty and hot outside and the air was sandy. The sunlight was different too, more yellow than in England

and, although the situation I was in was dangerous and unstable, I was still looking around me and taking things in.

Yusuf drove us to the apartment. There were lots of old cars and scooters and the traffic was crazy and I worried that some of the wacky-racers would crash into us. There were stray cats everywhere, crossing the streets and down alleyways and on the rooftops. They were light brown and dirty and skinny, as if they all came from the same tawny mother-cat. The streets were covered in dust and it was blowing about in circles like little tornadoes. Yusuf told us that beggars were part of the culture and it was rude not to give them a bit of money and we should have our spare change ready. The traffic slowed down as we drove further into the city and the beggars started coming up to the car and the guys I was with gave them a few *dirham*.

A really old man came up to my window. He was made of wrinkles and one of his eyes was missing; there was a big hole where his eye should've been and the socket wasn't sewn up or anything. I stared at him and he stared back at me. I was totally fascinated and wanted to take his picture. But the car drove on and he was lost.

Asif had told me he was going to Morocco with these Pakistani guys called Moz and Ramzan, who I knew from Stafford Road, and some black guy I didn't know at all.

'I want you to come too, Kate.'

'Why?'

'You like to see new places and people, don't you?'

'I can't afford it.'

'You won't have to pay for anything. You just need a bit of spending money.'

He told me they were going over to collect a van Ramzan had left there and, according to the law in Morocco, if he didn't pick it up soon, it would start costing money in tax. We'd fly over and drive back in the van, up through Spain and France and back to England on the Dover ferry. I thought it would be the trip of a lifetime and I'd see loads of stuff I'd never seen before.

Normally, a smart girl like me would've found that story a bit suspicious. And I did. But I was completely dehumanised by this time and the abuse I'd been through had totally messed up my brain. The world made no sense to me anymore. The place I was in was surreal and smoky and it was hard to see straight – and even harder to be as smart as I know I am now. Asif was still keeping the others away from me – even though he was always looking for a blowjob as a reward – and it was like I owed him something. I know if I'd said no, he still would've blackmailed me into going, if that's what he really wanted. So, even though I had a choice. I really had no choice.

I was still working part-time at Big-Burger and I didn't have much money, but I scraped together £120 to bring with me for 'spending'. They bought one-way tickets from Gatwick that cost £30 each with EasyJet, and we were to fly out at 7.30am on 27 August.

I travelled down to Gatwick on my own, so you can see I wasn't a prisoner or anything like that. People use that word 'groomed' like it's having your hair done and your nails painted and it's a misleading term: 'broken' would be a better word for me, or 'mentally dehumanised', 'spiritually deformed', 'brutalised'. I had freedom of movement in a physical way, but my chains were psychological. I was no more free than if I had a rope around my neck.

I sat next to Asif on the plane and told him I wanted to be a better person. I felt like I could trust him, even though I knew he was just using me. I wanted to talk to him about what had happened at the SAU and what was still happening. About how I was continuously being used and abused at the house in Stafford Road and other places. I wanted to talk about the demon Shahmeel had put inside me and how it was getting bigger and more evil every time they raped me. How I felt like I was going crazy and didn't know what to do about it. But he only wanted to talk about himself and how he'd escaped prison for drug dealing.

'I don't want to have sex in Morocco,' I told him.

'With who?'

'Anyone.'

'Even me?'

I didn't answer his last question. He knew I had no choice and if I said, 'Even you', it wouldn't mean anything. He'd just make me do it no matter what I said. He looked at the others and they grinned, like they knew something I didn't. At that moment I felt hated by everybody – and I found I didn't care anymore. I didn't have any respect for myself, so how could I expect others to respect me? I was worse than a whore because I did it for free. I wasn't even worth paying for – so what did that make me? There was no word for it, just an image inside my head: a diseased animal.

The apartment was in a large block and a few floors up. It was two apartments really – we had one and the Moroccans had the other, facing ours. It was tiled from floor to ceiling and had a lounge, two bedrooms, a bathroom and a separate toilet. I'd been in far worse places. The walls of the lounge were lined with big sofas and there was a round table in the middle, covered with a blue velvet cloth. Asif took £80 of my Big-Burger money to cover the rent, even though he'd told me the trip would cost me nothing.

I was the only woman in the room and, when the Moroccans came in, they shook everyone's hand except mine. Asif told me that, in

Islam, it was forbidden for men and women to touch a member of the opposite sex who they weren't related to – so, traditionally, they shook hands with the men and nodded to the women.

How hypocritical, I thought. *It doesn't stop them sticking their dicks up me when they feel like it, even though I'm not related to any of them.*

We drank Moroccan tea and smoked Moroccan hash and they cooked a big pot of lamb in the kitchen. Two of the Moroccan men were paying a lot of attention to me, even though they didn't shake my hand, and I knew what was on their minds. I just hoped Asif would keep them away from me. I was used to being ill-treated sexually, so I gave them one-syllable answers when they spoke to me, as a defence mechanism, and I didn't smile at all. To my relief, they seemed to get the message and left me alone after a while.

The next day was Friday and all the men went to the mosque. I stayed in the apartment on my own. I took a shower and sat on the balcony, listening to the *Adhan* – the call to prayer – echoing from somewhere I couldn't quite pinpoint. It seemed to reverberate through the whole city. I could feel the vibrations inside me and I wondered what I was doing in this strange place with these strange men. Why did they want me here? There had to be a reason and it wouldn't be a good one for me. I'd known it before I came and tried to understand what compulsion was forcing me to be so self-destructive. Okay, I liked to see different things that weren't part of my normal experience, but I'd been badly abused by these people and yet I was still here with them. I told myself if I tried to get away from their influence they'd come after me and kill me, as the others had threatened to at the SAU. But it was different now: I had freedom of choice since moving to Chelmsford, and I didn't have to keep coming back.

The thoughts began to resonate in me and I looked over the balcony wall, down at the stone courtyard below. It was calling to me, the hard ground, whispering to me. But, just then, an Arab man appeared on a balcony opposite with a prayer mat. I watched him and listened to the *adhan*, and a kind of peacefulness came over me. The feeling was significant in some way that I didn't understand, but the suicide spell was broken. The stones stopped calling.

The men were gone most of the day. When they came back, they had two Arab women with them who weren't very friendly to me. They were hanging on the Moroccan guys and one of them said she was an English teacher. When the lamb was ready, they served it up on a big dish. It was put on the table in the middle of the sofas and everybody ate from it using *khubz* – a coarse flatbread. Muslims only eat with the right hand because the left hand is used for wiping the bum. Yusuf said I could rip the bread with both hands but only put the right hand up to my mouth.

I'm left-handed, so I made a proper mess of this and got food all over my fingers and down my dress. But I was very hungry and the lamb was tasty, so I ate as much as I could once I got the hang of getting it into my mouth and not on the sofa. I was the last to finish and they said the last to finish had to clean up, especially as I'd made such a mess. I didn't know if this was a true tradition or whether they just made it up. The Arab girls didn't help me, and it just reinforced my feeling of being a servant to these men.

The next day we were all in Marrakesh and the lamb was doing the rumba inside my stomach. I spoke to Asif.

'I need a toilet.'

'There isn't one.'

'There must be somewhere…'

'Go and find it, then.'

And that's how I got lost in the side streets and bazaars and souks. I was wearing an ankle-length dress, but there weren't many tourists in that part of town and my red hair was conspicuous amongst the *hijabs* and *niqabs* and *khimars*. *Think, Kate, think! What's the French?*

'Où sont les toilettes?'

Responses came from some people who pointed in various directions.

'Sir nishan.'

'Dor 'al limen.'

'Dor 'al liser.'

But I didn't know any Arabic.

Meanwhile, I was clenching my bum cheeks tighter and tighter until, finally, I came across what looked like a market toilet in a kind of wooden shack. A couple of men shouted at me as I went inside.

'La tadhhab 'iilaa hunak.'

'Annaha laysat jayidatan bain sbt lk.'

I only got the gist of what they were trying to tell me after I saw the hole in the floor, overflowing with sewage. The stink was enough to make me go blind. I ran back out past the laughing faces until this guy caught hold of my arm.

'Toilet?'

He spoke English. Thank God!

'Yes, toilet, please!'

He took me to a place with a proper toilet, in a café. When I came out, he was waiting for me.

'You like some coffee?'

I was anxious to get back to the people I knew, even if they were criminal abusers.

'What? Here? No thanks.'

'Up there.'

He pointed to a window above the stalls.

'Definitely no thanks!'

'I buy you something.'

He took a long necklace off one of the stalls and put it around my neck. As he did so, he rubbed the back of his hand against my breasts. I pulled away, but the beads round my neck nearly choked me – I was like a dog on a leash. He pointed to the window again.

'I live there. You like to see?'

'I have bad diarrhoea… and my period.'

That didn't work with this guy.

'Come and see.'

Maybe he didn't understand the word 'diarrhoea' – maybe I should've used interpretive dance.

He grabbed my arm again, keeping a tight hold on the beads around my neck, and started to lead me towards his flat or apartment or shack or tent, or whatever he'd got up there. People around us didn't seem to mind, as if it was perfectly normal for him to be dragging a girl by the neck to somewhere she didn't want to go. Then, as luck would have it, the string holding the beads snapped and I pulled away from him. He came after me. I moved quicker – so did he. Then I was running, dodging between the stalls, looking back to see if he was still following. He was.

I saw a street that looked familiar and ran down it and found myself back out on the Jemaa el-Fnaa. I saw Asif and the others amongst the snake charmers, medicine men and tooth pullers and I ran across to them. The guy following me stopped. He stood on the edge of the square and looked across at me. His mouth was twisted in a snarl.

I wished I was stronger – but I wasn't strong at all. I was battered and broken inside and every time something like this happened it cut me deeper. I didn't tell Asif or the others about the guy who chased me. We got back to the apartment in the early evening and Asif came up to me casually. The two Moroccans were across the room. I assumed that, as the Arab women were with them, I'd be safe from them, but now they were leering over at me and it was unsettling.

****

'You got to choose, Kate.'

'Choose what?'

'One of them.'

'No!'

'Yes.'

All the time I'm thinking Asif will protect me, but he isn't going to. He's going to give me to them. I'm saying I don't want to pick one and Asif's saying they'll both rape me if I don't. I start to cry and they start to laugh, like it's a big joke to them. I don't want to choose either of the Moroccans – I don't want to have sex with anyone and I don't like the way they're leering at me. Asif and the others are grinning, like they knew all along this would happen; like they brought me, not to see any sights, but for their friends to fuck. I haven't seen any van yet and maybe I'm part of whatever deal they're doing? Maybe they're not going to take me back with them.

I start to panic and Yusuf comes over and grabs me, dragging me into the bedroom. I get the feeling I'm sinking, that my mind and my soul and my whole existence have sunk to the very bottom of a thick dark pool. I stop struggling in the bedroom because it's pointless and I'll only get hurt. I've been here before. I know struggling and screaming excites some men even more. I take my clothes off and just lie on the bed. I don't speak and I don't smile. I want him to know this is against my will, but I also know he won't care. He undresses and is about to get on top of me.

'Condom?'

'What?'

'You must use a condom.'

'No.'

I don't care anymore. I have no care for myself. I'm the dirty one and he's the idiot if he doesn't want to protect himself. If he had any idea how many men had fucked me – how many had raped me. I could have any kind of STI, or maybe he thinks Asif wouldn't bring him a girl with venereal disease. I take the pill, so I'm not going to get pregnant and with my polycystic ovaries, there's no chance of me falling for a baby.

I switch off while Yusuf is having sex with me. I think about my childhood and school and my family that's fallen apart and I feel so sad. So forlorn. When he's ready to ejaculate, he pulls out of me and comes all over my stomach. He obviously doesn't want me to get pregnant. He lies beside me and speaks to me in French – something about his wife and children and a farm they live on – like we're lovers or having an affair or something, not like he just raped me. I don't want to know.

* * * *

I felt like shit. Again. I told him I just wanted to be alone and he left the room. I went to the balcony and cried. Again. I felt I didn't want to live like this anymore. Again. The stuff that happened to me – the things I'd done. I shouldn't be alive. I should be dead. The men who raped me at the SAU should've killed me. They were cowards for leaving me alive – that was the worst thing they did to me. The human mind can only take so much; it wasn't supposed to cope with all this.

I climbed onto the wall and looked down at the stone courtyard below. I was barely able to breathe. It was a long drop and it'd definitely kill me. I imagined my body lying broken at the bottom and the evil thing coming out of me – rising out of my dead body like black smoke.

I'd be clean again. Myself again.

Could I jump without screaming?

The police would come and Asif and the rest of them would all get into trouble, get arrested, maybe go to jail. Maybe not. Maybe they'd say they didn't know me, that I was just some crazy tourist. Drunk. On drugs. I started to lean forward. Further. Further. I closed my eyes. Hands grabbed me. It was Asif.

'What the fuck are you doing?'

Yusuf raped me several more times while I was in Morocco, but it was just mechanical for me – something I had to do for being stupid enough to go there in the first place. A penance. On Saturday night everyone went clubbing, but I wasn't in the mood for dancing about and pretending I was having a good time. Asif was worried I'd go over the balcony so he left the English teacher who couldn't speak much English to watch me. He didn't have to – the moment was gone, and I wasn't going to try suicide again. At least, not here.

****

Around 11pm, the Moroccan who didn't get to rape me comes back alone. He tells the so-called English teacher to get lost. I run to the bedroom and lock the door. He's outside banging and shouting.

'Aftah albab! Aismahuu le fi!'

When that doesn't work, he switches to French.

'Ouvre la porte. Laisse-moi entrer.'

But I don't let him in and he gets violent and starts bashing at the door with a stick or something – I can't tell from inside the room. I'm praying the door doesn't give, but the wood is thick and, after a while, he gets fed up and leaves. I say a little prayer to myself, then I fall into a fretful sleep.

They return in the early hours and bring a young prostitute with them. They wake me up with their noise and I come bleary-eyed into the sofa room. The prostitute is young, no more than 15. She has long black hair, hoop earrings and tight clothes, and she looks scared. I can see Asif's angry about something – probably because I wouldn't let the Moroccan into the bedroom. He's bragging about how they all took turns with the young hooker in the back of the van. It's the first time this elusive van's been mentioned since we left England.

'Better than blowjob lips over there.'

That's what Asif calls me sometimes when he's angry – 'blowjob lips' or 'horse'. The others laugh. I don't care. I'm too tired to care. I feel sorry for the girl but there's nothing I can do for her. Then Asif orders me to perform with her while they watch.

'No!'

'Do as you're told!'

'No…'

He catches me by the hair and throws me onto the floor in the middle of the room. The young prostitute approaches and we perform in a 69 position and this gets them noisily excited – shouting and laughing and clapping. I can't remember how many times I'm raped that night, or by who. It's almost daylight when I crawl back to the bedroom and lock the door. The next day, the young prostitute's gone. I don't know where.

* * * *

On Sunday I was treated like a servant again. I carried some clean glasses from the kitchen with my fingers inside them and this upset the men, because it's considered dirty or unclean or something, and I had to take them back out and wash them again. I could see the ridiculous double-standards of these guys. They had all these 'cleanliness' customs from their religion, yet they'd fuck me without a condom, against their religion – a girl who'd had sex with more than 50 men. They didn't see the hypocrisy. I asked myself how I could have respect for people like that, but I didn't have respect for them. The problem was, I didn't have respect for myself, either.

Monday was the last day in Morocco and I finally saw the van. It had six seats and a sliding door and it looked more like a minibus. It was just an old banger and I couldn't understand why they needed to come over here and bring it back – it'd have been cheaper to just leave it. Asif said the Moroccans would get into trouble if they did that. I was physically and emotionally exhausted by now and I just wanted to go home. I told Asif I had a headache and he got out a packet of paracetamol and gave me one.

'One's not enough.'

'It is.'

What I didn't know was that the tablet was ecstasy, not paracetamol.

I sat at the back, behind the men – another custom. Like in the mosque. In Islam this is to respect women, as praying involves bending down and they have more privacy at the back. But some men misinterpret it to mean men are more important than women. I didn't mind being at the back, at least I wasn't being constantly pestered for sex. There was a light in the ceiling of the van, tinted red. I sat under it and they all laughed and made jokes about it being the 'red-light district'.

They said goodbye to the Moroccans and we made our way towards Tangier. After that we'd have to drive up through Spain and France to Calais – a total distance of 1,800 miles. A long way in a battered old minibus.

I watched the world go by through the window as we drove north through the Moroccan hills. The ecstasy tab was kicking in and I felt a sense of euphoria, like the world was really a beautiful place. The hills were a brownish colour, not green like in England, and there were sheep and goats and little hamlets with their own mosques. Shepherds tended to their flocks. I was fascinated by it all. *This* was what I'd come to see – real shepherds who seemed to be from a bygone age. It was dreamlike and otherworldly and full of wonder. I smiled inwardly and was glad I hadn't killed myself.

In Casablanca we stopped for something to eat at a shisha bar. It was an exotic place, full of rich colours and smoky outlines and Berber music playing in the background. I was still under the influence of the drug. They brought a big shisha pipe to our table. There was hot coal on the top and flavoured tobacco underneath with water in the bottom. You sucked the smoke through a long pipe, then passed it to the next person. They gave us a lighter to burn the mouthpiece after use, for hygiene purposes. None of the men used it – except after I'd smoked. As if I'd told them I had herpes.

'Blowjob lips has whore-mouth,' they joked.

'I have not!'

They laughed and thought it was funny. So I burned the mouthpiece after them.

'How funny is that?'

No one laughed, just scowled and looked sullen.

It was late when we left the shisha bar. Dark. There was a beggar woman with a baby asking for money. Asif shouted at her and drove her away. The ecstasy had worn off by then and the world didn't seem such a beautiful place anymore.

After Casablanca, we drove along the Atlantic coast, past Rabat and Kenitra and Larache. We stopped regularly at petrol stations; Asif wanted the rest of my money.

'I only have £20 left.'

'Give it to me.'

'You took most of my money for rent. You said I wouldn't have to pay for anything and I had to perform for your Moroccan friends and got raped by them.'

'It was part of the deal.'

'What deal?'

He threatened to trade me for a camel if I didn't give him the money. Was he joking? Maybe. Maybe not. He took what I had left and now I was penniless, and that made me feel more vulnerable than ever.

The closer we got to Tangier, the more worried I became. What deal? I was thinking they must be smuggling something – ecstasy in paracetamol packets? But there were only five pills in each packet: they'd need a tanker full to make any real cash, and Asif wouldn't risk getting caught for pocket money. It had to be something else. Back at the apartment, I'd overheard the two Arab women talking in French, and I'd thought they said the one who'd tried to break into my bedroom was a cocaine dealer. But I'd seen no cocaine the whole time we were there, just hash. I was really paranoid by the time we got to Tangier.

At the port, two customs guards came to check the van. We must've looked really suspicious to them: three Pakistanis, one black guy and a redhead, white girl. The guards pulled us over and told us to wait, then they went away. Asif started spraying aerosol deodorant all over the place, especially inside the suitcases. The guards came back with a sniffer dog and I was panic stricken. Asif told me to stay cool and keep my head down. Now, these guards must've had no sense of smell because the minibus reeked of Lynx body-spray, enough to cover the stink of a dead goat in a heatwave. It didn't faze the guards, but the sniffer dog started sneezing and nearly had a fit and it didn't find anything, not even the 'paracetamol' pills. I thought the sneezing dog would surely make the guards suspicious. If that wasn't enough to get us thrown into some dungeon, I didn't know what was. But I kept my head down like I'd been told.

****

The guards come and pull me out of the van. I'm screaming and calling to Asif to do something as they drag me to a wooden hut some distance away. Asif ignores me. Inside the hut, the two guards rape me – one after the other. I can smell tobacco and some kind of spice from them, I can feel their rough beards on my skin. Then they bring me back to the van.

****

Once we were clear, Asif said he had to give them a bribe, but he didn't have enough money – so he had to let them take me.

The ferry crossing to Gibraltar took an hour and a half and I don't remember it at all as I slept for a long time after the high of the ecstasy and the trauma of Tangier. When I woke, we were in a small Spanish town called Écija, to the east of Seville. The men were all flapping about and waving their arms and shouting at each other.

'What's wrong?'

'We never brought a map and we have no idea where we're going.'

I found an internet café and looked up the route, but they had no printer. Instead, I wrote down all the names of the towns on the way, so we could follow the road signs north, to France. I said I should sit up front so I could guide them, but they wouldn't have it. They were embarrassed by their own stupidity and my common sense. In their eyes it showed them up – and it was disrespectful.

'Women must sit behind the men!'

They took turns driving and, because they wouldn't listen to me, it wasn't long before they were going the wrong way, heading west towards Portugal instead of north towards France. I tried to tell them but they wouldn't listen.

We stopped at many garages for petrol and they scowled at me every time because I had no money left, and they couldn't sell me for sex as we were no longer in North Africa and they might get reported. They didn't want that because of whatever it was they were smuggling – they needed to keep a low profile and not attract attention. We ate at a fast food place and they all had vegetarian food because the meat wasn't halal. I had a normal burger to show my scorn for them not following my list of towns and going 100 miles in the wrong direction. In retaliation, the next time we stopped at a service station, they all had a shower and made me wait till last. When it was finally my turn, they said they didn't have time and they'd leave me behind, so I had to go without and stay stinking and sweaty.

We eventually made it to France and, at Calais, Asif gave me another pill. I didn't take it this time because I knew what it was and I crumbled it up and threw it away.

When we got clear of the terminal without any trouble, the men started celebrating and high-fiving each other. Asif said it was okay to tell me now that they'd managed to smuggle 25 kilos of cocaine into the country. I knew I was being given that information to bind me even closer to them. If I left them now, I'd leave with the knowledge that I'd been involved in a drug-smuggling operation that could send me to prison for a long time. However, as they didn't want me to know where they were taking the cocaine and I was no further use to them for now, they dumped me at Ashford train station without any money. It was very late and no trains were running. The place was deserted and eerie. I sat on a bench and waited.

I waited.

Waited and cried.

10

Reverting

When it came to writing this chapter, I felt anxious. I don't know what you, the reader, will make of it. But I wanted to express how lovely the religion of Islam is, and how close it is, still, to my heart. I wanted to express how much it helped me and how special it is – how passionate I was about it.

Being in such close proximity to Muslim men, I couldn't help but come into contact with their religion; even if some of those men weren't Muslim in the true sense of the word; even though they were rapists and racists who believed white girls were some kind of sub-human species.

When I first went to university, I learned a bit about Islam from the Jordanians in my halls of residence, and I became intrigued and wanted to know more. Maybe the cure for my abuse lay in the Qur'an. Maybe if I understood these people a bit better, I could stop what was happening to me. Maybe there was something I was missing, something I should know about. Maybe by understanding Islam, I could understand myself.

I noticed my abusers never spoke about their religion in front of me. When I tried to ask about it, because I'm a naturally curious person, they always got angry and told me to shut up. I found out later that all Muslims have the responsibility of *da'wah,* which means to spread awareness of the message of Islam so, by ignoring my questions, these men were actually doing wrong in the eyes of Allah. I came to realise they weren't true Muslims; they were just going through the motions, like how some Christians aren't really 'Christian' at all.

I'd asked Asif about it lots of times, but he always ignored me – like I wasn't fit to be talking about his religion. Finally, one day he turned to me abruptly, a frown on his face.

'Why do you keep asking about Islam?'

'Because I want to know.'

'All right, there are five pillars – *shahadah*, prayer, charity, fasting and *hajj*.'

Shahadah was the Muslim Testimony of Faith, and *hajj* was the pilgrimage to Mecca.

'What else?'

'That's all.'

He shut up, and I realised he didn't want me to know because knowing would make me human in his eyes and reduce his power over me.

One day I was walking along the street and felt like I was looking down on myself from high up somewhere. It seemed as if something was trying to tell me I needed more in my life, something outside myself, not inside me like the demon. It was telling me I needed spirituality, but not the conventional kind I was used to.

I knew nothing about Islam, but Ramadan was coming up. I knew from previous experience that the men who were abusing me would stop for that month. They'd go to have all their sins forgiven, and that annoyed me – how could their sins be forgiven, but not mine? It was like they could act holier than thou, while I sank, carrying the weight of their crimes. How could half the sin be forgiven, but not the other half?

I was socially and environmentally isolated, trying to survive within that isolation. This will sound crazy, but my isolation increased when my abusers stopped the abuse during Ramadan. My whole environment revolved around them and now even that tenuous thread of pseudo-reality was withdrawn and I was left with nothing but my own self-loathing. Not too dissimilar to drug and alcohol withdrawal.

The PTSD returned as well.

That particular Ramadan, I decided to try fasting, like they did, to see if that made a difference to the way I felt. I wasn't eating properly anyway, so I thought fasting wouldn't be a big deal. I expected it to be a passing thing: I'd try it for a day and see how I got on.

Around this time, I also tried doing a Rosetta Stone beginner's course in Urdu. It was only a little side project, but I'd learned so much about these Pakistanis, and I wouldn't learn any more or understand what was happening to me until I could understand the language. I believed it might help me with a couple of things. If nothing else, I could figure out what the sentences meant when they spoke, the significance of a pause, the grammar, nouns and verbs. And that would give me a better indication of their moods, their intentions towards me – maybe warn me in advance. But I was a complete beginner and I didn't get far with it. I was afraid to put too much effort into it because I didn't really understand my motivation.

I bought a book on Islam and read up about the rules and beliefs. The men started to come to me more in the run up to Ramadan – they wanted sex, as much as they could get, before they had to stop for a month. I told them I was converting to Islam and it'd be disrespectful and that stopped them in their tracks. They weren't expecting it. Then some of them tried to tell me it was alright to cheat on the religion, 'as long as we're both Muslim'. When I still said no, they tried to lie to me about Islam, saying we could have a 'temporary marriage' and other things that were totally made up.

I was still having a hard time keeping them at bay and I realised, if I was going to use their religion as a weapon against them, I'd have to know more about it. I wasn't really considering converting, at least not right then, but maybe it could give me strength – maybe I could finally have some power. It might make me believe in myself a bit more. Maybe there was a way I could stop them – maybe I could be a good person.

Maybe I could be a girl again and not this bad thing.

And that's when I started to feel normal again – while I was fasting, on my own at university in Chelmsford. There was a timetable for the five daily prayers, and another for when you could eat. Fasting started with *Suhoor*, which was a kind of pre-dawn breakfast, followed by the *fajr* prayer. After sunset, you first eat dates, because the Prophet Muhammad broke his fast with three dates. Then you said the *maghrib* prayer and ate the main meal, called *iftar*. I thought it was just food you had to abstain from, but it was drink as well – even water – and sex and smoking, and anything that could be classed as sinful, like backbiting, swearing, lying, fighting and so on.

It took me a while to find some dates, as all the stores had run out. This made me smile to myself because normally I'd never have noticed it, but it was Ramadan and now I knew why there were no dates. I'd never eaten dates – I remembered them as a kid, as something that was around at Christmas. But they looked like slugs to me, so I never ate them. I managed to find some in the end. I also bought a load of cheap two-litre bottles of water. I bought porridge and bananas for

Suhoor, so I'd have something substantial inside me during the fasting hours and that was it – I was all set.

My book told me that I should read the Qur'an, so I bought a copy of that as well. The Muslim calendar followed the lunar calendar, which was 11 days shorter than the Gregorian calendar – the calendar the West follows. So, every year, Ramadan started 11 days earlier than it did the previous year.

In Islam, your intentions are very important. It's no use doing something good if it's for the wrong reason – like giving to charity so everyone will think you're great.

I wanted to fast so I could discover how to be good so, for me, even the intention of fasting for Ramadan was giving me rewards I didn't know about. And one reward came in the form of self-control. Life control.

On the night before Ramadan started, I listened to Shaykh Ibrahim Mogra giving a 15-minute talk on the BBC Asian radio station. He had a soft voice, it was very peaceful and I listened to him again the following morning before daybreak, when everything was silent and peaceful. I thought, *If I get through the first day, I'll try it for a week.*

Thirty days seemed impossible so a week would be fine, if I could do it – just to get a feel for it, like an experiment. I ate my *Suhoor* of porridge and bananas and had a cup of tea and lots of water. I didn't know the *fajr* prayer, so I made up one of my own.

'God, I've no idea what I'm doing… but, hello, I'm here and I'm doing this for you.'

The point of fasting was to appreciate what God gave me as I'd been lucky enough to be born in a country where there was plenty of food and water. In some countries, there was no food and people were starving. In others, people had to hunt for their food – if the hunt wasn't successful, then they went hungry. Fasting gave me an idea of what it'd be like if God took the supermarkets away.

I have to say, it was hard in one way and it was easy in other ways. Of course, I was hungry and thirsty, but I was really motivated, and the motivation overcame the hunger and thirst. I went the whole day without eating or drinking; it was summertime, and the day was a long one.

Apparently, it was bad to delay eating after sunset because I should appreciate that God was now allowing me to eat and to delay was to delay my blessings. So, before it got dark, I prepared my *iftar* meal. I ate some dates and made up another little prayer and ate my *iftar* and listened to BBC Asian Network again.

I felt confident I could do this for the week, and I did. I realised I hadn't been looking after myself properly before. But Ramadan was forcing me to do that: to have two good meals a day. My body felt better and my physical health started improving. Maybe it was the dates, which I discovered I loved, and all the water I was drinking. I wasn't doing any cocaine, or amphetamine, or cannabis, and I enjoyed the week so much I decided to continue and see how far into the month I could get.

I was never really religious and I'd never done anything in the name of God before. Why would I? I would describe the feeling as getting a great present for your mother on her birthday and how happy that made you feel inside when she loved it and it made her so happy. It began to lift all the guilt off my shoulders that I'd been carrying around with me – about the sex, drugs, and the horrible, crazy up-and-down, out-of-control life I was leading. This was the first time in a couple of years that I felt like I had some control in my life, and it gave me back something that I'd forgotten about.

Self-respect.

I discovered a lot about Islam during the 30 days of Ramadan by reading the Qur'an and as much material as I could get hold of about the religion. It also gave me an insight into the psyche of the men who were abusing me. I realised they weren't 'Muslim' in the true sense of the word – just in name only. Islam had nothing to do with how they were, and their behaviour was contrary to the teachings of their religion. They were racists who thought of young white girls as being inferior to them and, therefore, they could do what they liked to them – but it had nothing to do with being Muslim or the religion of Islam. 'Muslim' and 'Islam' were the shields they used so nobody could touch them.

That period of fasting woke something inside me, something I thought was dead – a whole individual identity. Now I desperately wanted to change my life again. I realised I couldn't carry on with the crazy double life I was leading. I felt split in half: the good side of me was a student nurse at Anglia Ruskin University; and the bad part, controlled by the demon inside me, was a lost street-walker in Birmingham. I had to get away from the sex and drugs. If I didn't, I knew it wouldn't be long before I died an obscene and violent death. I longed to be a human being again. I wanted to have normal, healthy relationships with people. I didn't want to succumb to the power of my abusers anymore. So I made a conscious decision to convert to Islam.

The University of Essex was in Colchester and had an Islamic Society, which Anglia Ruskin didn't have. The university had a lot of international students and the Islamic Society had a lot of members as a result. I started going there for Islamic events and that's where I met Kaddi and other girls who'd reverted to Islam. I decided to join them. (I say 'reverted', because in Islam, they reckon everyone is born Muslim. But it's the same as converted).

The decision gained momentum after I attended Eid in Trafalgar Square in London at the end of Ramadan and met lots of Muslim women and made friends with them. I changed my phone number and, after Ramadan was over, I didn't go back to Birmingham. I established a new social network of converted Muslim women in Essex, and it felt like my abusers and my damaged mental state had finally lost their hold over me.

Kaddi and I got on very well. She was in her 40s when I first met her. She was English, but she'd travelled to various Muslim countries and had reverted to Islam a year earlier and begun wearing Muslim clothes and a *hijab*. Kaddi had a long history of mental health issues and she suffered from a sleep disorder and depression. As I was studying to be a mental health nurse, we were kind of drawn to each other. She'd met a guy called Morad online. He lived in Algeria and told her he was a doctor, but needed money because he was so poor. She started sending him money and then went to Algeria to meet him, where she reverted to Islam. She kept on sending him money when she came back to England and I could see he was just spinning her a load of lies. She eventually saw through him and stopped sending the cash, but she continued to practice the religion and didn't give up her faith.

I spoke to Kaddi about my experiences at the hands of Asian men. She told me I often repeated the same things over and over again. There was one time I came to her anxious and distressed because a man had looked at me at the bus stop. In Islam, direct eye contact with men was discouraged, but I'd accidentally met his stare.

'He wanted sex with me, Kaddi.'

'It was just a look, Kate.'

'It starts like that, I can tell.'

'Not everything's associated with sex. You have to let it go, Kate.'

And it was like that, we shared each other's trauma.

I don't know exactly what it was, but it seemed like the community of Muslim women united us and gave us support and friendship, and an active social life. There are so many women out there who are suffering from loneliness, who just need some company and someone to talk to. They end up going from relationship to relationship with men, trying to find someone who understands them and who'll listen to them. That's where abuse can manifest, breed and fester. We found that, when we had Islam, we didn't need any man. When you have so much support, it makes it easier to recognise an abusive partner. The people in your social circle don't speak to you like that, don't treat you like that, and you come to realise that your partner shouldn't either. There was no need to go to a mosque or speak to an Imam to revert to Islam. All I needed to do was say the words called the Testimony of Faith, *Shahada*, in front of witnesses.

'I testify *la ilaha illa Allah, Muhammad rasoolu Allah.*'

In the eyes of Allah, once I made the statement, I was Muslim and could choose a Muslim name. I chose Alia'a, which is the female version of Ala'a, which means 'exalted'. After I reverted to Islam, I decided early on that I wanted to wear the *hijab* – the headscarf. I don't know why – I guess I thought it would be protective in some way, that it would protect me from men. It was hard at first, because I had to deal with the sly looks, smirks and sniggers, not to mention the million questions I got asked about it. Quite soon after I started wearing it, I was sent on a work placement to an elderly medical ward in a general hospital. When the people who didn't know me there saw me wearing the *hijab*, they just took it in their stride and it was no big deal to them. But the people who knew me before I became a Muslim couldn't understand why I did it.

I loved wearing the *hijab*. It felt like a hug on my head all the time – a lovely, supportive hug. There were lots of different shapes, sizes and styles and each created a different look. It was great not having to do my hair every day – I could just wear a scarf. Kaddi and I used to experiment with different styles and we had such a laugh doing it. Sometimes we prayed together and made *wudu* in the women's wash area of the mosque. *Wudu* is like a type of ritual purification, where you wash your hands and mouth and nostrils and head and feet.

There's a concept called "the invisibility of whiteness". When a white person looks in the mirror, they see a "normal" person. All the things I'd been conditioned to believe were bad, were actually defined by my culture – a white girl from a rural English community. I was "normal" for the place where I was brought up. My abusers made me believe that was bad. When I reverted to Islam, I found another normality and discovered what they were doing to me wasn't "normal" within their culture. This helped me get my mind right to some extent and helped to counteract the brainwashing. Spending time with Muslim women provided me with much needed friendship and a form of therapy.

Being a Muslim was a serious thing for me – there were no half-measures. There was a decent halal butcher in Chelmsford and I got my meat from there. I asked them to put the meat through the mincer twice so it was nice and fine, for making Arab *kibbeh* and Turkish *lahmajoun*. Being around the different Muslim races for so long taught me a lot of dishes from all over the world, and the diet was no problem for me. Me and the sisters would go to halal restaurants and I loved the food, although they did use a lot of salt – my mother had avoided giving us salt when I was growing up because she was a nurse and it was bad for us – so it took a bit of getting used to.

Some mosques allowed women to pray in the main area with the men, as long as they were behind and the men couldn't see women's backsides sticking up in the air when in *sujud* – heads on the floor. One day, we were bending over in *sujud*, when Kaddi let rip with a loud fart – it was so loud it echoed around the mosque. We both burst out laughing and fell about uncontrollably. If you fart you're no longer in *wudu*, and you have to stop praying and go and do it again, apologising to Allah by saying '*Astaghfirullah*', which means: 'God forgive me for farting while praying – and for allowing myself to be distracted – and for being unable to stop laughing.' But we were in such hysterics that we couldn't say the word, and all we could do was giggle 'Shhh!' to each other and 'Stop it!' and we had to leave the room before they threw us out. After composing ourselves, we went through the ritual again and finished the prayers by saying goodbye to the angels. At least, I always thought of it as saying goodbye after finishing a prayer. Muslims believe we have an angel on each shoulder. The angel on the right is recording our good deeds and the angel on the left is recording our bad deeds. When we finish a prayer, we turn to each of them and say, '*Asalam alaikum wa rahmatullah.*' It means peace and blessings be upon you, but when I did it, I was saying goodbye to the angels, for the moment.

We went to lectures and they talked a lot about avoiding 'disbelievers' – in other words, don't do this or that because it's the way of the disbelievers. I always thought that was wrong. Kaddi was always putting forward questions in lectures and a long debate would follow that usually ended up with the whole audience clapping in agreement with her. But I was always shy and unsure of myself. I was afraid to look stupid because I was new to all this. In hindsight, I wished Muslim women were more forward and allowed to read the Qur'an out loud in public and could sing more. When they said 'disbelievers', they were actually giving a collective negative opinion of non-Muslims. It used to annoy me because they were referring to my family and I resented that. I didn't think they should be teaching reverts to separate themselves from their families. My family was important to me. Even though I was sort of estranged from them, I still loved them. There's nowhere in the Qur'an that says don't respect your family if they're non-Muslim, and I wished I'd challenged the lecturers more on the subject of disbelievers.

After I became a Muslim, I asked the university to house me with all girls because I was having nightmares about men climbing through my bedroom window. During the three years I was at Anglia Ruskin, I lived at four different flats across the campus. I had one flatmate called Tammy, a black girl who didn't like me being a Muslim. She'd string men along and use them to get what she wanted. It made me uncomfortable if she brought a guy back to the flat – it spooked me and made me nervous if I wasn't wearing a scarf. We talked about it and I didn't want to be confrontational, but it sparked a big argument and she ended up throwing some of my stuff about. I lived with another girl called Louise, who was a lesbian. I loved having her as a flatmate and we got on really well. She made me laugh. Another flatmate called Sookie was from Sierra Leone. She was Muslim too, and a bit younger than me. We used to pray together.

I'd pray anywhere, even on campus or in the middle of town – once it was time, I couldn't miss it. I carried my prayer mat and put it down in shopping centres and hospitals and parks and empty offices. I wasn't supposed to pray in a bathroom that had a toilet because it wasn't clean – it was being disrespectful to God. But I prayed in bathrooms when there was nowhere else available. The way I saw it was, God's supposed to be everywhere, including in the toilet. If he was watching me all the time like they said, he didn't stop watching me while I was taking a dump, so why did I have to avoid saying his name in there? It was the same for the men who were abusing me – according to their religion, God was everywhere. So, did they think he wasn't watching when they were raping me?

Being a Muslim worked well most of the time. Wearing the *hijab* helped me avoid men, and I didn't have to cope with them showing interest in me or coming on to me. I spent a lot of time with my new friends, going to dinner parties and Islamic lectures and classes at the mosque. I mainly went to East London mosques, like in Whitechapel, just a train ride away from Chelmsford. I learned how to pray to Allah and focused my life on becoming a better Muslim. I even took a course in Arabic and Tajweed and learned how to read the Qur'an in Arabic and how the Sharia law courts operate inside the UK.

But let me be clear, when I reverted to Islam it wasn't about giving up and giving in to the warped version of the ideology that was manipulating me. It was about trying to get myself back. My mind was chaotic – there were no rules – no structure in my life. Islam gave me that structure, something solid to hold onto when everything else around me was disintegrating.

My knowledge of Islam eventually exceeded that of my abusers and it helped to break their psychological dominance over me. I wore the *hijab* and prayed and meditated, and it helped me find a new kind of respect for myself. It allowed me to think for myself and stop being a slave to my neurosis. In my new Muslim community, I never talked about my life before I converted. This was called '*jahiliyyah*', which means 'days of ignorance' – that was the term used for the period before the Qur'an was revealed to Muhammad and Islam began, but it was also used by some revert Muslims to mean before they converted. That appealed to me because it meant the past was the past and now I was reborn, so there was no need to worry about the sins committed in the past because they were forgiven.

I had a clean slate!

And, after a while, the abuse faded from my mind.

11

Barak

I started a blog where I wrote about Islam and talked about how I fasted for Ramadan and became a Muslim. I started getting messages from a Syrian man called Barak who was living in Dubai. The name intrigued me.

'What, like Barack Obama?'

'No, more like Mubarak, which means blessed in Arabic.'

He said he wanted to send me money because he was touched by my story. In Syria and other Muslim countries, they bought brand new clothes for Eid and, because I was a poor student, he wanted me to buy myself a dress for the celebrations. I thought this was a bit suspicious and I told Kaddi about it – she'd been through something similar with Morad. These online men seemed to pick on Western women and fooled them. Although Barak was doing the opposite of Morad, offering money, we reckoned it'd soon turn the other way. I was extremely suspicious.

Kaddi and I vetted him as much as we possibly could. We spoke to him on Skype and tried to find out what his motivation was. We couldn't believe that he would just offer money without any strings attached. He said he was from a wealthy Syrian family, but that he was born in Dubai and had lived there until he was seven. Then he'd moved back to Syria and gone to university there, and now he was back in Dubai so he wouldn't get conscripted into the Syrian army for five years. He'd done a degree in computer science in Syria, where the state had paid for his education, and he was currently applying to UK universities to do his masters. The Syrian government was sponsoring him and paying his fees.

In the end, I decided to accept his money, through Western Union, which was a safe way of receiving funds if you didn't know or trust the person sending them. I'd just have to give my name, but nothing else. I couldn't find anything wrong with his gesture, but I stayed suspicious and as aware as possible that I might be getting myself into trouble again. I guess the way I looked at it was; these guys conned Western women out of cash all the time, so why not turn the tables a bit? If he did start asking for anything, then I'd drop him immediately.

After I Skyped him for a few months, he invited me to Dubai and offered to pay for the whole trip. Alarm bells started to ring, even though I was intrigued about going to the United Arab Emirates, which I'd heard so much about and would be a great adventure and an opportunity to expand my knowledge of Islam.

'I can't go without Kaddi.'

'Don't worry, Kaddi can come too.'

'Will you pay for her trip as well as mine?'

'Of course.'

We made sure Barak was telling the truth and there was no hidden agenda by checking the flight tickets, checking the hotel online, and deciding what we needed to do if we got into trouble – where the British Embassy was, and details like that. Going to the United Arab Emirates was a risk, but I'd led a risky life already – so I didn't think it through maybe as much as I should have.

Kaddi and I flew out to Dubai together – it actually turned out to be Abu Dhabi, which was the capital and second biggest city of the UAE. We flew with Etihad Airways and it was the poshest and most comfortable flight I'd ever been on. The hostesses had these really interesting hats that had a drape down one side, almost like a *hijab*, but not quite the same. The plane had a mini television for each seat and everything was included. Meals and drinks, even alcohol, was free, but we didn't have any of that. I just had unlimited cups of tea during the seven-hour flight.

At the appropriate time, we said *salah*, the ritual prayer. Kaddi had her head down for so long the hostess asked if she was alright because she looked like she was unconscious or something. They were about to check her pulse when she straightened up and said '*Salam alaikum*' to the angels on each side of her shoulders and wondered what the fuss was about. The hostess got such a fright and we burst out laughing when she left.

Barak wasn't at the airport to meet us. Instead, he sent a car from the hotel, which was a huge five-star place, paid for by him. There was an arrow on the ceiling of our room, pointing towards Mecca. This confused Kaddi.

'Isn't Mecca in the east?'

'Not here it isn't.'

We didn't meet Barak for several hours, after we'd unpacked and settled into our room. I'd seen him before on Skype and, when he did finally arrive, he was just as I'd expected him to be. He was pale-skinned and very good-looking, with brownish, copper-coloured hair and hazel eyes. He had a funny accent and you could tell he'd learned English as a second language and been taught by Americans, because the accent was kind of American English, with some Syrian thrown in. Kaddi and I were still trying to suss him out, but he seemed sweet and innocent and shy.

Abu Dhabi was very hot – nearly 40°C. I couldn't step outside the hotel without putting factor 50 on my exposed skin. I was glad I was Muslim and could cover up most of my body. The city felt very manufactured. All the plants and gardens were watered by foreign labourers who wore identical blue jumpsuits and looked a bit like clones. They did all the menial jobs, like litter picking and window cleaning and bin collection. We asked one of the blue jumpsuit workers what his name was, but he only spoke Hindi and we couldn't communicate with him. I wondered if these people were being exploited. Where did they live? How much did they earn? If they didn't speak English or Arabic, they must've been easy to exploit.

Barak drove us to Dubai from Abu Dhabi and arranged for a friend of his to sneak us into the Burj Al Arab Jumeirah hotel on Palm Island. It was a very expensive place, for celebrities and rich people, and you couldn't just walk in there. We had a look around and I wanted to have tea, but it was £35 a pot. There were wall-to-wall fish tanks downstairs and men walking around with huge platters of dates – Barak said they were the most expensive dates in the world. There was an amazing waterfall display, with lights and spouts of water that shot up in time to classical music.

We saw some celebrities but I wasn't sure who they were, just that I'd seen them somewhere before. The women's toilets were so luxurious, with mini showers and bidets and big mirrors and vanity tables and a very posh chaise longue. Sneaking us in there showed that Barak had a bit of a rebellious side.

When we got back to Abu Dhabi, he took us to a zoo in a little town called Al Ain. It was a quaint sort of place and the penguin enclosure had air conditioning so the birds didn't get too hot. We bought umbrellas at the zoo shop to shade us from the sun and there was a little mosque which we visited when the *Adhan*, the call to prayer, started. Unfortunately, I slipped on some leaking water and fell on the stone steps. Barak and Kaddi rushed to help me. It was a bit embarrassing, but I was okay and sprang back to my feet in as ladylike a manner as I could manage.

Barak was a proper gentleman and very respectful. He was 27 and I was 20 at the time. He only ever met us in public places and drove us around wherever we wanted to go, like shopping malls and markets. All Kaddi and I wanted to do was ride on a camel and he was bemused by this – most women he knew just wanted to go shopping all the time. We were strange to him, not impressed by the glitter of the shops and just wanting a desert adventure. Camel riding was touristy and Barak wasn't a tourist. He didn't know how to go about it. There were no camels in the zoo because they're wild in the UAE, so there was no need to have them in an enclosure. We never did get to ride on a camel, but we were appreciative of the free trip.

It was great being Muslim in a Muslim country – where it was normal, even though they sometimes thought we were weird because we were English. We went to Sheikh Zayed Grand Mosque, a big place of worship. It was huge and beautiful, made of white marble, gold, semi-precious stones, crystals and ceramics. It took my breath away. Barak had very fair skin and, next to me and Kaddi, looked just like another Western person. The guard asked him in Arabic if we were Muslim, him included.

'Of course we are!'

I was wearing a full-length dress, but the guard told me it was too short and I'd have to wear an *abaya* – they had some spare ones on a rack and I picked the longest, which drowned me when I pulled it over the top of my dress. Being a young white woman was probably the worst thing I could be trying to get in there. But he let us in eventually.

We stayed in Abu Dhabi for six days and I had a beautiful time. Barak was very innocent for his age and still a virgin at 27. He was never disrespectful to me or Kaddi, and he never tried to take advantage of us, even though we were in his country and he probably could have if he decided to. I'd never known this before – a man who didn't want sex from me and who wasn't two-faced and treacherous.

During that short stay, I found myself becoming attracted to Barak – in a spiritual way, in a way that was new to me and so very refreshing. I think I was falling in love, even though I'd never been truly in love with a man and didn't realise it at the time.

All too soon, it was time to say goodbye, and Kaddi and I flew back to Britain, leaving Barak in Abu Dhabi.

I spoke to him every day on the phone after I got back. He found a place designated for foreign students at the University of Salford and arrived in Manchester to study for his master's in computer science and I went up to see him. He was living in student accommodation near the university and I stayed overnight there.

The flat had one bedroom and was newly built. It was self-contained, with a nice kitchenette and a flat screen television. I thought he'd want to make love and I'd have been happy to do it with him, but he said he wanted us to be married first. Even though I was nearly 21, I didn't know what real love for a man was – I'd never experienced it. The only man I'd ever loved was my father, and that was completely different. I loved Barak, really loved him. He was a beautiful man and, in some ways, so innocent and naïve. He was fascinated by England and learning the language – certain words intrigued him, like 'shattered'. Every now and then he'd just say, 'I'm shattered' and burst out laughing.

When we went out on Friday night, we didn't go into any of the clubs, just watched the people. There were lots of drunk students and Barak had never seen anything like it before. There was a girl sitting in the street while her boyfriend was trying to get her to stand up, but she kept falling over. Barak was concerned.

'What's wrong with her?'

'She's drunk.'

He was shocked. He'd never seen how alcohol could affect people like that.

I went to the shops one day and, when I came back, he was crying. He'd been watching an episode of *Jeremy Kyle* on the television and was touched by a story of a mother and daughter making up after years of turmoil and care system involvement. Barak wasn't used to Jeremy Kyle, and the story really affected him.

At the end of September, Barak and I had an Islamic marriage. The Imam at Manchester Mosque knew his family in Syria, and we signed the marriage contract there in front of two witnesses. We wanted to have a party, but neither of us knew anyone in Manchester so we just went out for a wedding meal together. We went to an Arab restaurant and I wore a special dress for the occasion. Barak bought me a beautiful engagement ring so I could tell my family I was engaged – it was gold with three diamonds, a big one in the middle and two smaller ones either side. He knew I wasn't a virgin and he was okay with that and didn't judge me in any way. But I didn't want him to know how much sex I'd had or how I'd been raped by so many men. I tried to act shy in bed, even though there was nothing sexual I hadn't experienced. I hated myself for that, but Barak showed me nothing but love and respect and our coming together intimately was refreshing and beautiful.

I went up to Manchester every second weekend and he came down to Chelmsford every other weekend. We saw each other as much as we could. We wanted to be together all the time, but we both had to study and the weekends worked well for us. It was like being young again, properly young – young and in love, the way it should have been, instead of getting raped all the time. The plan was to be married under Islamic law for the first year, then register the marriage under civil law after 12 months. At that time, I could tell my parents and we could be a normal couple in a normal relationship. When we both finished university, we could get good jobs and get married with a proper ceremony. It would be like a fairytale come true and we'd live happily ever after.

Barak was a lovely man and I never told him about the SAU or my demented trips to Birmingham. I dealt with my feelings alone. I wanted to be a good wife to my husband and a good person generally. We loved each other so much and I didn't want him to think badly of me or to know about the things that had happened to me. I felt terrible about it, like I wasn't being truly honest with him when he loved me so much. I felt like I was an imposter. I did tell him that sometimes things made me cry at night – sometimes I had nightmares and felt afraid. He accepted that. He never argued with me or found fault with me, and he tried to help me every way he could. He was always thinking of ways to make me happy. He'd take me out to dinner if I felt down, or take me out jogging with him if he saw I was getting depressed. He encouraged me to come out of myself when the demon called to me from the back of my mind.

I felt better than ever during the time I was a Muslim with Barak.

I was on a university placement with the Criminal Justice Mental Health Team in Chelmsford and I'd just finished a placement with the Drug and Alcohol Team. I wore the *hijab* the whole way through these placements and I'm sure it helped me connect with patients because they assumed I was a good girl who knew nothing of drugs and alcohol and mental illness. How wrong they were about that.

Being in love, and life being so good, and working in such close proximity to legal teams, I felt I should go back to the police and re-report the first abuse. And, after going to a MAPPA (Multi-Agency Public Protection Arrangements) meeting in Essex, I found the courage to do it. I felt I had a duty to do so as a nurse, a Muslim and a human being – and maybe it'd give me some kind of closure. But I was still in two minds – people would find out if I went to court. Barak would find out.

I still wasn't totally convinced by the end of the day, I was walking along in a kind of daydream, wondering if I should or shouldn't do it. I wasn't paying attention to where I was going and suddenly realised I'd been walking in the wrong direction and was now climbing the steps of Chelmsford police station. I stopped dead in my tracks. Was I really ready to do this? I decided that where I'd found myself was a sign from Allah and reporting it was the right thing to do. He was leading me to my destiny. So I said to myself: 'It's now or never.'

I carried on into the police station because I knew if I turned around and went home, I would never come back. If I'd known what was ahead of me, I probably would have run back down the steps. I spoke to the police receptionist:

'I have something to report.'

'What is it?'

'I don't want to tell you, unless you're the person who'll be dealing with it… because of its nature.'

At that point I started crying.

'I don't want to have to say it more than once.'

She went off and got a male police officer from somewhere. He took me into a room and sat me down.

I told him I wanted to re-state a rape I'd already reported. I said I felt guilty for saying it was consensual in my original statement, because it wasn't and a lot of bad stuff had happened to me afterwards because of that. I felt I had a duty to re-report it because I thought they might do it again to someone else. He asked me what I was talking about – what rape, and what happened afterwards? He wanted names, and I told him about Shahmeel and Imran and Ali Sultan and Hakim and Uncle Nabi and the dangerous-looking Turkish guy and Tamjeed and the rest.

During it all, the police officer got confused – too many names. He wrote them down but then told me he didn't hold out much hope of getting any of it to trial because it was historic, and I'd been over 18 at the time. Same story as before. But, the difference between then and now was before I was terrified to go to court. Now I wasn't. I didn't wait for him to ask me.

'I'm willing to take this all the way. I'm willing to give evidence in court.'

He said he'd contact Telford police and see what they had to say, then he'd be in touch. He clearly had no idea of the response he was going to get.

Neither did I.

Once I got out of the police station in Chelmsford, I thought I better call Barak and let him know what I'd done. I didn't tell him the full extent of the abuse, just the original rape. I mean, how could I tell him everything? He said I should've let him know I was going to re-report it, and he'd have come with me. He seemed disappointed, like he'd been let down, and I didn't blame him. Maybe I should have let him know what had happened to me, but I just couldn't see a good way of explaining it. That's because I didn't really know what had happened to me – not the full extent of it. I had never heard of words like 'grooming' or 'sex trafficking' or 'serial abuse', and I didn't know I was part of it. I thought it was just me this happened to and it was mostly my own fault that it did. I'd been telling myself I was just a drama queen and it wasn't really all that bad. I didn't know why I was still having nightmares and flashbacks and depression about it.

Two specially trained female officers from West Mercia Police came down a week later and I did a seven-hour-long videotaped interview with them. I wore a *hijab* and I cried through most of it. It was difficult, reliving that first rape all over again in such detail.

That was in June 2009. In August, I got a four-week placement in the low-security mental health unit at a hospittal in Manchester and moved in with Barak. We bought a big road map of Greater Manchester and put it up on the pinboard because neither of us knew the city very well. I put a pin where we lived and a pin where the university was and another pin where the hospital was. It worked well for us and we had a good time together, despite the fact that he was still disappointed that I hadn't spoken to him first, before going to the police.

Around this time, my mother got married to her boyfriend and I was getting more and more anxious thinking about the police investigation. I was scared now. I reported all these violent gangsters and the police had taken me seriously this time. I kept thinking about how the rapists were going to be arrested and questioned about me and reminded of me, when I'd convinced myself they'd forgotten me and weren't looking for me anymore. Now I was going to be at the forefront of their minds and I was really worried.

What had I done?

I kept having little panic attacks every now and then when I thought about it. I was racking my brains to make sure they wouldn't be able to find out where I lived. Some people at the SAU knew I was going to uni in Chelmsford and that frightened me. Then again, I was doubtful they were going to come down and wait outside for me. It would take them a long time to bump into me, and they would be wasting a lot of money trying to find me. No, I knew they couldn't get to me, but it didn't stop me from fretting.

I wished I could have got hold of a gun; I wished I could have shot the lot of them – I wouldn't have minded going to prison for it and being labelled as a mass murderer. At least those rapists would be dead and they wouldn't be able to destroy anyone else's life. It was distressing to think I could kill people, but I began to feel strongly that the justice system gave me no other option. How could people like middle-aged male judges appreciate what was going on at street level? How could they put themselves in the place of a girl like me, experiencing a horrendous wait while old Pakistani men had a conversation in a foreign language about who was going to rape me first?

I came to the conclusion there was no one to defend me. Not even the law.

I was told that there were several investigations going on into Asian gangs grooming young white girls. What was actually happening was starting to leak out and would soon be all over the news. Every day. Over and over. Different cases of underage girls groomed and manipulated and raped and treated as if they were vermin, victims of abuse and racial hatred by Pakistani gangs. It sparked off another horrible whirlwind of recurring nightmares, but without me being the victim. Instead, the images of these little girls, some as young as 11 and 12, tortured my mind. It became more than heartbreaking, it was soul destroying.

And the worst part about it was, people knew – many, many people knew.

By now, West Mercia Police had been given extra funding and drafted in extra officers. They launched Operation Chalice to investigate the grooming gangs in Telford and other areas after they'd ignored it for years. Young girls had been abused by the same men who abused me, even before I went to live at the SAU. The police had known about it and done nothing. I would've been safer sleeping under a bridge than I was at the SAU, *and everyone knew that* – the police and social services and even the staff at the SAU. But nobody told me. And when I found out the hard way, they blamed me, and I had to stumble out of it on my own.

However I looked at it, it seemed to me that the only one who hadn't known about the extent of the grooming and abuse was me, and now that I did, it made me feel so guilty, because maybe if I'd spoken out sooner, it might've helped some of those kids.

I remembered when Imran brought the young girl to my flat at the SAU three years earlier. I never thought it was part of something so widespread. I felt bad about it at the time, and now I felt even worse. Poor little kid. I remember she said she'd been with him since she was 12. I wished I could go back to that night and take her away from him. I didn't know how bad it was, that this stuff was going on all over the country. I should've gone back to the police earlier – I should've done something. Maybe if I had, it wouldn't have got so bad.

My whirl of thoughts at the time brought the demon out from the back of my mind. It grabbed hold of me again and shook me till my very soul rattled – just when I thought I'd got clear of it for ever. I was retraumatised.

I couldn't find solace in Islam for this. It wasn't like anyone had any wise words they could give me. All those lecturers going on about disbelievers, but nothing to say about abusing children – nothing to say about that. There was nothing Islam could offer to make me feel better about this. Nothing at all.

I started having flashbacks again and needed counselling. I kept having night terrors where I'd wake up in a cold sweat, hallucinating and seeing a young girl sitting on the end of the bed in my pyjamas. I decided to shave all my hair off. I talked to Barak about it and he supported me, like he always did.

'If that's what you really want to do. Let me help you, I don't want you to hurt yourself.'

I chopped it all off with the kitchen scissors and he helped me shave my head with his razor. I shaved off my hair because I hated everything. I hated hair. What was the point of it? It just got dirty and you had to wash it just to make you look attractive. I didn't want to look attractive. I wore the *hijab* anyway, so it didn't matter. I didn't care what I looked like when innocent little girls were being used and abused like I'd been – degraded and dehumanised. Maybe even worse than what I'd gone through and was still going through. The thoughts of other girls' pain and suffering really affected me.

Shaving my head had a kind of symbolism to it. If you strip someone of their external individuality, what are they left with? Their internal individuality. Their humanness. Their thoughts and feelings and morals. Humans in their most basic form, not obsessed with their external selves to the point of not knowing who or what they really are any more. The reality of being human, the reality of freeing what's underneath, is what matters most.

Sometimes I just felt plastic. I felt like a fake, like I was walking around pretending to be human, pretending to be a person, and I was getting sick of it. Sick of feeling like I was pretending. So, I don't know, maybe I felt my hair was a pretence, a trivial thing, skin deep. Maybe it was a physical representation of my mental state.

I felt out of control at that time and didn't know what was important anymore. I didn't feel in touch with myself or what the point of anything was.

Why did I shave my head?

I don't know – maybe I just needed to change something.

12

My Puppet Role

To make matters worse, they brought me back to Telford from Manchester to do an ID parade at a police station and pick out some of the men I'd told them about. On the outside I probably looked fine, but you don't want to be brought face-to-face with the people who raped you. You don't want to have to look them in the eyes again. I was relieved when I found out it was videos and not in the flesh, so to speak.

I was taken into a room and a couple of cameras were focused on me. There was a man controlling the recording and writing stuff down. The line-up was a series of images on a computer screen. They showed me videos of nine people, each one with a number. One of them was the suspect and the other eight were just people who looked like him. I had to wait until the end of the video, then they showed it again and then I had to pick one of the people and say his number three times. I found it really hard because I only met some of the men once, over three years ago, and then maybe only for an hour or even just a few minutes.

I failed to pick out the dangerous-looking Turkish guy – I thought it'd be easy, as his appearance was so menacing. But when they put him next to eight other dangerous-looking Turkish guys, they all looked the same. I felt really nervous – if I'd met any of them on the street, I'd have run away and had a panic attack, and dealing with them now was just as bad. I picked the wrong one. The same with Bazam. I'd only met him once and they put him in a line of chubby Pakistanis of the same age, and I couldn't identify him. Everyone knew who he was: they'd arrested him and questioned him, and the police knew. But he couldn't be prosecuted because I wasn't able to pick him out in the ID line-up.

I had to attend more ID parades after that – a whole series of them over the course of several months, I think six altogether. I was asked to pick out Ali Sultan, Hakim, Mike Nolan and Shahmeel. I remember having to organise days off from my placement in Manchester so I could take the train to the police station. I found it easier to tell the truth to my mentor at the hospital so she understood the situation. I didn't go into too much detail; just said I was a victim in a police investigation and I had to do ID parades. They were all very supportive on the unit and I can't thank them enough for that.

I was recruited into Operation Chalice. They were doing 'sweeps' of arrests. They'd already done the first sweep and were about to do the second. They decided they'd arrest and question Shahmeel in the second sweep. He was still in prison, so they had to 'produce' him, then arrest and question him. It was important to do each sweep all at once, so the suspects couldn't talk to each other and come up with cover stories, or warn other criminals so they could escape arrest.

I'd already sent the police a picture of Hakim that I got from Facebook, to help them identify and arrest him, and I was able to successfully pick him out at the ID parade. He'd aged a lot in the three years since I'd seen him, more than you'd expect. He'd put on a lot of weight, but I still picked him out – how could I forget him? I also successfully picked out Ali Sultan, but Shahmeel's identification was harder than the others. It was like he was looking back at me through the glass of the screen; it was like he was there, in the room, even though he wasn't, and he could see me and was grinning at me in that evil way. I wrote a poem about it afterwards.

Here I am
Looking through the glass
In nervous anticipation
As I look from one to one
I see you there
Looking back at me
And something inside me changes
Like old strings tightening
A shudder sweeps down my wooden spine
A familiar feeling
A familiar fear
I fit back into my puppet role so snugly
As if I'd never left.

Shahmeel was number six in the line-up and I had to say his number three times: six, six, six. It was the devil, the demon, looking at me from the other side of the glass screen. And I knew what he'd put into me was still there.

By the time I did the line-up for Mike Nolan, I was a bag of nerves. I knew which one he was straight away and it gave me a sinking feeling in my stomach. But I had to ask them to show me four times because I didn't want to get it wrong, especially after failing to ID Bazam and the Turkish man. He didn't look well – he had big dark circles under his eyes and he looked really menacing. It scared me. I wondered what would happen if he got found not guilty and came after me for reporting him?

I began having a recurring dream, that Imran and some other men were chasing me. I was in the back of a 4x4 vehicle and Barak was there and someone else was driving. For some reason, the car would be going very slowly and Imran would be catching up, even though he and the others were on foot. It was in a residential area with lots of houses and gardens. We went around a corner and decided to abandon the car and make a run for it. That's when Barak and the driver disappeared and I was on my own – and the 4x4 wasn't a car at all, but a little pink tricycle. I didn't want to leave the bike there, but I had to. Then I ran behind some bushes but this woman saw and started shouting:

'What are you doing here? You don't belong here! Get out! Get out!'

I try to say I'm just hiding and could she be quiet, but no words would come out of my mouth. Then I see Imran and the other men running towards me, so I give up and emerge from the bushes to face them. Imran comes up to me and punches me in the face.

And that's when I wake up.

During their investigations, I was assigned two female STOs – specially trained officers. One of the things we had to do was revisit where I'd been. They drove me around in the back seat of a car with blacked-out windows. One of the women had a camera and was filming my response as I directed them around the areas of Telford where I was raped.

I took them to my flat at the SAU but didn't get out of the car – I couldn't go near it. I took them to Shahmeel's house and Ali Sultan's house and the doss-house next door. I pointed out the places from the car, never getting out. I took them to the flat where Hakim raped me;

and to places like car parks where I was forced to give people blowjobs; and once, behind a church, where Imran made me give him a blowjob with a 10-year-old boy standing guard.

I started having dreams about that too – being in the car with the policewomen, doing the drive-by again. We are driving in the area where I was first abused and this time I have to get out of the car and go right up to Shahmeel's house. I was afraid. I ask the policewomen:

'Is he in prison or is he here?'

Then he'd come out, but it wouldn't be him: it'd be a monster with three sixes on its forehead and it would try to get inside me – through my mouth and my ears and my nose and my vagina, and I try to stop it.

I wake up screaming.

After my placement in Manchester was over, I had to go back to university in Essex. When I got back to Chelmsford, and I was alone again, I really started to struggle and go downhill once more. I missed Barak's support so much and I got depressed and cried all day. Even walking to the shops was hard – I'd move like a zombie and slow to a halt and just stand there, wondering how I was going to get home.

That's when I got a call from Hak, asking if I wanted to come up to Birmingham and hang out. I felt the urge again – the urge to go back, but I didn't want to. It started pulling at me and I tried to pull in the opposite direction, away from it. But, slowly, it started to get the better of me – the urge. I kept saying to myself, over and over: 'Don't go back! Don't go back! Don't go back!' But I didn't want to stay on my own in Chelmsford, and where else could I go?

Barak?

I couldn't ask a man like Barak for anything, like a family, because I wasn't worthy of anything. That's why it always came down to the sex thing, because I didn't have the right to ask for anything else. If I asked someone to commit to me, I'd feel like I was asking for something I wasn't entitled to. More and more it began to seem like this feeling was my home now – I could go on holiday to a nice place for a while, but I'd always have to come back home, where the weather was shit.

I wrote in my journal that I was just a doormat, and doormats weren't good for anything else because they're too dirty. I couldn't change. I tried, but I couldn't do it. Even if I did change, I'd be pretending to be something I wasn't. You hear about domestic violence in relationships, how some men beat their wives and girlfriends – I thought that might be a welcome change from what I was experiencing. At least it'd be something I understood.

About a month after I shaved off all my hair, I got a call from one of the specially trained officers assigned to my investigation. She was concerned about how depressed I was and she made an appointment for me with my local doctor's surgery. I wanted to see a female doctor, but there wasn't any, so I saw the nurse, who put me on Prozac. I was still only 21 and the leaflet the drug came with said it wasn't recommended for people under 25, as it could give them suicidal thoughts.

A couple of weeks after starting on the Prozac, my mental health deteriorated. I wanted to jump on a train and go back to the seediest part of Birmingham I could find and let myself be gang-raped by the worst criminals in the city.

I had a dream about being murdered by a Pakistani. He was dressed in a surgeon's outfit, with gloves and a mask, so he wouldn't get contaminated white-girl blood on him. He tried to dispose of my body in a sewage plant, where I belonged, but I wasn't dead. So he tried to choke me to death with his penis and that's when I woke up, coughing and spluttering.

This poem is underneath that entry in my journal:

Please take my ears away from me
Take my eyes so I can't see
Take my voice so I can't speak
About the secrets that I keep
I hear the things they say to me
Please take my ears away from me
I see the things they do to me
So take my eyes away from me
Please take my mind away from me
And take my memories from me
Take my soul away from me
Take everything I have from me.

My situation was so distressing that I tried to overdose. I didn't want to, but my mind was driving me to it. I hated myself for feeling the way I did – it wasn't natural. *I* wasn't natural. I was on pain medication for a back injury I'd sustained while moving my stuff from one flat to another on campus. I'd been prescribed a large amount of it and I popped out 60 tablets on the table in a pile. They were big, round pills, not easy to swallow, so I got a pint of water and started taking handfuls of them. Shoving them into my mouth and drinking the water to get them down. I needed four pints to swallow them all and I started to feel dizzy before I'd even finished. I got into bed and lay down. It was like I saw myself from above – a bird's-eye view.

It looked so sad, the ending of my life.

I must've passed out, but I suddenly felt somebody slapping me across the face, and I briefly came to. One of the other students was sitting beside me on the bed, shaking and slapping me. There was a knock on the door and she went and let some people in. They were ambulance men, who took me to hospital. I knew who they were and I didn't want to go, but I was too zonked to resist.

When I got to A&E, they put me in a side room and hooked me up to a blood pressure monitor that was attached to the wall. I knew they weren't going to let me die like I wanted. I tried to escape so I could find some place to hide and curl up and die alone, but I was so dizzy and disorientated I couldn't run and the sister caught me and took me back to the room. A doctor came and he stroked my head.

'Why did you want to do this to yourself?'

'I don't want to live any more.'

Then I started crying and I couldn't stop. I was attached to the wall by the blood pressure machine and it felt like I was chained up. I couldn't escape. Eventually, I fell into a heavy sleep but woke shortly after with an overwhelming urge to throw up – I don't know if they gave me something to make this happen but, if they did, it worked! There was a healthcare assistant in my room and he ran off to get a sick bowl, but I didn't have time to wait for that. I flopped out of the bed and stumbled across to the sink and vomited like that girl in the *Exorcist* film. I couldn't stop throwing up after that – it was fluorescent yellow bile and it tasted like paracetamol. I was just sick and sick and sick and sick, until I thought my insides were going to come up. They took some bloods and did an ECG and said the paracetamol levels were now safe and they put me on a drip.

I was so angry. I was trying to kill myself and all I did was make myself violently ill. I couldn't even do that right.

What a failure!

The next morning my mother arrived. She'd driven all the way from Shropshire. She was really upset and wanted to know why I'd taken an overdose. I couldn't keep the truth from her any longer. I told her I was involved in a police case and that I was both a victim and a witness, and that it'd all got too much for me.

'But, Kate, what's it actually about?'

'Multiple cases of rape.'

She was shocked. Just like me, she knew very little about what had been going on. She said she had an idea I wasn't happy, from the times I'd come home briefly, but she'd never realised things were so bad for me. I think she was really sorry about that disagreement we'd had when I was 18 and left home to go live at the SAU. It had always upset me that I'd lied to my parents about where I was and what I was doing. I'd be in Birmingham or other places, and I'd be on the phone to my mother.

'Yes, things are fine. I'm at the university.'

I'd be lying. Sometimes I thought, if I died or was killed and my body was found in Coventry Road or Green Lane or Alum Rock or Ladypool, my mother would never know how it got there. It would be found in some horrible place, full of dirt and filth and faeces. But the phone had been a lifeline. Even if I didn't tell her the truth, the sound of my mother's voice on the other end of the line would always bring me back to reality.

Until I hung up.

And now she knows. And my father would know too; and my brother and sister; and the rest of my family. What would they think of me?

The hospital wouldn't discharge me until I had a mental health assessment. When the nurse came, I tried to be honest. I tried to tell them everything, about being raped in Telford and the Asian gangs and everything. I didn't say how I thought there was a demon inside me and I didn't really know myself what was wrong with me at that time. I was still vomiting and had to stop mid-sentence to be sick into one of the cardboard bowl things. So they stopped the assessment halfway through and said they'd come back later that day. Which meant I couldn't leave.

When I was finally assessed by a mental health team, they cleared me to go home to Shirlett with my mother. They didn't understand the extent of my problem, and I couldn't explain it to them. One of the nurses told me that I wasn't sectionable. I was willing to be sectioned and I would've agreed if they'd asked me, just to stop me going back to the abuse. But they didn't think I was a high enough risk. I realise now I was a very high risk and I'm lucky to still be alive. Back then, I could've done with at least a couple of weeks as an in-patient, just to keep me off the Birmingham streets and out of danger.

My mother took me back home from Chelmsford. I couldn't really call it home because it wasn't my house, and it seemed to me that nobody wanted me to think of it as my home. So I just called it 'Mother's house'. I tried to tell her how I felt – I said I found it hard to live just because I didn't want to hurt anyone by dying. But it was difficult. I wished people would want me to die, then I could do it without worrying about leaving hurt behind.

She tried to understand.

I didn't take another overdose, but I wasn't safe and I wasn't fully right in my head until I was diagnosed and began therapy in 2015. I had no feeling of any kind. I was in a constant state of numbness where I didn't care about anything anymore and couldn't feel anything anymore. I also thought what an idiot I'd been for trying to kill myself. Death was the end, the last thing on the list to do. I tried to fight the urge to go back to Birmingham by suicide, but going back to Birmingham had to be better than death. Didn't it? I felt like I couldn't fight the demon anymore. But I knew what would happen if I went back to Birmingham and I couldn't do it while I was with Barak. I was having all these horrible thoughts I couldn't control and I didn't want to destroy him like I was destroyed. I could never find a way to explain to him what I was feeling – I couldn't explain it to myself or to anyone else.

So I gave up.

Again.

That's when I left Barak.

I left Barak because I didn't want to be with him while I was doing what I was doing. I didn't want to hurt him, but I couldn't love him the way he deserved to be loved. I couldn't stop myself – I couldn't fight what was inside me. Looking back now, I realise it wasn't a good time to be making life-changing decisions. I should have been in hospital for my own safety and to stop me ruining the rest of my life. But 'to stop you ruining the rest of your life' isn't a valid reason for admission. Whatever way you look at it, I needed help of some kind because my mind wasn't right. It was like something had been killed inside me.

Barak was a good man. He was kind, honest, gentle and emotionally open. He was safe to be with. But I didn't fully understand him. He may have been autistic and processed trauma differently to me. That might explain why he seemed so faultless. It confused me, how nice he was and I placed him on a pedestal. He was something I thought didn't exist – a perfect man. Everything about him had meaning and that attachment was part of my trauma. When you've lived with extreme harm, safety can be overwhelming and you cling to it like a limpet. It's a tactic used by torturers – they inflict obscene pain, then send in a 'nice guy'. The tortured person is so desperate for any kind of relief that they embrace the gesture and capitulate.

I called Barak and told him about the overdose. I told him it was a drug thing, because I didn't know how to explain it any other way. How would he have understood? I cried on the phone when I told him it was over, but I had no choice because I had to be alone and not belong to anyone to do what I was going to do. This was what I deserved anyway. I was a sex slave and that was my true calling. Trying not to be was impossible.

I only stayed with my mother for a day, and then I went back into Birmingham.

****

I'm supposed to meet Hak, but he's not around and this guy called Shaweer, who says he's a friend, picks me up from the station. Shaweer doesn't take me to Hak's place in Billesley, but to this dosshouse on Wormwood Road in Alum Rock. There's about half-a-dozen men there, all dressed in their religious clothes – white, loose-fitting trousers and tunic tops – and I make a joke that they look like Jedi Knights. They don't laugh. They've come from celebrating Eid al-Adha, which is a Muslim festival, with their families. The one who owns the house is called Mamu and he's an old man with a thin strip of hair round his head. They're cooking a big pot of curry and smoking marijuana.

As soon as we're inside the door, Shaweer hauls me up the stairs to a small room at the back of the house. There's no covering on the floor, just creaky wooden boards with big gaps in between, a boiler that leaks and a metal-framed single bed with a nasty-looking, stained mattress. The men queue up and take their Eid clothes off – I can see that some of them have genital warts. They want to show respect for their white clothes, so they fold them neatly and carefully. Then they rape me, one at a time and sometimes two or three at a time. They do everything –

anal, vaginal, oral. One of them sticks his penis into my mouth after it's been up my anus, while I struggle and some of the others hold me. I throw up on the floorboards.

Afterwards, I'm in the living room with them and they're eating the curry. Despite going there willingly – or maybe compelled to by the strange compulsion in my mind – I now need to get out of that place, so I say I want to go to the toilet. The front door is locked, so I go into the loo and sit on it to urinate. Just then, one of them bursts through the door to check that I haven't run off. I have my trousers and underwear around my ankles so I can't get away from him. He pulls his penis out and starts shoving it into my face. He grabs my head and forces it towards his penis. I keep pulling my head away and moving it from side to side and eventually he gives up and goes back to the others.

When I come out, they're sharing the food from several large bowls, but there's a smaller bowl in front of my seat. No one wants to share with me because they consider me to be dirty. They speak in Urdu or Punjabi, which I can't understand, and I'm wondering how I'm going to get out of there. I keep thinking Hak must know where I am and he'll turn up soon and take me to his place in Billesley, but he doesn't.

Eventually they begin to leave, one by one, until there's only me left and the old guy who owns the house, Mamu. It's very late and I'm exhausted, and he takes me to a room with a made-up double bed. His English isn't good when he speaks to me in a low voice:

'You sleep. I take you home in morning.'

I'm badly messed up, so I just fall on the bed and kind of pass out. A little later I wake to find old Mamu beside me, trying to have sex with me. I jump out of the bed to run, but he's surprisingly fast for his age. He grabs me by the hair and screams.

'You bitch!'

He pulls my head back and starts punching me in the face. I fight back and manage to get free. I run downstairs and find the front door unlocked. It's 4am and very cold, but luckily I'm still dressed. I woke up as he was trying to take my clothes off. I can hear him coming after me, screaming and swearing in Urdu.

I don't know where I am, so I just run down the deserted street until I'm sure he isn't following anymore.

* * * *

I called Hak and he came and picked me up. I was really angry at him for giving me to his friends – at least, that's what I believed he did.

'I had no idea they were going to do that, Kate.'

'Oh, no? And I suppose you told them I was a whore?'

'I didn't…'

'Just get me to the station.'

I stayed at Birmingham New Street station for the rest of the night and caught the first train back to Chelmsford in the morning.

13

Going Crazy

Barak was staying in a hotel in Leeds, which was something to do with his computer course – he may have had an interview or something, I can't remember. I went up there for one day, so I could end it with him properly. I was crying on the train. The woman beside me was crying too, and I asked her what was wrong. She said her dad had died. I told her I was breaking up with my husband. We cried together.

I went to the hotel in Leeds and Barak wasn't angry. He was never angry with me. He just listened. I don't remember what I said exactly, because it's all a blur. The anti-depressants I was taking must have had something to do with the numbness I felt. I told him I didn't want to be a Muslim anymore, I didn't have any religious feelings anymore – it was all gone, just an empty space in my mind where it used to be.

I didn't have any feelings at all. Which wasn't true, because I still loved him. But how could I love him and do the stuff I was doing? It was crazy – I was crazy. And getting crazier.

I cried when I spoke to him, I remember that. He cried too. It was heartbreaking for both of us and we cried together all night. I loved him, really, and he loved me. We loved each other and leaving him broke my heart as much as it broke his. But I felt like I had no choice.

If I stayed, the demon would destroy us both. It was bad enough it was destroying me, I didn't want it to destroy him as well.

It was a parting of indescribable sorrow.

Instead of going back to Chelmsford or Shirlett after being in Leeds with Barak, I went to Birmingham and just wandered about, not doing anything in particular – just trying to figure out what was wrong with me and why it made me leave the only man who loved me. I got the last train back to London that night, but I arrived too late to link up with the last train to Chelmsford. I was stranded in London with nowhere to go. I didn't have any money for a room or a taxi, so I telephoned Hak in Birmingham and asked him if he knew anywhere in London I could stay for the night. It was late, about 1am, when I was approached by a man who looked Asian.

'Are you Kate?'

'Yes, I missed my train.'

'Where do you live?'

'Chelmsford, in Essex.'

'I can take you there.'

The guy told me his name was Ravindu and he was from Sri Lanka. We left the station and went over to a car parked by the side of the street. It had three men inside.

'What's this?'

'It's all right, they don't speak English. I have to drop them off at London City Airport, then I'll take you to where you want to go.'

You see, this is how I found myself in serious situations very quickly. Anyone else would've walked away, but I got into the car and we drove to a Travelodge near the airport. They all got out and went into reception, while I stayed in the car.

A few minutes later, Ravindu came back out and asked me to come inside for a few minutes. Again, any woman with an ounce of sense would've stayed put, but I followed him into the lift and we went up to a room on the third floor. The other three men were inside the room and Ravindu shut the door.

* * * *

As soon as I arrive they all start grabbing me and pulling at my clothes. Then an argument breaks out between them, and Ravindu tells them to back off, in Sri Lankan – at least, I assume that's what he says, because that's what they do. The other three leave the room and he grabs me and is all over me, kissing my neck and chest and trying to get my top off. I don't know what to do; if the others are outside the door or what. I'm trying to push him away and he's going;

'Why, honey? Why don't you like me?'

In my stressed-out state, the fight or flight instinct tells me to fake it – then he'll relax and let me go. So I go completely limp.

'I do like you, I'm just shy.'

It works and he lets go of me and I make a run for the door, hoping the others aren't outside. They're not. I run to the lift and push the button, but he's coming after me and he grabs my arm. I shake him off.

'Get away from me!'

I run down the corridor to the stairs. As I spiral down and down, on every floor the stairs are facing the lift and I can see the numbers descending and I know he's in it.

When I get to the bottom, I realise I'm in the basement and there's no way out. I need to go back up to the ground floor. But wait, he won't be expecting me to be down here. So I hide in the basement until I think it's safe to move. Then I climb back up to reception and look through the double doors to see if the car's gone. It is.

I heave a huge sigh of relief, but when I try to breathe again, I can't. I'm trying to force a breath into me but I can't control it. The receptionist comes to help me and gets me to sit down and tells me to stay calm and concentrate on my breathing. It takes me ages. He gives me some water to drink. It's hard to regain a steady breathing rhythm and I have to concentrate and keep focused until the panic subsides. By now there's a few people around me and they're asking if I'm all right. I nod.

'Are you asthmatic?'

I shake my head.

'A panic attack?'

I nod again.

'What happened?'

* * * *

I can't tell them. How can I say I don't know why I keep doing this to myself? Why did I get in the car? Why did I go to Birmingham in the first place? Why do I continuously get myself into dangerous situations? One day I won't be so lucky and they'll find my body in a ditch somewhere and they'll never catch my killers.

The room was paid for, so they let me stay there for what was left of the night. I could make my way back to Chelmsford in the morning. While I was lying in the bed, wondering if Ravindu and his friends would come back, I kept asking myself the question: what's wrong with me? Am I crazy? Did I not think I was worth enough to feel scared about what might happen to me? Was I too numb inside to feel fear?

Not strictly true.

Part of me was afraid the people from Telford who I was reporting to the police would be able to find me in Birmingham. Part of me hoped they would find me, so I could kill them. I weighed up the possibilities of it happening. The only connection between the Telford gang and the gangs in Birmingham was through Tamjeed, to Cemal and Hafeez. The police had decided not to investigate Tamjeed, so it was unlikely he'd be looking for me, though not impossible. In any case, the Pakistanis always used to tell me: 'We don't have friends, only family.'

When I first started hanging out at Hak's, I half expected someone from Telford to turn up one day, but they never did. So, the probability of any of the guys I was reporting actually coming across me in Birmingham was pretty remote, but if it happened it happened – that was the way I saw it.

Barak tried to call me after I got back to the university, but I wouldn't answer the phone. I went cold inside. He left messages asking me not to do bad things, but it was no use trying to get through to me because I was deformed inside and words just bounced off me. They couldn't penetrate the deep scarring. I should've gone to him – I wanted to go to him – but I'd done too many bad things. It was too late. I thought maybe he'd come to me, like a knight in shining armour to rescue me. But he didn't. I couldn't blame him for that.

Barak was one of a kind and no one else could live up to the memory of the time I spent with him. I left him to protect him from the life I was leading and it was probably the worst decision of my life – but what else could I have done without hurting him deeply? Not go back to the abuse would be a fair comment – and it's something I don't have a comprehensive answer for. I felt I had no control over what was happening to me. I was so emotionally damaged – the men made me feel like I had no right to say 'no' to them. They believed it themselves; they believed I had no right to say 'no' and they made me believe it too.

I gave up fighting it. Fighting against it was too traumatic – it was easier to give up. Looking back now, I'm proud of the times I did try to fight, even though the memories of those horrific events are still very painful. But I don't blame anyone who gives up. The psychological violence is so exhausting that sometimes you just can't do it – so you blank it out and let it happen. I'm not saying you should actually give up completely – never give up completely on yourself, even when you feel like you're at the end of the road and can't go any further. Just go to sleep for a while to get your strength back. But keep waking up!

In the weeks that followed, I was taken to many other towns and cities in the West Midlands to be used for sex. A particularly horrific incident involved 10 men in one night. I was so convincingly groomed and brainwashed that I believed it was consensual. I knew no other method for healthy sexual activity. I found myself back in the cycle of self-destructive abuse and this way of life became normal again. Very few women would describe such an experience as consensual and it wasn't. It was intimidation. It was control. It was *rape*.

Worse still, I believed I was complicit in my own destruction and I didn't care, it seemed like it was destined to happen and there was nothing I could do to stop it. I was completely isolated in my mind, cut off from normality.

My abusers were my family.

My raison d'être.

The rapes at the SAU groomed me, traumatised me and created the me I became then. By the time I escaped to university, I was a fully fledged 'p***-shagger', shaped exactly as they wanted me and passed on to the next group. I was ready for the Birmingham gang because I was already conditioned to believe I was good for nothing else. I was passed around by one group to another as a 'favour' to their mates and not for money – at least, I never saw any money change hands. I think it gave them a feeling of status and made them popular with their peers. The serial rapes destroyed my limited support systems and I became completely isolated, even at university. I had nowhere to go, life became an endless series of abuses and humiliations, with surreal interludes of my sessions at university drifting in and out like ghostly shadows.

I was almost completely destroyed as a person.

Almost.

Bru, who used to supply me with cocaine, called me and I went up to Birmingham to see him. He picked me up and, as we were driving, another car with three Asian men in it pulled up beside us. I didn't like the look of this, but Bru seemed to know them so I wasn't all that scared. I trusted Bru, he'd 'looked after me' when I was really in a bad way and he'd always treated me with respect. So, when Bru got into their car, I went with him.

We drove to a block of flats in Highgate. The guy who owned the flat was called Khalil, who the others referred to as Big K and, after we were there for a while, more men started to arrive. They began piling in one by one, bringing big black sports bags with them. Big K took a large mirror off the wall and laid it across two stools like a table. They took out eight little weighing scales and opened up the black bags, which were full of white slabs. I asked Bru what it was.

'Heroin.'

That freaked me out and I wanted to leave, but Big K got really agitated and said I couldn't. I was getting scared now and I think he would've hit me if Bru hadn't got between us.

'Don't worry, she'll stay.'

I didn't want to be there or be involved, but it was like being kidnapped. Once Big K backed off, Bru told me I couldn't leave because they were afraid I might go and say something to someone and, if the police turned up, they wouldn't have time to get rid of the evidence. That really worried me. Did they know I was talking to West Mercia Police? Did they know I was part of Operation Chalice? I guessed if they did, then I'd be dead by now, so I sat down and kept my mouth shut.

The weighing of the heroin went on all night, for hours and hours, and these guys were smoking weed and taking lines of cocaine and they were very jumpy. There was a lot of cash going around as well – every man had his own stack of money and Big K was hiding bundles around the flat. I never helped them bag up or do anything; I just sat and watched, worrying in case the police raided the place and I'd be implicated and probably go to prison for a long time.

I took out my phone to play Candy Crush to calm my nerves and take my mind off what was happening around me. As soon as he saw the phone, Big K came at me with a knife.

'What're you doing? Who're you texting?'

Again, Bru jumped in to save me.

'She's cool, she's cool.'

He took the phone off me and showed Big K that I was just playing a game.

'She's not going to snitch. Leave her alone.'

Bru told me to be more careful. He said Khalil had done time in prison and he was a violent guy. In fact, he'd spent most of his life in prison for smuggling heroin from Afghanistan. He stabbed someone while he was inside and he was a bit unstable because his mother had been murdered a long time ago and he saw it happen.

'Why'd you bring me here, Bru?'

'I didn't mean to. I had no choice.'

* * * *

Once they finish weighing the heroin, the men want to have sex with me, as I'm the only woman there and they're all high by now. So they start getting their penises out and trying to make me suck them. Bru tries to stop them, but they just push him away. I'm screaming at them to leave me alone, but they just laugh and take me to the bedroom and I end up being raped by all of them.

* * * *

I tried to think of ways of controlling my mind without going to Birmingham. I needed to figure out what a normal life was again, because I was doing it all wrong. I'd never gone to a party or had a girly night out. I'd never had anyone to get ready with and dress up to go out with. I didn't even own any clothes to go out in. There were a lot of normal things a girl of my age should be doing that I didn't know how to do. I had to try to discover myself, or rediscover who I used to be, but it was difficult and lonely. I never knew what was right to wear. I didn't want to look horrible, but I didn't want to look like a tramp either – like the tramp I was. I was afraid to look nice in case someone decided to rape me and I'd get anxious about it. I worried about that a lot – that if I did this or if I did that, someone might rape me. I was also afraid to admit to a man that I'd been raped, in case they might think it was an opportunity to do the same. Maybe they'd think I'd be less likely to report them because it had happened before.

They would have been right.

I wanted to figure out how to be around men without it turning sexual straight away, so I decided a dating site was the best way to do it. I wrote on my profile that I wasn't interested in anything sexual and I just wanted to go out on dates with someone, like to dinner and the kind of normal things other girls my age were doing. But I soon discovered that most of the men on dating sites were just there for sex.

I met this guy called Gula, who turned out to be Kurdish, although I didn't know that before I met him. He looked Italian and he had lovely eyes. We got on well to begin with and eventually it led to sex, which disappointed me in a way, but I was trying to be normal and that's what normal girls of my age did – wasn't it?

He said he liked my 'posh accent'. I'd read a book or two and my vocabulary was wider than his. I'd use words like 'established' or 'necessarily' or 'discrimination' and they were the biggest words he'd heard a girl use.

'You are the most educated girl I have met.'

He used to say he liked me because he could have an intelligent conversation with me. But paying me compliments was part of his own grooming process, nothing else. All he wanted from me was sex and he turned out to be as bad as the Pakistanis. Gula lived in a shared house and one night he asked me if I'd sleep with his cousin. Any normal girl would've been appalled by this request, but I was so used to being disrespected by men, I didn't even know what respect was, so I wasn't insulted. But I said I didn't want to. He kept insisting for a while after, and I finally started to think it was time for us to part company. So I arranged to meet him one night to break up with him.

* * * *

When I get to his place, there's a group of men there with two young blonde teenagers. One of the girls is all over Gula and he just laughs at me when I ask him how old they are. Then this old ugly guy comes up to me and asks me for sex.

'No!'

'I'll tell Gula. Gula will tell you off!'

What? He's speaking to me like I'm some scared little girl or something. I feel sick; I could throw up thinking about what they might be saying to the two young blonde girls. I decide I have to get them out of there, but they don't respond when I try to talk to them. I want to help them but they don't want help – or they don't seem to. It's very difficult. I give them my number, but I know they'll never call me – and they never do.

The ugly guy starts to drag me into the bedroom, but I get away from him and try to leave. They stand by the door and won't let me go and I'm thinking I'm going to get raped again now. But I'm not going to let them think it's consensual this time.

'I'm not going to have sex with you.'

'Why?'

'Because I don't want to.'

'Why?'

'Because I don't want to and I don't have to and if you make me then it's rape and I'm calling the police if you don't let me go.'

The word 'rape' gets a reaction and one of them says 'Whoa!' and their expressions change to fear. They try to convince me it's not rape, because that's what rapists do – they try to convince their victims it's not rape because that makes them easier to control. But I stand my ground.

'Yes, it *is* rape. You can't have sex with me. I'm saying "no".'

One guy is still standing by the door.

'Can you get out of my way, please?'

I don't know why I say 'please'.

'Don't be unreasonable. Calling the police is unreasonable.'

'Well, let me go then, and you'll have nothing to worry about.'

'But it's late at night. We can't let a woman be out alone at night.'

This makes me laugh. These guys are about to rape me and now they're worried in case I might get raped out on the street! They let me leave and that's the last time I see Gula. Or use online dating.

* * * *

After my overdose, I came to realise that the biggest threat to my life was myself, what I was doing, not these men. Okay, they might be the means that justified the end – but I was my own killer. I'd stopped being afraid. I'd stopped caring. Rape didn't scare me – death didn't scare me. That's a very dangerous state of mind.

I spoke to my STO about Gula. I gave her his address. She said I could report it if I wanted to because, although they didn't rape me, they blocked my exit and, technically, that was kidnap, or holding a person against their will or something. But I decided not to – how would I explain why I was such an idiot for getting involved in the first place?

I know I have to take responsibility for my actions. Sometimes I was innocent and it wasn't my fault, but sometimes my actions led me to those dangerous situations I found myself in. Though that's no excuse for anyone to rape me. No matter what the circumstances, if a man knows a woman has said 'no', then he knows it's rape. And a man who's raped before is likely to rape again.

I can't remember how I came into contact with Kaliq; I think it was through Hak, but I'm not certain. He was in his 30s, short and bald, and he wore a beanie hat. Kaliq wasn't interested in having sex with me and that's probably why I trusted him.

What I didn't know was, he was a pimp and he tried to set me up as one of his string of prostitutes. He took me to a little B&B one night, without telling me where we were going, and said he had to get something from a room.

I thought he wanted to have sex with me and I wasn't falling for his line, so I tried to think of reasons I could give him as to why we shouldn't have sex. But there was another man already in the room when we got there.

* * * *

Kaliq gets out a bag of cocaine and chops up a line for me. Why don't I try to get away? Because I believe it's futile – again. What's going to happen is inevitable – again. And to keep fighting against it only makes it worse. So I just let the numbness envelope me – again.

All this time the other man's watching and it's a weird situation and, even though I feel numb, I don't want to do the cocaine because I'm not into cocaine anymore. Kaliq chops the drug in a big rush, like he wants to get out of there. He has the line laid out on the bedside table and he orders me to do it.

I reluctantly crouch down low to sniff the cocaine and, when I straighten up, Kaliq is gone – but the other man's still there. He's big and muscular and I have no idea who he is. He looks dangerous and I know it's another desperate situation I've gotten myself into.

'Strip.'

This is an order, not a request. I don't want to do what he says, but I'm afraid not to. I strip off my underwear and now I'm naked. He pushes me into the bathroom and tells me to get on my knees, which I do. Then he sticks his penis into my mouth and violently thrusts in and out, hitting the back of my throat each time. It's so violent, I realise I have to keep really still to prevent myself from getting hurt.

This is no blowjob – this is what they call a 'face-fuck', and I'm getting really scared. It's violent porno stuff, making the woman choke on the penis. The point is to hit the back of my throat, that's what turns him on the most. It's meant to intentionally make me choke because that's what he likes. It's making my eyes cloud over – I can't breathe and my eyes are streaming. All this is getting him more and more turned on and I'm gasping by the time it's over.

Afterwards, he tells me his name is Nadhir, like he's my friend. Like what's just happened is normal.

'I'm a pharmacist.'

He seems to think I'm impressed.

'I bet you didn't expect me to be a pharmacist.'

As if I'm a prostitute and not used to this class of client. I don't care who he is or what he does, I just want to get out of there. Kaliq comes back soon after. I think Nadhir hands money to him, but I can't be sure. Nadhir leaves the room in the B&B and it's not long before there's a knock on the door. Kaliq opens it and another guy comes into the room.

It dawns on me what Kaliq is doing and I wonder how many more are waiting outside? I haven't time to put my clothes back on and now I'm in the bathroom again with this guy called Itsaf. He's all over me before I can do anything. He wants to sniff a line of cocaine off my chest and then he wants me to sniff a line off his penis. He does this all in a rushed way, clumsy and awkward.

He tells me to suck his penis while he's leaning me over and pushing my back down, so I'm arched and my bum is in the air. Every time he pushes my back down, his penis slips out of my mouth. Then he's grabbing my head and trying to put his penis back in and he's saying it's my fault and I'm not very talented.

He obviously thinks I'm a whore and I should know how to do this stuff. In the end he just bends me over the bath and has sex with me that way. The whole thing is gross from start to finish.

As we come out of the bathroom, Kaliq is standing in the room with another man for me. I can't believe this. This guy's name is Wassim. I tell Kaliq I'm not a prostitute and he says he was told I was.

'Well, I'm not!'

'OK, just do this one and we'll call it a night.'

Wassim just wants straight sex with a condom. I'm completely exhausted and I know it's useless to argue. He's taking ages to come and I'm feeling sick by now and ready to throw up on him. I don't wait for him to orgasm – I just get up and put my clothes on and he looks at me confused. I walk out of the room and onto the street. It's late and I don't know where I'm going. I think I end up getting a cab to the station – I can't remember.

* * * *

I tried to stay clear of Kaliq after that. He managed to contact me and offered to set me up in a flat in Birmingham and we'd go 50/50 on the rent.

'What about the money you'll be making off me?'

'What money?'

'Fuck off, Kaliq!'

I ignored all his calls after that and he eventually gave up on his plan to pimp me out to all and sundry.

14

Twisted Thoughts

It doesn't take much to ruin someone's life, does it? Or maybe it does. Maybe what happened to me really was as bad as I believed it was. As if one day I woke up and the world was totally different to the way I thought it was. When I was going through one of my 'reminiscences', I found what helped the most was playing music. I remembered doing that when I lived at the SAU, playing it loud with my headphones on so I couldn't hear the banging on the door, or the shouting. I'd say to myself:

'Press the stop button, let's play a different memory.'

I was able to shift bad thoughts like changing a music track. It worked for me – sometimes.

The other thing was God. As you know, my parents were pretty liberal-minded, to say the least. They were both brought up in Christian families, but they decided they'd let their kids choose their own religion. So, when I was young I guess I was a bit confused – whether to believe there was a god or not. As a teenager, I came to the conclusion that I didn't know one way or the other, but that I'd better be a good person, just in case. Since then, I've experienced times in my life where the only option I had left was to pray to God to help me, any god – Allah or Brahma or Gaia or Kali or Pan or Yomi or any deity who'd listen. I needed God to hear me when nobody else could – at the times when I felt everyone hated me and nobody believed or understood that the horrible things I was doing to myself weren't on purpose. God was the only one who could look inside my soul and know I really didn't want to do those things and that I wasn't in control of myself. There were times when I felt so alone and it was just me and God and we'd get through it together.

He was the only one I could ask for help.

The behaviour of someone suffering with PTSD can seem very confusing. It doesn't make rational sense why an abuse victim who escaped one situation of being abused would have irrational urges to go back to the source of that abuse. Does it? Yet these abnormal and maladaptive thought processes occur behind the facade of normality and can be psychologically debilitating. I didn't want to do what I was doing, but I was powerless to stop myself. I couldn't ask for help because I knew no one would understand why I kept going back. It's hard for me to understand it myself, even now after all this time – after all the counselling and training I've had as a mental health nurse. I knew that, if I hated myself for what I was doing, other people would hate me even more if they found out. I made a lot of mistakes because I had no one to turn to and because it was so difficult to understand. But I'd like to assure anyone who might be going through what I went through that there is always someone you can talk to – always someone who will understand. Someone like me!

Through all this there were so many times I wanted to quit my studies – times when I hated it and couldn't see the point and couldn't cope and had enough. But I stayed. And the reason I stayed was because my life without university was literally a simple step away from becoming a prostitute. I knew, without uni, this would become my life. It was carry on studying or become a professional whore, not just a free trick. So, I stayed and made myself go every day – forced myself to keep going.

I was spending half my life in the company of rapists and gangsters, who were about more than just sexual gratification – they wanted to hurt me, they wanted to disfigure my mind – and I let them do it. But I was spending the other half in the relative sanity of study and, despite the mental trauma, I was still better at my assignments than a lot of people in my class. I began to make a chart, showing how the men in the grooming gangs were connected through social circles or family, and this helped me retain some semblance of sanity by trying to understand what was happening to me and how they were doing it.

Nobody knew where I was. Nobody could help me. As time went on, I came to realise that the only person I could rely on was myself. I managed to remain objective. I used what I learned on my course at university to develop my own self-help techniques and understand how I could break the cycle of mental illness and abuse that I was caught up in. The stuff I'd studied helped me to understand the gang culture I was immersed in and why I kept going back to it. I was desperately trying to utilise what I'd trained for in uni to break the psychotic stranglehold of the four years of abuse. I tried to recognise and understand what was playing inside my mind, over and over again. I was still experiencing abnormal thoughts, but I tried to understand and control them. This helped me to hold on to my tenuous sense of 'self' – who I really had been, once upon a time.

Gradually, the person I am today began to emerge.

I thought of my mother and how strong she was when she was bringing us up on her own. I began to draw on the memory of my mother's strength. I was beginning to come to grips with my mental state and how I could break the psychological hold the gangs had over me. I didn't really know what triggered a bad memory. They came at random times, just like the images of penises and similar flashbacks I had had before. But, after talking to a counsellor who was part of the ISVA (Independent Sexual Violence Advocacy) for Chelmsford police, I felt better. I believed there was a good chance she could help me understand what I was going through.

Once my mother found out about what was happening to me, after the suicide attempt, it was inevitable that my father would find out too. She had no alternative but to tell him and he would've been very upset if she hadn't. After all, he was still my father and we were very close once. We made contact and I asked him to come with me to a session with the counsellor. Once he found out about the abuse, he tried to be understanding. I guess he must've blamed himself for a lot of what happened – maybe if he and my mother hadn't split up? But I didn't blame him – I didn't blame anyone, except the people who took advantage of me.

In the counselling session, we talked about self-preservation and how I didn't have any sense of it. I described my compulsion to go back to the gangs as an extreme sport because of the risks involved. I believed I deserved to be treated the way I was because of the bad things I did. The counsellor helped me realise I didn't need to take those risks and I didn't deserve to be treated like a dog. She helped me focus on new goals: like finding self-worth and self-respect. I'd tried that before, with Islam and Barak, but I always failed in the end. I decided to try harder this time and figure out where I could find those things and keep them inside me, instead of the demon.

After talking with the ISVA counsellor, it confirmed something I'd been thinking already – that more victims still lived in Telford and other places, and they probably weren't able to get away to university, like me. They had to get on with their lives, so I should be able to do so, too. I wondered how many other victims were still suffering, like me. Had they been able to deal with it? Was I the only one still going crazy?

If you're a woman and you've never been raped, then you're lucky. In the course of my profession, I've met so many rape victims and so many rapists, that I've come to the conclusion that any woman who's managed to avoid being raped, in one way or another, is very lucky. I hope if girls and teenagers read this book, they'll be able to understand how easy it is to get caught up in a cycle of grooming, sex, alcohol, drugs and mental instability. I hope they'll be able to avoid taking the first step into that cycle. I learned that the old saying 'knowledge is power' is true. I was weak because I didn't know anything about Pakistani men or gangsters or their grooming tactics, and I didn't know the extent of what was going on. I believed I was isolated and alone.

You're never alone!

I believe the dangers of grooming and sexual abuse should be taught in schools as part of the sex education curriculum, particularly in relation to different ethnic groups – and without being racist in any way. I believe the records of successful trials and convictions could be used, and maybe books like this and visits from police and social welfare experts. Anything would be better than nothing at all.

After the counselling sessions with the ISVA lady, I wanted to figure out a way of gaining back my self-respect and rebuilding my self-esteem. Everything I'd tried so far had failed. Respect is something that's earned, even respect for yourself. I decided the only way to do it was through achievement, and that meant staying in uni until I qualified as a mental health nurse.

As part of my training, I was sent on another work placement module with an NHS mental health facility. I was assigned to an eating disorder unit (EDU), which was mostly populated by women and girls. For the first time, I started to feel like a mental health professional, but I was still young enough to see things from a teenager's point of view.

The first thing I noticed was the staff speaking to the girls as if they were five or six years old. When I saw these teenagers, it brought back my own experiences, but I wasn't sure if comparing their personality traits with my own was such a good idea. One patient hardly ever made eye contact and the staff assumed she was being rude and told her off. It made me angry because they were supposed to be helping these girls and they didn't seem to be. All my emotions are inside my eyes and if I look at someone I feel exposed and believe that person can see into my soul, leaving me weak and vulnerable, which I hate.

It's an irrational thought, but many emotions are irrational. That's what the police counsellor said after I had the sessions with her, and it made me think – that little phrase could help me understand the actions of people, including myself. Emotions are irrational! I was a student nurse, but it wasn't so long since I'd been a teenager myself, and I could still remember what it was like. It was important for me to remember that, otherwise I might lose the ability to communicate with these girls and end up speaking to them like the staff did.

In the EDU, the crazy hang-up was with food. Food is a part of everyday life, so it affects every day of their lives. They had to change so much regarding the way they thought about, coped with, and viewed the world in relation to food, which was really difficult for them. In my own case, I realised, you could substitute the word 'food' with the word 'sex', and it was a similar scenario. They didn't want to face this problem – it was so hard and scary to do and staying the way they were was safer. They didn't know how else to cope with the irrational emotions of their situation.

Neither did I.

They needed another way.

I could relate to that, like the craving inside me to go back to the abuse. Unlike the girls trying to purge themselves of food, I was trying to gorge myself on guilt – the guilt I felt for agreeing to that word 'consensual' when I first reported rape. In a convoluted and perverted way, I was going back to prove to myself it was consensual and, consequently, I shouldn't feel the guilt. But it never worked, I just felt worse and worse. These girls needed positive thoughts all the time because what was wrong with them could kill them. They didn't want their lives to be like this, but they didn't want to die either. The same as me. I didn't want my life to be the way it was, but I didn't want to die, either. I felt like I wanted to die many times and even tried to die a couple of times. But, if I'd really wanted to kill myself, I could've done it.

This was the first time I even considered that I might have PTSD. All this time I was blaming this and that for my behaviour and the demon inside me. I never imagined that the demon could be a mental disorder – me, a mental health nurse, being crazy myself? People would fall about laughing, wouldn't they?

We all have an inner voice, so why don't we regard people who speak to their inner voice as being unhappy and needing help, and not as someone to be feared? And who could say what was mad and what was sane, anyway? We should just normalise what's seen as the signs of madness. I was reading the notes of a patient and I suddenly started thinking; *this could be me, they could fit me into one of these places no problem.* I felt safer around mentally ill people than I did around so-called 'normal' people. What did that tell me?

It was the first time I started to consider that maybe I had a mental illness. Maybe that's what I'd been fighting for so long? And that's why it's been so hard? I started to ask myself questions – if I was fighting a mental disorder, was I winning the battle or losing it? Did I need help, or was I coping with it on my own? I couldn't tell if I was getting better or not because, when I was happy and content, I felt I was okay and I always had been. But when I felt low and depressed, it seemed like I made no progress whatsoever and was depressed all the time, never really happy. I would push the bad feelings to the back of my mind for a while, but they always escaped from there and returned stronger than before.

When I was depressed, I knew these feelings were never going to go away – that I'd feel like that for the rest of my life. This scared me and made me feel negative about everything – myself, my future. It didn't matter where I went or what I did or who I talked to, the problem would never go away. But when I was up I felt fine, and the way I felt when I was down didn't make a single bit of sense to me.

I went back to Essex to finish my work assignments. I was given a drug and alcohol placement, where I learned theories of addiction and treatment models. There are many forms of addiction and obsession; I was addicted to and obsessed with returning to the scene of the crimes that were perpetrated against me, even though I hated it and tried not to do it. It was such a strong compulsion that it was difficult for me to fight against, just like alcoholics and addicts keep relapsing, even though they hate themselves for doing it.

Then there was my fear – my weird, irrational, unnecessary fear – at least, that's how it seemed to me. Every now and then I had to stop and remind myself I wasn't living at the SAU anymore. But my physical location didn't matter. I still felt a kind of craving to do what

I had been doing in Birmingham – almost like I needed to give myself a reason for feeling the way I did. It was a form of self-harm because I didn't care about myself or what happened to me. A form of self-rape!

I'd known for some time that something was very wrong inside my head, but now I began to see it more clearly. I was two people, living two completely different lives. I decided to go back to the mental health team who assessed me at the hospital. They hadn't been in touch since my overdose, even though they should have followed up and kept an eye on me.

A Greek social worker called Alta was assigned to me and I attended counselling sessions which were helpful. She was the only one who really tried to find what was going on with me. She came to see me at my flat in the halls of residence at uni, and she had a way of understanding me that others hadn't. She told me she was going to put me on the vulnerable adults list, because of the high risk of me returning to Birmingham and the abuse. She encouraged me to go to my GP for antidepressants, and they prescribed sertraline. Alta then arranged for me to see a psychiatrist. I requested one from outside my catchment area, but that couldn't be arranged, so I had to see someone I knew on a professional basis from being a student. He diagnosed me as being bipolar and prescribed quetiapine.

Quetiapine is a mood stabiliser you have to be weaned on to slowly. The side effects could be very strong and he kept wanting me to increase the dosage to get the full therapeutic effect. He said I should be taking 600mg a day, but even on 200mg I was sleeping 16 hours and feeling zombified when I was awake. I tried to increase to 300mg, but that just made me sleep for 20 hours instead of 16.

It made me look as though I'd put on weight, even though I hadn't. It was as if the weight I already had seemed to hang differently:

saggier, baggier and bloated, and my face looked puffed out. Another side effect was my memory. I kept leaving stuff behind. I'd be in town or on a train and I'd realise I didn't have my handbag and couldn't remember where I'd left it. Some things I never found again if I left them on a bus or in a café. Once I left my laptop in the train station and, when I went to lost property, they'd scanned it as a bomb and I had to pay £20 to get it back. I was on quetiapine for eight months. After that, I assessed the medication myself and decided my quality of life was better without it.

Finishing university was a struggle. I failed my last assignment, which was very frustrating, but understandable. They allowed me a second attempt, and I also had to work on my undergraduate major project, which was a 10,000-word assignment, and do a final work placement. My father said I could move in with him so I wouldn't be distracted, so I went to live with him in Kent, which was about 70 miles from Chelmsford. It was okay because I only had to do my major project, which was a dissertation on 'the role of physiology in occupational therapy', and I didn't have any classes. I studied at my father's and used books at Canterbury Christ Church University.

My father was very supportive when he learned about how I was abused at the SAU and the pending court cases. He helped me with a lot of the police stuff and I'm very grateful to him. The police wanted him to appear as a witness in two of the cases because, when I was at the SAU, I told him some guys were bothering me, without telling him the full story. Being a witness took a toll on him because he doesn't cope well with stress – when he gets emotional, the stress gets worse. He's not very nice when he's stressed, and he started saying things like 'fucking p***s', which he'd never said before. He's very liberal-minded and certainly isn't a racist, but what happened affected him more and more as time went on. Being racist or blaming an entire community for the actions of a minority doesn't solve anything and he knew that. He's an intelligent man and he eventually apologised for his behaviour. He tried his best to cope, despite all the stress.

I lived with my father until September 2011. I was with the Canterbury and Coastal Community Mental Health Team until January 2012. They were very good and I attended a bipolar group, which I found really helpful. I was assessed by a psychotherapist, which consisted of weekly 45-minute sessions. He was the top psychotherapist there and we discussed whether it would be better for me to be assessed by a male or female. He decided to do it himself, which was a good decision, as I needed to learn how to relate to men in a normal way. I felt a woman wouldn't understand me, unless she'd been through what I'd been through, and that was highly unlikely. I'm not sure to this day whether or not I was actually bipolar. I don't need medication for it anymore and all my 'bipolar' symptoms can be explained by post-traumatic stress disorder.

My father had an active social life when I went to live with him – lots of house parties and raves in the woods, which was fairly typical of him. He took me to them and I met Alvin O'Rourke there. Me and Alvin hung out together while I lived with my father and we became good friends. He was probably my best friend in Stodbury at that time.

I went back to see a hippie woman at Super Spirit called Willow who was still supervising young girls who were coming to camp – girls who were at the right age to become victims of grooming and abuse. I didn't want to spook them; I just wanted them to know what their options were, so I asked Willow to speak to them. She asked me if I'd like to go on a 'hypno-journey', like she used to do when we were young at camp. Back then it was to find our 'purpose' or 'what we stood for', and I thought it might help me find an answer to why my life was as it was.

I went into my journey knowing I might not find what I was looking for. I wasn't even sure what it was. I lay on the floor inside the dome tent and closed my eyes. Willow said to relax and imagine I was going on a journey downwards. I could hear her voice growing fainter and further away as I went deeper and deeper.

'Light, love and joy is a person you can speak to, in the comfort of the arms of Mother Earth.'

I imagined Mother Earth as my own mother and light, love and joy were pure emotions that ebbed through me like the sea – they flowed into me like a wave and then retreated again.

I believe this is what emotions are supposed to be because we're not meant to be happy all the time. Light, love and joy come and go – come and go – come and go.

I looked for the 'thing' – the demon they put inside me – the feeling that wouldn't go away. I didn't want to speak to light, love and joy. There was another emotion I wanted to speak to. I wanted to know its name. I wanted to see what it looked like. When I found it, it was dark and I couldn't see it clearly.

It wasn't a ball of stinking maggots like I thought it would be, but it was moving, it was breathing. Strangely, I began to feel a sort of connection with it. I could see it breathing like a human being or an animal or some sort of living creature, and I gave it the respect I give to all living things. I felt excited – anxious and desperate to speak to it.

'What are you?'

It breathed in, like it was going to reply, but then it started coughing. The cough was black and phlegmy and sticky. I felt annoyed because

I thought it was refusing to answer. When it stopped coughing, I asked again.

'What are you? Why are you here?'

I was desperately trying to see what it looked like, but I couldn't. It sounded as though it was trying to answer, but again it just coughed and coughed and coughed, so much it couldn't get a breath to speak.

And I felt pity.

I realised it wasn't answering because it couldn't, and I wanted to do something to help it breathe. Then Willow began to bring me back – but I didn't want to leave it. Back past light and love and joy – but I didn't want to feel them. I had so much to ask it.

Back into the arms of the Mother.

15

Giving Evidence

The train journey between Chelmsford and Birmingham was long and boring. It took between three and four hours; that's a lot of thinking time. To pass the time, I used to write down my thoughts and experiences.

One time I was waiting for a train in Birmingham, going back to Essex; it was a time when I was very down and wanted to die. I wished I could just sit on the track and let the train run over me. I knew I couldn't, because someone would stop me. Or, if I jumped in front of the train as it came in, I might not be killed outright, just horribly disabled and disfigured and I'd be in a worse position because I wouldn't be able to finish the job. I might be paralysed – mutilated inside and out.

I got on the train early and started writing down my thoughts. Sometimes I'd cry as I wrote. The train started to fill up with people, but I didn't care who saw me crying or writing or even who read what I was writing. I half hoped somebody would, so they could rescue me from my life.

The train became so full there were hardly any seats left and, eventually, a man sat beside me. I didn't care, I just carried on writing – wondering to myself what I was doing here and how I'd got myself into this state – how much I hated myself and how much I wanted to die. I had an idea to put everything into a little notebook and leave it on the train for random passengers to read. But I was afraid it might be thrown away as rubbish and never read by anyone, so I didn't do it.

As we travelled down through the country, I wondered if the man sitting next to me was reading the stuff I was writing – I assumed he wasn't. But, when the train pulled into one of the stations on the line, before he left, he turned to me and said:

'Take care of yourself.'

He must have read a little bit. It must have upset him and somehow he thought of the perfect thing one stranger could say to another. It was a small gesture, but I still think about it to this day.

Memory fades, especially after trauma. Writing my experiences down allowed me to reconnect with parts of myself that might otherwise have been lost. In that way, my writings weren't just about what had passed – they also helped me to understand who I was, then and now. Eventually, I gave my writings to the police, and they said they could use my thoughts as evidence when I went to court to give evidence against Shahmeel on 8 November 2011.

The trial began on Monday 7 November, but I wasn't required on the first day because they were swearing in the jury. I stayed at my mother's house during the court case. I came up a week beforehand and my father came up a week later and stayed with my grandmother – I wasn't allowed to talk to him because he was being called as a witness. The prosecutors were also calling some of the people from the SAU as witnesses, my counsellor from university, and the police I first reported the rape to. Also, a social worker from the criminal justice mental health team who'd brought me to the MAPPA meeting that led to me re-reporting the rape. There might have been more witnesses, but the police told me very little because they didn't want to be accused of prepping me.

I had a million questions, but they couldn't answer them. They did let me visit the court before the trial, so I wouldn't freak out when I had to go in there. It was Shrewsbury Crown Court and it was huge – it looked like a building from medieval times. The ceiling was really high and reminded me of a cathedral. I had no idea what to expect. I'd been trying to prepare myself by watching rape cases on *Hollyoaks* and *Law & Order: UK* on the television. I remember asking myself: 'Are the barristers that horrible in real life? Surely they're not allowed to say those things?'

How naïve I was!

I asked a friend of mine who'd been to court – for throwing a cigarette butt on the street – what it was like.

'They'll try to lead you into a trap with their questions, Kate.'

'How?'

'They'll encourage you to say something that's not true, so they can turn around and call you a liar.'

I knew then that I had to tell the truth, the whole truth, and nothing but the truth.

'Don't rush your answers, and don't let them make you say "Yes" or "No" if the question needs a longer explanation.'

I wouldn't let them do that. I'd be brave. I'd be strong. But all the time at the back of my mind I thought, how was I going to feel when this trial was over? What if they couldn't get a conviction? Maybe if they could convict one – just one – that would indict the rest. But I knew my case would be very hard to prove because I was 18 at the time – I was regarded as a woman in the eyes of the law, even though I wasn't.

My relationship with my family was improving and my mother and sister came with me for support. They were allowed to stay with me in the little witness room before I was called in. When it was my time, they would go and sit in the public gallery.

They had to clear the court before I was called – the jury, defendant and public all had to file out before I was brought in. I sat behind a little black curtain where Shahmeel couldn't see me. Then the whole court had to watch the 90 minutes of my police interview on a big flat-screen behind the witness box. It had taken seven hours on the day and they had to edit it down, but it still made me cry when it came on. I cried watching myself cry on the video. I didn't make any noise, just sat there with the tears silently streaming down my face and dripping off my chin. I had a tissue that was ripped to shreds by the end.

After the video, the judge called a break and everyone had to leave first, before me. All this time, tension was building inside me and my nerves were at breaking point. I felt like running out of the court and down the street and never coming back. But I couldn't do that. I had to face what I'd been running from for so long.

When we came back, I was again behind the curtain and Shahmeel's barrister started to cross-examine me. She was a young woman in her early 30s with long blonde hair – exactly the type of woman Shahmeel hated. He'd have raped her if he got the chance!

'You had a bit of a reputation, didn't you, Kate?'

I immediately burst into tears and found it hard to speak.

'Not then… I hadn't done anything…'

The judge let me sit down during the questioning and I sat there and cried the whole way through. Shahmeel's barrister tried to insinuate that I was in love with him and had made the rape up because he rejected me. I'm sure that's what he must've told her and she was representing his lies. I could hear his voice coming through her mouth.

They were his words and I couldn't understand how an educated woman like her could believe her client's lies – if she did believe them.

I cried all the way through her cross-examination, which lasted the whole day. The judge offered me lots of breaks, but I was so upset I didn't know if I needed a break or not – I knew I was going to cry either way. During one break, Shahmeel's uncle burst into the courtroom after everyone else had left and saw me. I don't know why he wanted to take a look at me; maybe to see if I was wearing a *hijab* like I was in the videotaped interview. I wasn't. He was probably wondering to himself, 'Is she a Muslim?' and was reassured when he looked, probably saying to himself, 'No, she's just a white slag.' Or did he take a look so he could be sure he knew who he'd be searching for on the streets? I don't know.

The barrister said I was an attention seeker and that I must have been flattered when he told me he'd buy me a car and a house, but I said no.

'It was scary and weird and I knew it was bollocks,' I said.

I shouldn't have said 'bollocks' in court – I swear I could hear it echoing around the cathedral-like walls and up to the high ceiling and back again, and it seemed like the whole court went quiet. But the judge didn't say anything, so I reckoned I might've got away with it. I don't remember much else of what happened, but it's all on record.

The barrister also had my mental health assessments and medical records which she tried to use against me. By this time, I was almost qualified as a mental health nurse and it was something I knew more about than she did. I kept saying to myself: 'Don't let her lead you into a trap with her questions.'

'You had a mental health assessment, didn't you?'

She wanted me to answer with a simple 'yes'. I didn't.

'While I was in A&E after I took an overdose.'

'The jury don't need to know that.'

Yes, they did!

She asked me to read what was written down, that I'd been 'gang-raped'. I explained that I said I was 'raped by a gang' and that I was being sick into a bowl while I was trying to talk, and the hospital staff had typed up their interpretation of what I said when they got back to the office. Again, she said the jury didn't need to know that. They did. They needed to know the difference between what she was insinuating and what was the truth. She was comparing the reports from different professionals, concluding that what I said to them varied, so I must have been lying.

'Like you're lying now.'

I wasn't lying. I tried to say that they were trying all the men separately and, even though this trial was just about Shahmeel, there were other men involved. The judge stopped me talking about that in case I told the jury something they weren't supposed to know. The jury did ask questions: was Imran one of the men involved? Was Ali Sultan one of the men involved? They were told they weren't allowed to know. I wanted to scream: 'Yes, they were involved!'

But I didn't. I couldn't understand *why* the jury wasn't allowed to know. The fact was, I was set up by the Telford gang when I was raped by Shahmeel and I knew they told him to do it. They were all part of it, all connected, and the jury should've been told that. But the law's a strange thing – it makes me wonder sometimes if the judicial system needs to be reviewed so abused women don't need to be violated again in court by defence barristers.

It also exposes you to your abusers. The judge actually mentioned that it was my birthday and I'd be 24 in two months' time, right in front of Shahmeel and his family. I'd felt reasonably safe up till then, but that, coupled with the fact that my surname had also been used in court, meant I felt vulnerable once more.

My cross-examination stretched across two days. At the close of the first day, I knew I had to go back for another grilling. I think the jury must've found it difficult to watch – I was a bit of a state in the witness box.

When the defence barrister was finished with me, the prosecution barrister asked me a few questions. The questions were difficult and upsetting, but I knew he was just trying to show the jury that I was genuinely distressed by what Shahmeel did to me. I don't remember all his questions – it was much shorter than the defence cross-examination – but I do remember the last one he asked me:

'Why didn't you tell your mother?'

I just cried again.

'I don't know. I don't know why I didn't tell her. I wish I had.'

Although I was only required in court on two separate days, the trial went on for two weeks. The rest of the time, the police told me not to sit in the public gallery because it could affect the jury's verdict. The reason it went on so long was because of the number of witnesses they had, on both sides.

Shahmeel had his stepmother and sister as character witnesses. They said I showed my vagina to a child and my breasts to another child, on separate occasions. Instead of a victim, they tried to make me out to be some kind of paedophile exhibitionist. Shahmeel showed no remorse in court.

In the end, he was found guilty of raping me three times. He was sentenced to three concurrent 10-year prison terms, to be added to the end of his existing sentence for serious robbery. It would be at least 2020 before he could even apply for parole. It was denied.

Hakim got away with what he did to me, even though maybe he was the worst and even though I picked him out in the ID parade. They couldn't find a single eyewitness to say that we'd ever met. They said there wasn't enough evidence to prove we knew each other, so Hakim was never charged and never came to court. Nothing happened to him and he got off scot-free – which made me think I should never have told the police about him. I should've killed him myself and there would've been no evidence to prove we knew each other.

Imran and Uncle Nabi were arrested, but they made out that the sex they had was consensual, so the police and CPS dropped it. The dangerous-looking Turk got away with it too, as did Bazam and Tajammul and Gazi Amir and a lot of others.

I wished I'd killed them all!

Everyone said I should try to move on after the Shahmeel trial – that winning in a court of law was about moving on and not letting what they did to me ruin the rest of my life. But even after I moved on, I still remembered the ones who got away. It tainted and destroyed my teenage memories. Me trying to move on like it never happened felt more like a form of denial. Who would it help? It wouldn't help the other girls they'd raped since, or the ones they would rape while they were walking free.

I don't forgive the police for advising me to say that Shahmeel's rape was consensual, the first time I reported it to them. Rape is rape, and it doesn't matter if you're underage or over 18. I told them, and they let me go back. They knew what was going on back then, and I didn't. I didn't know about the widespread abuse of white girls. I thought I was the only one – alone, isolated, imagining things, going crazy. I did the right thing; I was trying to be a good person. They gave the rapist the benefit of the doubt, just because I was over 18. If they hadn't done that, things might've been different. I'm not saying they would've been – but they might have been.

In January 2012, after Shahmeel's trial, I actually moved to Birmingham. I got a job with a hospital close to the house in Stafford Road where Asif used to take me when I was desperate. By this time, the house had been renovated and rented out to a family. The battered old cars were gone from outside and I imagined a nice, loving family living inside, although I never went to check.

I don't know why I felt the need to return to Birmingham and actually live there after all the abuse I suffered. I think it was a healing thing, a way of conquering the place. It seemed to give me a sense of triumph over the abuse and empowerment over the past. I thought I felt strong enough to resist and have nothing to do with my abusers, even at close proximity.

One day I found myself in Green Lane and realised I was walking past an old, converted pub where I'd been abused one night when I had nowhere else to go. I'd spent all that night saying 'no' and fending men off as they tried to have sex with me. That time I managed to escape and didn't know where to go, but now it was as if I knew exactly where I was and where I wanted to go. It was a healing emotion in a way, because now I felt in control – even though I really wasn't.

Taking the job at West Whitchurch Hospital may have been a product of the PTSD, I'm not sure. I just know I was happy working in the catchment area of the Pakistanis who abused me. They thought I was nothing but a dirty tramp and here I was, probably looking after some of their family members. If they knew I was doing that, it would probably offend them – maybe it was a way for me to get even?

But why *was* I still preoccupied with that stuff? Why did I let it influence decisions on where I worked? Why couldn't I just let it go?

Even though I felt in control at last, I guess I was still lost, not knowing where I belonged. I still resented Essex because I felt trapped there and I still couldn't go back to Telford or Shirlett. I tried living with my father, but that didn't work out either because I was studying by myself for the most part and found it hard to make friends.

The job was a zero-hour contract as a healthcare assistant with the Heart of England NHS Foundation Trust, across three hospitals – West Whitchurch, Solihull and Good Hope Hospital in Sutton Coldfield – and I loved it. I loved working hard for the patients. I was on the 'bank' and if one of the wards was short, they got a nurse from the bank – which was a bit like working for an agency. I was moved around different wards a lot and I loved being versatile.

I finally graduated in March 2012 with a 2.2 BSc (Hons) in Nursing (Mental Health).

I found myself a one-bedroom flat in Yardley – near the dual carriageway part of Coventry Road, where I used to get dumped. I wasn't afraid, I was defiant. After a few months of living there I started to recognise things – they started to come to me out of the blue, like shock realisations. Maybe these shock moments were also part of the PTSD, the way memory didn't come straight away, but then hit me like a ton of bricks and made me jump out of my skin. Maybe it was some kind of anxiety, but I wasn't afraid. I felt empowered. I wasn't lost and confused any more.

My friends were women who were also reverted Muslims. We went to the revert group on Stratford Road and I hung out with them a lot when I wasn't at work. We went to the mosque together once a week and I even held a women's Qur'an class at my flat. The girls would come round and set up a buffet of food and sit in a circle on the floor and we'd all read a page of the Qur'an out loud and then discuss what we'd read. We'd practise reading it in Arabic to improve our Tajweed skills. We'd go to the Muslim shops on Coventry Road to buy scarves and books and ornaments and prayer beads, then we'd go and have coffee and cakes. I loved it.

I was very wary of men at this time, but I met a Yemeni guy at the mosque and he seemed very respectful. He reminded me of Barak. We got on well and he used to come around to my place and we'd chew *khat*, a shrub that has the same effect as amphetamine, and smoke *shisha*, tobacco sweetened with molasses, through a water-pipe or *hookah*. He introduced me to a group of Yemenis he associated with. They were more respectful than the Pakistani men I'd come into contact with and didn't expect to have sex with me, so I hung out with them and chewed the *khat* and smoked *shisha*. It was all very platonic and I learned a lot about their culture. We talked about Islam and exchanged ideas and opinions. I never had to have sex with any of them, and it was nice to be able to chill out with that group. It was reassuring for me to know that not all Asian men were rapists and abusers.

I never seemed to have any money, no matter how many hours I put in. I tried budgeting and I should've had some wages left over but I didn't. Then they increased my rent and the flat got overrun with mice from the empty shop below. I'd come home from work and there'd be three or four rodents running around, and a chocolate bar would be half eaten and there'd be mouse droppings in the rice. When I tried to sleep it was like they were right under my bed, but they were actually in the floorboards.

I caught one by trapping it under a scarf and I put it in a Tupperware box. I took it on the bus to get it as far away as possible, then I released it into a park. I caught another one by the tail, but it tried to bite me so I dropped it. I tried poison and found one dying on the bathroom floor – I didn't want to just throw the poor thing away, so I made a bed out of cotton wool for it to lie on until it was fully dead.

When the Yemenis came round, they always sat on the floor. I remember once, when a mouse ran out, they all screamed in a kind of Mexican wave and jumped up on the sofa. I never saw them after that. In the end it got too much and the flat was too expensive, so I moved in with my grandmother, Elizabeth, in June 2012. She was my mother's mum and she lived in Walsall, as did my other grandmother and I got on well with each of them. They knew a bit about the abuse, but not the full details, as that would've upset them too much. I vowed not to have any contact with my old abusers and I started wearing my Muslim *hijab* again. Then, one day, I accidentally bumped into Asif.

'Kate, how are you?'

'I'm well.'

'You look great. You want to get some food?'

'No, thank you.'

'Something else?'

'No!'

'Come on… for old time's sake.'

'Goodbye, Asif.'

I walked away. I never saw him again.

I didn't have Kaddi anymore. After I finished university, she got married and moved to Saudi Arabia with her husband, who was Syrian. She lived there as a teacher for a while, teaching English to schoolchildren. But living in the Saudi culture was too hard for her, so she got divorced and returned to the UK. Later, she went on a trip to Gambia to do charity work, helping children to get sponsored and go to school. She eventually moved out there and started her own charity, helping the less fortunate. I went out to visit her once, and I stayed for two weeks. I spent a few days in a hotel and the rest of the time with Kaddi in Serrekunda.

It was a mind-blowing experience and I could write a whole book about it! The effects of slavery were still very obvious and the poverty was shocking, as was the lack of healthcare facilities, and potholes in the roads so big you could fit a bus into them. If you got run over there was no ambulance to take you to hospital and, even if you got there, they wouldn't treat you if you couldn't afford it. The average wage in Gambia was about £35 per month, yet the restaurants were all overpriced and only tourists could afford them. I ate street food with the locals, who were nice enough, but the men were all looking for western wives so they could support their families.

Once, when I was eating at one of the street-food shacks, I met a man who said he was an undercover cop. He showed me pictures of a drug bust they'd done where they'd found kilos of cocaine, enough to fill the back of a pickup truck. I wondered why all the slabs were black.

'Because they were wrapped in rubber to stop them getting wet. Then they are hidden in rice or water to be smuggled.'

I asked him why Colombian cocaine would be distributed through West Africa. He said it was an easier route to Europe than going through Central America and Mexico. The trade was controlled by corrupt politicians who got filthy rich, while the people they represented stayed dirt poor.

The government cut the water off during the day, so I had to fill up lots of buckets during the night, to wash with and flush the toilets and for cooking. I couldn't drink the tap water and kids sold sachets of clean water on the streets that I tore the ends off with my teeth. The electricity would go off at random times which was really annoying at night when it was dark. I'd have to rely on torches and little gas fires to make a pot of *attaya*, which is a kind of Gambian tea. Malaria was rife, so I had to be careful with the mosquitoes – the homeless people would cover themselves with a big piece of material like a sarong that even went over their faces.

Kaddi worked in the countryside, known as 'the bush'. The women carried huge loads on their heads and had big bulging back muscles like you wouldn't believe. They walked around topless and breastfed in public, and this was viewed as perfectly normal. It was interesting for me in the beginning but, in the end, what I saw there was so mind-altering and stressful that I didn't feel mentally well enough to handle it, so I never went back. Kaddi stayed another five years, before coming back to the UK.

I joined another revert Muslim women's group and met some good people and went to classes in the mosques. My friends were Lisa, Louise and Marie, all Muslim reverts. They were the highlight of my day and they brightened my life. We went everywhere together: mosques and lectures and the *khutbah* (public preaching) on Fridays, and the revert group at Green Lane Masjid. I started wearing a *niqab* – I wore it everywhere; I felt safe and thought no one would recognise me.

Wearing the *niqab* brought its own social difficulties. I experienced a lot of racist aggression, from black women in particular. They'd make comments under their breath as they walked past me, or start arguments with me or bully me, not letting me pass. I also had a couple of bus drivers shout at me. One of them told me off for not moving to the front of the bus before it stopped to get off, even though that was against regulations. I guess he was just racist and didn't like what I was wearing.

Another time, when I was wearing a full veil and gloves, some teenagers threw white paint on me – they obviously didn't know I was white because they could only see my eyes. But the worst was foreign, not British, Muslim men who wouldn't leave me alone. They stared at me and followed me down the street and tried to start up conversations with me. I guess maybe a white woman wearing a *niqab* was a turn-on for them – how they knew I was a white woman I don't know, they just did. Maybe it was my blue eyes, or because I was on my own, or the way I walked. That's when I decided that wearing a veil, or even a *hijab*, was actually having the opposite effect to what I wanted, and I was now at risk of getting abused again.

From my short experience of wearing the veil, I can honestly say that it's people and society who oppress women who wear it, not the *niqab* itself. The veil's just a piece of clothing and it represents submission to God, not to men. But men hijacked that concept and I hated them for it. I hated the thought of any man coming near me, except Barak – and Barak was gone. I felt I couldn't trust any of them and I just needed to be left alone and allowed to live my life the way I wanted, not the way someone else thought I should be living it. Is that too much to ask?

I felt fairly confident that the old feelings wouldn't come back but, just in case, I signed up to a GP clinic straight away and asked them if they could put me in touch with the local mental health team. They never contacted me, so I went along to community mental health and spoke to a duty nurse, who wrote a few things down. But I never heard from them again either, and I was pretty much left to my own devices. I believed I'd become a strong person, but I was only just about coping on my own and needed some help.

The Mike Nolan trial was coming up in a couple of months and, gradually, the feelings of depression and suicidal thoughts started to come back – getting stronger and stronger until I was left in a general state of wishing I was dead. I felt like that even when I was happy so, if something happened, like a bad day at work, it became even worse. In this state, it didn't take much to make me feel really suicidal. On top of this, I wasn't sleeping well on the day shifts, so I switched to nights. I'd come home starving, but I'd be so tired I'd just sleep instead of eating, then I'd wake up at 5pm and feel depressed.

I was away from the abuse, but my mental state was deteriorating again and I needed to be strong enough to stay away from the Birmingham gangs until I could sort myself out. The coming trial was on my mind and I didn't know how I was going to get through it or how I was going to cope with the hostile cross-examination again.

Giving evidence in court was one of the most distressing things I've ever done. But I had to go through it, there was no way out of it. Yet I'm glad I did it. I was able to tell the truth and that mattered to me. I didn't want to survive by staying silent. But it was a very tense and topsy-turvy time.

16

Moonrocks

I decided to wear the *hijab* when I went to court to give evidence against Mike Nolan. My barrister said it'd be interesting to see how it would go with me being Muslim and Mike Nolan being a soldier. I still don't know what he meant by that. It was 2012 and the trial went on for three days. In hindsight, I think I shouldn't have worn the *hijab* but, at the time, I felt that not wearing it would somehow be dishonest – that it would be manipulating the jury and that would be wrong.

I know now that juries are there to be manipulated, by both sides. Even if you're telling the truth, you have to tell it in a way that's going to be believed. If you're lying, you have to lie convincingly. Both sides are trying to impress the jury: one with the truth and the other with lies. The side that manipulates best, wins. I failed to manipulate the jury into seeing what a horrible crime Mike Nolan perpetrated on me.

There were a thousand things wrong with that trial. It was in Shrewsbury Crown Court again, but this time I was treated unfairly from the very beginning. I felt I was discriminated against because I was wearing the *hijab*. The judge looked at me with clear disapproval and wouldn't let me sit down. I tried to, but he told me off – that was a bad start. I had to stand the whole way through, which I found really hard. I felt awkward and exposed and it felt like I was the one on trial. Again, they played a shortened version of my videotaped police interview to the court.

The defence barrister was a middle-aged man this time, and I'm sure he was paid for by the army. The first thing he said to me was:

'Don't worry, I won't ask you for details of why you got kicked out by your mother.'

He told the jury that Nolan went to the same college as me and he asked me if I'd met him there. I didn't even know he'd been to the same college and I certainly didn't meet him there. But the barrister insinuated that that was how I picked him in the line-up.

I said in my statement that Nolan was in the army when he raped me. The barrister said that was a lie: he was working in a bar in the area and only joined the army after that time. Again, he insinuated that I could've met the defendant in the bar. But I didn't drink and rarely went to bars – he didn't mention that. I said Nolan was in the army when he raped me because that's what he told me when we were introduced. By now my head was spinning, but I didn't cry like I did at Shahmeel's trial. I stayed as cool as I could, trying to answer the questions in a truthful and honest way. In the police interview, I'd said that Mike Nolan had a 'problem' and by that I meant the crazy way he acted when he raped me, how he was out of his head on something. I felt he had some serious psychological issues – as do all rapists. It was just an observation, but the defence tried to make it lurid somehow, like I meant he couldn't satisfy a woman. How would I know that if he didn't have sex with me? It was just farcical!

I should've asked for a break, but I didn't. I just kept going.

The taped police interview was cropped in such a way that the jury were confused. They weren't given the full story. For example, in the interview, the policewoman asked me:

'Why didn't you tell us this before?'

'Because I didn't think it was relevant.'

What wasn't made clear to the jury was that this was my second interview. They didn't know that I'd already given a seven-hour interview about Shahmeel and the others, and that I had to come back to do this one a few weeks later because I forgot about Mike Nolan. It seemed to them like I'd just made the complaint on a whim. This time I was cross-examined for less than an hour. I think the defence barrister kept it short on purpose, as he saw it was going well for him.

The prosecution barrister was the same one as in the Shahmeel case. He asked me some questions but I can't remember what they were. I think he was trying to clear up some of the misconceptions set out by the defence. By then I was confused, and my head was reeling. I just wanted to go home.

Mike Nolan gave evidence and said he wasn't denying that I was raped, only that it wasn't him who raped me. I'd mistakenly picked him out of the line-up because we went to the same college. He didn't mention that we were at college at different times, so it would've been impossible for me to have met him there. The prosecution team only produced one witness and that was the guy who introduced me to Nolan. The defence barrister discredited him and insinuated that he had a grudge against the defendant and that he concocted the rape charge with me to get even. Josie, my friend at college who saw the bites and bruises that Nolan had inflicted on me, refused to give evidence for the prosecution. She said she didn't remember anything and she wouldn't even answer the calls from the police because she wanted no involvement whatsoever.

So, between the sketchy evidence provided by the prosecution and the complete pack of lies convincingly presented by the defence, the jury probably thought I was either telling the truth about the rape but had accused the wrong man, or that I was lying for revenge. There was reasonable doubt.

Mike Nolan was found not guilty.

It was all routine for the barristers – another day at the office. They knew each other and joked together and it was like a game of chess for them, and I was just a pawn. The verdict was very hard for me to take as it made me out to be either stupid or a liar.

I was heartbroken.

And there was still Ali Sultan's trial to come.

While I was waiting for that, I passed a compulsory basic training programme so I could ride a scooter. I used to belt round Birmingham on a black and white Peugeot Vivacity that had flowers on the side. It felt good to begin with, having a bit of independence, and it was fun riding the bike – it released some of the stress inside me. I'd go for trips, just to get to know all the roads, and I'd get lost and have to keep checking the map on my phone. But I was constantly getting forced out of my lane by car drivers who came up really close beside me. I even got driven off the road once and had to go down a side street that wasn't where I wanted to be. It was very dangerous and it freaked me out in the end. When the bike got stolen, I didn't get another one.

My graduation was in October 2012 and there was a ceremony at the campus in Chelmsford. They had a huge marquee – I'd never seen one so big. My mother and father and grandmother, Eleanor, came with me. I collected my gown from a leisure centre and had my photo taken there. Then all the graduates had a parade to the graduation venue. Afterwards we went to a sports hall on campus for free champagne.

I'd like to say here that I'm very grateful to all my lecturers who were so supportive, even though they didn't fully know what was going on with me. They did a really good job and managed to keep me on the course and all the way to graduation. Even when I took an overdose and had to tell them what happened, they were still supportive. I'll never forget them for helping me through, despite my mental health problems at the time. They are true examples of what the mental health profession is all about.

Due to Operation Chalice, Ali Sultan, along with six other men, were arrested in November 2012. He was found guilty in May 2013 of raping two girls, aged 13 and 16, and he was sentenced to seven years in prison, which meant he'd be out in less than four years if he was found not guilty of raping me. Seven years for all the crimes he'd committed was nothing, but it was all they had evidence to prove, so they were hoping my case would keep him off the streets for a while longer. I'd already picked him out in an ID parade, and the police interviewed me about him again when he was arrested in November 2012.

Ali Sultan's trial for raping me was first scheduled for May 2014. The police didn't actually arrest him for my rape until after Operation Chalice was over because they didn't want anything to jeopardise the big investigation. They decided it was best to wait until he was charged with the other rapes before interrogating him about me.

The police support service sent me a reminder of my pending appearance in court every month from January – about four altogether. After the two previous trials, I really wasn't looking forward to it and it was starting to affect my nerves. I called them up and asked them to stop sending reminders, but then I'd get another a few weeks later.

I'd saved up a bit of money while I was living with my father, and my bank told me I was entitled to a graduate loan after I finished university. So I put a deposit down on a flat and moved out from my grandmother's in Walsall, to Moseley in south Birmingham. I was upgraded to mental health nurse status at the hospital once my pin number came – a unique registration number with the Nursing and Midwifery Council. This meant I had to be ultra-flexible and available to work shifts at any time. It was like being on call 24/7. But I had a nice little flat all to myself and was my own person and could live the way I wanted to.

After I qualified, I applied for NHS jobs all over Britain. The interviews were nerve-racking and used 'competency based' questions, which involved saying specific key words. I did very well, but the feedback was always that they picked someone with more experience, as I was newly qualified. Nursing is a very localised profession. Nurses usually train at their local universities and then apply for jobs in areas where they know the services because they've been on placements there as students.

I probably went for 30 NHS interviews and every time I didn't get the job I lost more confidence. I finally got a post in a care home, but carried on with my contract job at West Whitchurch while I was applying for work in my actual field of nursing – mental health.

The pending Ali trial was playing on my mind and that really depressed me. One job interview was very close to the court date, and it was all I could think about – not the interview. Memories of the SAU made me cry and I just got up and left. I sat outside and cried for ages before getting a bus home.

The old feelings of fear and uncertainty came back once again. I had near-constant flashbacks to the other trials and I was worried about what they'd ask me and what they'd say about me. What if nobody believed me and the jury just decided that I was nothing more than a slag? I was working a lot of nights and spending all day in bed, feeling shaky again. I just kept holding on to the thought that, once it was over, that would be it and everything would be okay and I'd never have to think about it again.

Then, the Friday before the trial, the police called to say the case had been adjourned because the defendant had to have an emergency operation – he'd be on morphine after the operation and unfit to stand trial. I don't know what was wrong with him and the police weren't allowed to tell me. I thought to myself, *'What about me? I'm unfit to stand trial, but I still have to do it!'*

The trial was put back to September and now I had to keep myself together for another four months. I tried to contact mental health services in Birmingham but, like I said, I kept getting fobbed off and sent from here to there, and nobody really cared. They were unwilling to give me any therapy because 'I was still involved', which meant stuff was still happening in my life and they don't give you therapy while things are still happening. So, I was left with no treatment at all. I did get to see a psychiatrist, but he wouldn't give me antidepressants because of my bipolar diagnosis, and he said I wasn't depressed. No, I was distraught – it was like torture. During those four months I was at my most vulnerable, with panic attacks and flashbacks and the same horrific old, distressing episodes I'd had before.

I was a fully qualified nurse now – isn't that ironic?

I'd been taught how to help other people, but not myself. I'd stopped wearing the *hijab* because it wasn't safe for me to do so in Birmingham. Just like when I wore the *niqab*, I'd been sexually harassed, and I believed sexual assault was the next step. I asked some of the men who approached me in the street why they thought they could speak to me like that – what gave them that right?

'Women who wear the *hijab* are sluts – they wear the scarf during the day and go clubbing and drinking at night.'

I believe these sorts of men have low self-worth themselves. They want to keep women covered up and controlled because they're afraid they can't compete with other men if the women are allowed to express themselves and their sexuality. Their disrespect for independent women is really their inferiority complexes showing through their machismo. Having said that, some white guys are no better. If you're a single woman going to a club or party on your own, it's very likely that every man in the room will hit on you at some point or other. They seem to think a woman on her own is fair game, and they take rejection badly when they go too far.

So, the *hijab* wasn't doing it's intended job because other people weren't following the rules. I thought it was probably better for me to stop trying to be what I wasn't and just be me – the real me, whatever that was. I decided again to try and have a normal social life, like young women of my age do, to get me to stop thinking about it all the time.

I met a guy called Jay who was fun to be with. He didn't want sex from me and we weren't a couple or anything; we were just good friends and it was nice to have a male escort like that, who kept the lechers away from me when we were out somewhere. One day he brought a friend of his called Dave around to my flat and we had a few drinks and talked and listened to music. Dave was American and very charismatic, and we became friends too. He said he was from Syracuse in New York State and he'd been involved with gangs there. He'd been kidnapped twice and spent seven years in prison. A red flag?

The reason Dave was in Birmingham was because he was born in Sheffield – he'd been deported back to the UK while the rest of his family lived in Australia. I didn't know if any of this was true so I took it all with a grain of salt, but it was exciting to listen to instead of alarming, as it should've been.

My ridiculous simple-minded naivety again.

He began coming round regularly and then staying over and, eventually, it seemed like he was there all the time. I was getting worried about the situation and, when he asked me for £200 to buy drugs, I told him to leave. The next day I was doing some food shopping in the Co-Op in Moseley when Dave appeared behind me and offered to carry my bags. When we got outside, he pointed at two men standing across the road and said we owed them the money for the drugs and, if we didn't pay, bad things would happen. We? I should've tried to call the police, but I was scared he'd implicated me in something dangerous. He took me to a nearby ATM and stood over me while I withdrew the money for him to give to the 'drug dealers'.

He came back to my flat with me afterwards and I couldn't get rid of him. When I asked him to leave, he'd beg me to let him stay because he'd be killed on the street, or some other excuse. He didn't seem to have any place to go or any job, and his charisma soon wore off. His presence, and the pending trial, were having a detrimental effect on me and I just wanted him out of my life.

Dave had been back in the UK for several years, going from job to job, before he met me. He wasn't on benefits and he had no money and he kept leeching off me.

Like I said, I was in a very vulnerable mental state and it got to the point where I started to hate him. I went from being intrigued and captivated by him in the beginning, to absolutely despising him. His

American accent would get on my nerves and it just sounded whiny all the time, like how a little kid whines when they want something.

I was doing nights at the care home with my friend, Lisa. I felt very isolated there because there were only two nurses, one on each floor, with three carers. The carers didn't like the nurses for some reason, and they weren't very good with the residents, either – they did the minimum amount they could get away with – and it was a constant battle every night to get them to do their jobs properly. I'm a perfectionist when it comes to my profession. I take pride in being a nurse and I won't tolerate incompetence or laziness. Just because I couldn't cope with the interviews didn't mean I couldn't cope with the work. When I was at work, I felt such a sense of fulfilment and responsibility that it gave me confidence; I really knew what I was doing. The residents needed me to keep the carers in line and that's what my job was about – taking care of people.

On this particular night, an agency carer came running to get me while I was doing the medication round. She was worried about a resident who she thought was in septic shock. Septic shock is a life-threatening condition that happens when blood pressure drops to a dangerously low level after infection. It reduces the amount of blood and oxygen reaching the vital organs and can lead to cardiac arrest and death.

I raced to where the resident was. The man was in a bad state, hyperventilating and distressed. I immediately rang 999 and calmed him down and gave him some water and reassured him that he was going to be okay. I checked his observations – blood pressure, pulse and respiration – against the day shift, but they weren't recorded. The day nurses who'd handed over said he was sweaty and they'd showered him a few times, but they hadn't taken his observations. When I took them, after dialling 999, they showed he was very close to cardiac arrest and I prepared to use CPR and asked the carers for help, but they were more concerned about getting the other residents into bed so they could take it easy.

The paramedics arrived quickly and took over. They gave the man an injection to stabilise him until they got him to hospital. They told me I'd done a good job in keeping him alive and, after they left, I sat in the office for a while, shaking and breathing heavily. Once I gathered myself, I gave the carers supervision instructions and carried on with my medication round. I realised that if I hadn't acted quickly, the man would have died. But he'd survived, and I'd saved his life. It was a euphoric feeling.

I spent the rest of the night on my own. After I finished medications and the residents were settled down, it was quiet, and I sat in the office in silence, writing up reports and notes. By the time I got the bus to go home in the morning, the feeling of euphoria had faded and I was physically and mentally exhausted.

When I got in, Dave was smoking something that someone had given him. He was puffing at it from a miniature brandy bottle that he'd knocked a hole in the bottom of. There was some kind of gauze in the neck, with a little rock of stuff on top of it. He was heating it with a lighter, holding his head back while he sucked smoke through the hole.

'What are you doing?'

'Smoking.'

'What is that stuff?'

'It's nothing… it's called a legal high. It just lifts you up.'

'Are you sure?'

'Sure I'm sure. Take a hit, you'll see.'

I needed something to lift me up after the night I'd had, so I took a long puff of the white smoke from the hole in the bottle. I sucked it into my lungs and held it there for as long as I could. I felt my heart beating harder, like it was going to beat right out of my chest. I breathed out and it hit me. It took my breath away. The feeling was so strong it blew me off my feet – blew my head off. I fell back onto the sofa and gasped. It felt like when I sniffed cocaine for the first time with Bru, but a million times stronger. I lay there with my eyes closed and I thought to myself, *'Oh my god, what is this?'*

Whatever it was, I knew I'd want more.

You can be addicted from the first time you do crack cocaine, even if you don't know it. If you like it and you want to do it again, you're addicted.

I looked over at Dave, but he was busy doing his own 'blast' – which is what it's called. I looked towards the kitchen and saw a bent spoon and bicarbonate of soda, crack paraphernalia. My mind was racing.

'Oh my god, this is crack!'

I knew then why people were willing to kill for this stuff. I knew then why crack addicts became thieves and muggers and ruined their lives over the stuff. I tried for years not to become a 'crack whore' – and now I could literally see my life falling apart before my eyes – everything I'd worked so hard for. It was the worst and best feeling in the world, like a ride on a roller-coaster, the ultimate adrenaline rush, while still being aware of what's happening.

The high lasted about half an hour then, when I was finally able to speak, I said to Dave,

'This is crack cocaine.'

'It's not crack.'

'It is, Dave.'

'Stop calling it crack.'

'That's what it is.'

'It's blasting coke.'

That's what he called it. He wouldn't admit it was crack, even though I knew it was. When the hit wore off, I was scared. More than scared, I was terrified. I never wanted to do it again.

'I hate you, Dave. I hate you. We can never do this again.'

But, by the end of the day, I was back puffing at the hole in the bottom of the brandy bottle.

After all the bad things men had done to me, this man did the worst thing of all.

We started buying cocaine and turning it into crack with bicarbonate of soda. Dave cooked it, not me, because it was a big secret and, even among cocaine users, cooking crack was a massive taboo. I kidded myself that once the Ali Sultan trial was over with, I'd be able to deal with the crack addiction, which was getting worse by the day. I got a sick note from my GP for stress – the only sensible thing I did as I couldn't be a nurse and a crackhead at the same time.

We did the 'moonrock' whenever we could, at least a couple of times a week. Each time it cost me between £250 and £400. I was spending all my money and falling into debt. I called my bank and increased my overdraft and spent that. I couldn't even afford to buy food anymore. I had some electrical stuff like a Digibox and Nintendo DS and I sold them for £25, which was enough to do a bit of food shopping.

We'd be up all hours of the night. Once, we walked to a 24-hour garage to get a can of beer and, on the way back, we saw this guy walking down the street. Dave was craving the crack so much he wanted to mug the guy. I was horrified.

'If you mug that man, I'll call the police and testify in court against you, Dave.'

And I would have, I was still a nurse and I still had a duty of care to the public, even if that didn't extend to myself. It stopped him mugging the guy. Dave never had any money, so we bought the cocaine with my cash. But he'd take control of it and be sniffing 'bumps' of it off his hand while he was cooking the crack. I wanted to stab him when he did that – it was *my* drug, not his. I paid for it!

The crack became my lover and I loved it in return, in a deluded way that was caused by the effects of the drug. I developed a way to hold it in my lungs for longer. I'd breathe in as much as I could and hold it until my lungs were almost bursting, then I'd let out a tiny bit of breath and suck in some oxygen. I'd do that again and again until I'd hurt from stretching my lungs too much. I'd pick up the homemade pipe after we'd run out, just to see if there was a tiny bit left.

I'd pull out all the bits of gauze and lick the inside of the neck of the bottle that was all black and scorched – it was like licking an ashtray. I'd lick the kitchen surface when Dave cooked up. I was turning into a crackhead. It had me hooked, good and proper. I loved and hated it at the same time, because I knew it'd kill me. I could've done blast after blast and died of a crack overdose and I wouldn't have cared.

I was losing weight from lack of food. I didn't care much about my appearance and my hair looked unhealthy. I was pale and drawn, sweaty and clammy and twitchy when I was coming down from a high. My lips were starting to blister. Crack interferes with the way the brain processes chemicals and you need more and more of the drug just to feel 'normal'. You get addicted very quickly and you just lose interest in everything else.

Dave was crazy. The skin on his fingers was falling apart from years of handling cocaine without gloves. He kept coming up with these 'really good' ideas, like growing his own coca plants, which was impossible in a flat in Birmingham. I mean, we weren't living on a plantation in Colombia or anything. Then he wanted me to start doing phone sex, which I refused to do. Then he was going to write a book called *Rapping for Dummies*, which was a complete joke because he was a shit rapper and didn't know what he was talking about.

I wished I'd never met Dave. I wished I'd made him leave when I wanted and not listened to his excuses. I considered calling the police but I knew Dave would turn on me if I reported him. And I was worried I'd be implicated and treated like a criminal because I was taking an illegal drug. I might lose my job, my career, and everything I'd worked so hard for would evaporate before my eyes. Society would judge me and I'd be reduced to nothing.

I didn't understand my crack abuse, it certainly wasn't 'recreational'. I wasn't trying to have fun. I was just chasing the high and, when I thought about it, I didn't get any real satisfaction from it. Afterwards, the crash was horrific. I felt empty, couldn't think, couldn't feel. My mind switched itself off. It was like the distress I felt had nowhere else to go. The drug forced it out and the aftermath left me numb and disconnected. This created an addictive cycle that made me feel horrible.

Then I started to cry – all day and all night. I wanted to kill myself again. The flat I lived in was on the ground floor of a huge, converted mansion. It had communal stairs and you could climb right up into the loft. It had big old rafters and was a spooky place. I thought I could hang myself up there.

The maintenance man would be the first to find me and he'd be able to deal with it, not my family. I thought more and more about the rafters and it became almost romantic to me, like a ghost was calling me up there to do it. How had this happened? I felt like a hopeless, helpless addict and it made me cry with shame at how I'd sunk so low.

I was on my knees.

17

Addiction

My life was spiralling out of control again, both physically and mentally. I'd hit a new low as a crack addict. I was no longer being exploited by grooming gangs, but was now being manipulated by a failed gangster from America. I was desperately trying to make it to trial day. At first, there were weeks to go, then just a few days, then one more day, then it was here. I just wanted to get the Ali Sultan court case over and done with, and then I could deal with the crack problem. I knew I had to sort it out soon because I kept going up to the loft and looking at the rafters. I'd even picked out the beam I was going to hang from.

Ali Sultan's trial came up in September 2014. I took the bus to court on the first day. Before I left, Dave wanted money from me for food because he said he was starving. But I needed what little I had for fares and stuff. He said I was being selfish. I was facing the ordeal of cross-examination by hostile barristers and he wasn't even coming to support me – and it was me who was being selfish?

My friend Lisa and grandmother Eleanor met me there and we waited for hours in the witness room. Then my barrister came to tell me the defence barrister had called in sick because he had food poisoning. I couldn't believe it. This was a high-profile case because of

Ali Sultan's previous convictions; it'd been in the newspapers and on television as the final part of Operation Chalice. I'd psyched myself up for the ordeal ahead of me, and now I had to wait another day. I reckoned the defence barrister wasn't prepared enough and he was just buying time to gather more evidence or something.

But the prosecution barrister said he went to law school with him, so he knew the food poisoning excuse was genuine. That really annoyed me – they all went to law school together and it seemed they were all mates and, once again, these court cases were just a big game to be played.

I could've cried.

I could've literally jumped out of the window.

After a wasted day in court, I caught the bus back home. I sat on the top deck and the bus was still moving when I came down the stairs to get off. I felt a little unsteady from the disappointment of the court and I think the crack was affecting my bones. I was also weak from the lack of proper food. I don't know what happened, but I twisted my ankle as I got to the bottom step. It really hurt and I grabbed the rail and pulled myself up. It was very painful and I had to limp all the way to the flat. When I got there, the maintenance man gave me a pair of crutches he had in his van in case of an emergency. He said I could borrow them to get to court tomorrow.

After she finished work, my mother came round to find out what had happened at the trial. She took one look at my bruised and swollen foot and shook her head.

'That's broken, Kate. You have to get it looked at.'

I was exhausted from waiting in court all day and I had to leave early in the morning to get back there. So I just took some anti-inflammatory medicine and some paracetamol and lay down to rest my foot.

I went back to court the next morning on crutches and wearing a strap on my ankle that I'd bought from Asda – only to have the case adjourned again. This time it was the prosecution barrister – he wanted to check legal precedents on whether he could use Ali Sultan's past convictions in court, about whether the jury should be allowed to hear them or not. So the trial was put back again – this time until March 2015.

Almost a full *year*.

It was a massive blow.

The adjournment really brought me down. I felt utterly defeated. I went to hospital the next day and they confirmed I'd broken the navicular bone in my left foot. I'd never broken a bone in my life, and now I do nothing and break my foot. I put it down to the crack, it must've weakened my bones and made them susceptible to stress. They put my ankle in plaster and I could barely move it, so I had to catch a taxi home with my last bit of money. No food again.

I had to go back to the orthopaedic department the following day and they gave me a plastic boot with padding inside that you pump up to make it tight. The doctor told me he was puzzled.

'It's very strange how you broke your foot that way.'

'I have a lot of stress in my life at the moment. Maybe I was walking funny or something.'

I didn't mention the crack. But I couldn't wait another year to kick the addiction. I knew I'd be dead by then, one way or another. I tried to think what to do, but my brain was all over the place. When I worked with the Drug and Alcohol Team in Essex, I'd visited a few charity-run services in the area that had addiction programmes, and I thought I could find something like that in Birmingham. I asked Dave to come with me, but he wasn't interested.

'It's not crack, Kate. I told you that!'

But that's what addicts do. They defend the drug and go into denial about being addicted.

I found a place in Highgate, right where Asif's garage used to be. They booked me an appointment and I went along. I told them about everything that was going on in my life and they were 'concerned about my situation'. So was I!

I went to my first Narcotics Anonymous meeting the following Monday. I wanted to be able to eat and not be skinny and ill-looking. I didn't want to jump from the rafters in the loft with a rope around my neck, or ruin everything I'd worked so hard for. I wanted to be a nurse again, not a crackhead.

There was a large reception area in the building, with posters that said things like 'Please respect the people who are trying to give up and don't bring illegal drugs onto the premises'. In the NA meeting itself, the chairs were arranged in a circle. I was nervous because I didn't know what to expect – the place was packed and very intimidating. Someone explained what it was all about and, after reading a bit from the 12-step NA book and talking about it, there was a pause for anyone who wanted to share their daily struggles. It went silent for a while, then some guy stood up and started to speak.

'I'm Jack and I'm an addict.'

I can't remember what he talked about – anything really – whatever he wanted to share. Anyone who wanted to speak after that had to stand and say their name and, 'I'm an addict'. I was so nervous about doing that; I guess in case anyone reported me for taking an illegal drug as a nurse, even though I wasn't working and was off sick. But it was all very confidential, like confession in the Catholic Church.

Still, I was determined to do whatever I had to, to get myself off crack. One woman burst into tears and cried so hard I couldn't understand what she was saying. But it encouraged me to talk and I ended up bursting into tears as well and spilling my guts out to everyone, about the rapes and how I couldn't recover from them. How all I needed was a positive social network, so I could do non-sinful things and boost my self-esteem and self-worth, but I couldn't get it, couldn't find it. No one would help me, and I ended up being victimised over and over again. Afterwards I felt so embarrassed and ashamed, but the people there were very nice. They all gave me their numbers and told me to contact them if I needed help or support. They closed the meeting with some reading and I left feeling drained, but positive.

On the way home, I called my father – I couldn't call him from the flat because Dave was there. I get emotional when I'm trying to explain something upsetting, so I hid behind a bush when he answered, because I didn't want people on the street to see me crying. I told him everything.

'I'm coming to get you, Kate!'

It was a four-hour drive and already 11pm, so I persuaded him to wait until morning. He asked me to tell my mother what was happening because she needed to know. So I did.

My father came for me the next day. Dave was out at the time and my father took me back to Kent. We talked about what was the best thing for me to do: either stay in Kent with him and get a new job, or stay in Birmingham and find a new flat. I was concerned about leaving my job. Dave didn't know where I worked so, if I just found a new flat, I could keep going to NA and get myself straightened out. In the meantime, my father and mother and brother went around to my flat in Moseley and threw Dave out and changed the locks. I was worried that, even if I got a new place to live, Dave would still be a problem and I might bump into him on the street and he'd try his hardest to manipulate me back onto crack. So, in the end, I decided it was best to move back to Kent, at least for a while.

Over the next couple of weeks, I sold £1,500 worth of my furniture for £400 on eBay, put the rest of my stuff into storage and went back to live with my father in Stodbury. I attended two more NA meetings in Birmingham before leaving, and I went to a number of others around the Stodbury area when I got there. Some did the 12-step programme and assigned you a mentor, but I didn't really connect well with the text.

The first thing was to 'admit that I'm powerless over my addiction, that my life has become unmanageable'. I pretty much agreed with that and took it very seriously, but not the bit about being powerless. I wasn't powerless – I could fight this thing. The next three steps were all about God. Despite being white and English, I never properly understood Christianity and I found this religious stuff a bit strange. Step four was about taking stock of myself, which I was prepared to do, and the next three were back to God again. Steps eight and nine were about making amends to the people I'd harmed – I reckoned my crack addiction had harmed nobody but myself. Step 10 was taking personal inventory and admitting when I was wrong. Eleven was about prayer, and 12 was to carry the message to other addicts.

After being to a few NA places, I finally found one in Canterbury that suited me. In Birmingham, whenever you spoke you had to say your name and 'I'm an addict'. I'd found that hard, as it made me not want to speak because I hadn't wanted to say that. I'd wanted to say: 'I'm Kate and I don't want to be an addict.' Or: 'I'm Kate and I'm not an addict anymore.'

The Narcotics Anonymous meetings in Canterbury started off with someone being the host. Everyone there was an addict at different stages of recovery. I felt a bit of a fraud when I first started going; I mean, here were all these people who'd been struggling all their lives with drug addiction and here was I pretending to be a crackhead after only a couple of months on the stuff. I felt like an imposter and that, if they heard my story, they'd fall about laughing and ridicule me for not being a real addict. But luckily, I didn't have to talk about any of that. Everyone took turns talking about something, anything, they liked. They didn't have to talk about drugs and nobody said what they were addicted to or for how long, just what they were doing and how they were coping. They talked about their thoughts and feelings and things that bothered them – a kind of a verbal diary, I suppose.

They were all very friendly. It was a big group, with three or four newcomers, like me. They had a keyring reward system. The first was a white one with 'Welcome' on it, and 'Just for today' on the back. The next one was orange and said 'Clean and serene for 30 days', then green with 'Clean and serene for 60 days', then maroon with 'Clean and serene for 90 days' – and so on, until you got to the black one which was for two years. And every year after that you got another black tag.

I really liked the keyrings – they gave me a goal to reach for. I wanted to get to 30 days and, once I'd got it, I didn't want to lose it. If you did drugs you had to go back and start all over again. I went to the NA meetings twice a week and got three key rings, as far as 60 days, then I stopped going. By then I felt I was free from the addiction and I didn't need it anymore and it was reminding me of being on crack, which I didn't want to think about. I knew I could go back at any time and would've been welcomed by the people there who'd got to know me. I'm really grateful to all of them, because I never went back on any kind of drugs. Narcotics Anonymous got me clean. It gave me my life back.

It wasn't all easy. I experienced withdrawal – at first it was exhaustion, nightmares and shaking, followed by paranoia, mood swings and depression. I cried at night and experienced cold turkey but, gradually, it got easier. I remember going out to dinner one night with my father. When the plates were taken away, there was a bit of white flour on the table and I automatically dabbed it with my finger and licked it. I'm just glad it was only flour and not cocaine.

Telling my family was another good move. I promised my parents I'd never do cocaine again and, if I did, I'd be betraying that promise to them. They helped me when I asked for help and I owe them a great deal.

While staying with my father, I regained about 40lbs over three months, which I needed to do. I got an agency job to begin with, while my foot was still in the cast. It paid well and weekly, and that helped me get my finances straight after the money crisis during the addiction.

Because of the year I'd lived with my father in 2011, I tried to contact some people I'd known back then, to see if I could have a normal social life, without the extremes of abuse and addiction. But most of them had moved away, to France or London, and others were backpacking. My best friend back then had been Alvin O'Rourke and I'd been in touch with him on Facebook six months previously. I sent him a few messages, but he didn't reply – so I asked my father about him.

'Is Alvin still around?'

'Haven't you heard ...?'

'Heard what?'

That's when I found out that Alvin had killed his mother. It was such a shock and I didn't believe it. My father showed me the article in the newspaper and I read about it for myself. Even then I felt they must've framed him for something a burglar did. He was such a nice guy, never violent or even aggressive. But he liked to party and he did a lot of drugs.

The details of the crime were horrific. She was stabbed while she slept in bed then strangled. She was also sexually assaulted. It sounded like a surreal, frenzied attack – but why? Why did he do it? The judge said the attack was an example of 'the destruction caused by the use of drugs', and that he didn't doubt that 'Mr O'Rourke would not have acted as he did, but for the ingestion of drugs which disinhibited him.'

After killing her, he took her bank card and her car and ran away, but he crashed the car in Devon and was arrested. I spoke to him on the phone from prison and he told me he'd had a drug-induced psychosis and had no memory of the murder. He said he'd taken cocaine and mephedrone and spice and he was also very drunk. He was sentenced to 30 years in prison and the judge said there was no guarantee he'd be freed even after that sentence was served.

It made me cry a lot and think about my own mother. When she'd asked me to leave, it wasn't her fault. She believed I'd be fine. I believed I'd be fine. Lots of 18-year-olds leave home and are fine. Neither of us knew there were so many rapists in Telford. It seemed like a nice place and we thought we knew it. Even though I struggled to connect with my mother and struggled emotionally when I went back home to see her, I loved her and still love her and I couldn't imagine killing her. I couldn't comprehend it. It was totally outside my sphere of understanding. I stayed clear of cocaine and crack forever after that. I hate it now – it's a soul-destroyer.

When my foot was better, I got a permanent job in a charity disabled-living care home. I was rebuilding my life again. I told them about the pending Ali Sultan court case when I started, so there'd be no problems when the time came. The court paid for my loss of earnings, but only for the days I was required – not any time that might be needed for recovery. I took unpaid leave on the days the court paid for and two weeks' annual holiday for recovery, which I reckoned I'd need if it was anything like the Mike Nolan trial.

It was much better staying with my father in the weeks leading up to the trial because I had someone around to stop me getting low enough to attempt suicide – I had someone to distract me. My father did everything he could to be supportive. We went out to dinner a lot, to Zizzi and Prezzo, and the pub, and a very posh upmarket Indian restaurant called the Krishna, which cost a fortune and you had to book a table. We took it in turns to pay for the food – I had a decent amount of spare money now, which was a change for me. I had no car and rent at my father's was cheap. It helped my self-esteem, being able to take my father out to dinner. Much better than spending the money on crack.

18

Is This The End?

My father drove me up to my grandmother Eleanor's and we stayed there for the weekend before the trial which had finally been scheduled to begin on Monday 2 March 2015.

While I was staying there, two STO police came round. They wanted me to clarify the evidence in some social media conversations between me and Danielle Rizzo, who lived at the SAU at the same time as me – I'd given them my computer's hard drive. Dani and I had been talking about a man called Ali and the police wanted to know if that was Ali Sultan. Some of the conversations were about him and some weren't, they just wanted to clarify which were relevant.

When I woke on the morning of the trial, I wished I could just go back to sleep and not have to go to court. But it was here now, after all the waiting, and my stomach was churning. Lots of memories had been going through my head over the last few days. I felt very angry about everything.

I hated Ali Sultan for making me have to do this as well as raping me, for making me go through it all over again. I wished he was dead, then I wouldn't have to be in here. I felt very angry towards all the men who raped me. I felt angry for what they did to me, for the way they made me feel like it was my fault. For the way they knew what they were doing, because they'd done it to other girls before me. Ali Sultan's previous sentence was nearly served, but the police had decided to keep him on remand until my case was heard. If he was found not guilty, he'd walk out of the court a free man.

When I got to the court, it was the same as with the other cases – I had to enter through the back door, as if I was sneaking in. Then I was taken straight to the witness room along with my mother and my friend, Lisa. My father was a witness so he had to stay away until it was his turn to give evidence.

Once again, I had to watch the videotaped interview I gave to the police when I reported the rape. After almost five years, there was stuff on there I'd forgotten all about.

People from the witness-support charity came in to talk to me, and they brought William and his girlfriend with them. He was a witness too, so he wasn't supposed to be in the room with me. It was a long time since I'd seen William face to face, but I knew this could ruin the case.

'Hello.'

William's voice was quiet and friendly, but I panicked.

'No, no, no! You can't be in here! Get him out!'

I felt really guilty afterwards. I didn't mean to be so rude, but I was afraid we'd bugger the case up. I never managed to get in touch with William afterwards, to apologise, to tell him how grateful I was for his support and his bravery in coming forward to help me get justice for what they did to me. I hope he's okay and he's doing well. I think there were other cases going on that day and they were running out of rooms to put people in.

When it was my turn, they took me through a corridor where all Ali Sultan's supporters were sitting, watching me go past, into a little room connected to the court. I could see some of the men who'd been given short sentences during Operation Chalice, who were back out by the time it had taken for this case to come to court. It was really frightening. I was accompanied by a volunteer from the victim-support charity when I left the little room. She was a young girl and I tried to make her feel comfortable with me – I guess that's the nurse in me, trying to make others feel comfortable while I'm facing stress myself. But it helped having her there, because it took my mind off the situation.

There was a huge floor-to-ceiling curtain that ran all the way from the door to the witness box, which meant I could go straight there without walking the length of the court and everyone having to leave. I felt a lot safer behind that than I did behind the little face flannel of a curtain in the previous courthouse.

I vowed to myself that I wouldn't let what happened in the Mike Nolan case happen again. I'd concentrate. I'd be brave. I'd be strong. I'd address the judge as 'Your Honour', I'd ask questions if I needed clarification, and I wouldn't give one-word answers, even if that's what the defence barrister was trying to get me to do. I'd explain everything clearly so the jury got a correct picture of the truth. That's it, I'd paint them a picture in their minds. I'd explain everything and describe it in all its depraved detail.

After the police interview video was shown, as soon as the defence barrister asked her first question, I started to cry.

So much for my strong resolutions.

The defence barrister wasn't the same one who had food poisoning a year earlier; neither was she the one who'd defended Shahmeel – but she was almost identical in every way: a young, blonde woman. Maybe they thought if they had a young white woman defending them against another young, white woman it'd lessen their guilt or make them seem less culpable in the eyes of the jury? After all, if a young, blonde, white woman was prepared to defend them, how could they be guilty?

Ali Sultan was accused of three counts of rape – two oral and one vaginal, and one attempted rape. The police asked me how many times he made me give him blowjobs, but I couldn't remember. They said 'roughly' and I said 'five', though it was probably a lot more, so they decided to group them all together into one count of rape. I was okay with that because I just couldn't give them specific details of every single time. I remembered the first blowjob and the last one, where I refused to do it anymore and he tried to force his penis into my mouth, then masturbated all over my face and hair – that was the attempted rape.

The judge let me sit down and I started to cry as soon as the cross-examination began. The barrister was asking me upsetting questions about the time Ali and Bazam came to rape me, a time when I was mentally traumatised having just been raped for the first time by Shahmeel, only days before. A time when I was stressed because I was doing my A levels and was estranged and rejected by my family. I was so vulnerable when they pushed their way in and forced me to give them blowjobs. It was what caused me to give up on myself – to lose hope – like I was dying inside and had become worthless and nothing.

That was when they destroyed the me I was before.

The defence barrister used more evidence than in Shahmeel's case. She tried to say it had never happened; not that it was consensual, but that it had never happened and I was a liar.

'I put it to you this never happened!'

'It did.'

Then she said I was in love with Ali and was doing this out of revenge because he'd rejected me – just what they'd said about Shahmeel.

'You loved him, didn't you?'

I couldn't help it, I laughed. Then I was annoyed with myself because she'd provoked a reaction and I wished I hadn't. But I just couldn't help it. It had taken me so much by surprise because it was so ridiculous. I knew she was trying to trick me and I knew I had to be watchful of what I said and consider my answers carefully – but that's easier said than done in the cauldron of a criminal courtroom. She asked me about Bazam.

'Do you recognise the name Bazam Rehman?'

'Maybe.'

She repeated the question.

'Do you know someone called Bazam Rehman?'

In my head I was thinking, *is she talking about the Bazam who raped me? Everyone knows who he is but I failed to pick him out in the line-up. What if Bazam Rehman is someone else and not him?*

'Do you know Bazam Rehman?'

'No, I don't know who Bazam Rehman is.'

'But you said you did.'

'I said I know a Bazam, but I don't recognise the surname.'

'Well, I put it to you, Miss Elysia, that this Bazam never existed.'

'Well, you seem to know him…'

She blinked a few times but said nothing in response, then she changed the subject.

She got to the social media conversations between me and Dani – we'd been having an argument at the time and Dani was being aggressive, insinuating that I said Ali Sultan had a big dick and he didn't rape me. I was saying back that it was called denial and I was trying to cope with what had just happened to me and that he'd raped me. I thought it was strange evidence to use, because the court could actually hear me saying he *did* rape me when she made me read the text out.

The barrister referred to them as phone conversations, but I corrected her because I'd promised myself I'd paint a picture of everything as it actually was. This was an incorrect fact and needed to be put right. I was very polite.

'I'm sorry to correct you, but these conversations were through MSN on the internet.'

She accepted my correction but then asked me if I'd seen those conversations since the incident. I didn't want to lie, so I told her the police had shown them to me the day before.

'What?'

I was panicked now – what had I done? She spoke to the judge and asked to have some kind of legal conversation, so the usher took me back to the little room. I kept saying to myself: 'Shit! What if I've totally screwed up this case? Shit, shit, shit, shit!'

I wanted to put my ear up to the wall to hear what was going on, but I knew it'd be no use because the wall was about 6ft thick and soundproof. I'd just wanted to tell the truth and not lie, but what if I'd caused the whole case to collapse? Panicking wouldn't solve anything – I had to think of something to distract myself. Then I thought, *If the room is soundproof, it means they can't hear me, either. I might as well sing.*

I love singing, but I only do it when I'm alone and no one else is listening. I tried to think of a nice song and I came up with a reggae tune by a female artist called Etana – the song is called 'I Rise'. I didn't think of it intentionally; it just came into my mind.

I was singing and smiling to myself because the words fitted my situation. She sings about being born strong and the trials she faced that pushed her to her limits. I am strong. I will fly away from all this. I finished the whole song and hoped they didn't have a microphone in there or something and could hear me out in the courtroom.

The usher came after about 15 minutes and took me back in.

It soon became obvious that I hadn't crashed the case because the defence barrister started asking me questions again about the MSN conversations with Dani.

'So, you told Dani that Ali had a big penis?'

'No.'

'Are you sure?'

'I wouldn't have said that.'

'Why not?'

'It wasn't big.'

A ripple of laughter went round the courtroom and I thought the judge was going to get cross. But he didn't. Every time she mentioned the conversations she called them phone conversations – she kept getting it wrong, and every time I corrected her. I couldn't let her confuse the jury, whether she was doing it deliberately or as a genuine mistake. It happened so many times that she was getting visibly irritated with me. The last time she said phone conversations I repeated: 'Internet conversations.'

'Whatever!'

She said that like a spoiled teenager who wasn't getting her own way.

Then she tried to get the jury to believe my hard drive was 'seized' by the police, in some kind of bad way, like they raided my flat and took it from me by force or something. But I gave it to them voluntarily, so I had to explain that too.

Again, after the defence cross-examination, the prosecution

barrister asked me a few questions to clarify some things and finish up – and again I can't remember what he asked me because my head was spinning.

William was up next and I was allowed, but not advised, to stay. So I left. It wasn't worth risking influencing the jury in a negative way.

Danielle Rizzo gave evidence for the prosecution the next day. I wasn't in court and neither were any of my family. But one of the STO police told me she totally backtracked on her original statement and turned on me in court. When she was originally asked to provide a statement, she was probably excited about it. Dani loved to be the centre of attention and it would've appealed to her to be a heroine, standing up in court and giving evidence against the bad guys in front of everyone. She would have lapped up the attention and probably would have stayed strong if the case had come up quickly. But, over the months of delay, she'd had time to think about the implications and I guess she wasn't as brave as she thought she was; the novelty would've worn off for her and she didn't want to do it – but she had to, or she would have been held in contempt of court. What she didn't have to do was completely turn against me and try to destroy my character – maybe someone got to her, I don't know. Anyway, the prosecution barrister had to pause the trial to have one of those legal consultations with the judge. She was declared a hostile witness and the prosecution got to cross-examine her and ripped her concocted story to shreds.

The trial lasted a week altogether. My school friend, Andria, was called as a witness. She had to go to court on her birthday and I was so grateful to her. I bought her a Pandora bracelet as a birthday present and sent her a thank you letter. They asked her about my character and she told them about how she saw a big change in my personality after I went to live at the SAU. I didn't remember myself before the

SAU and I wondered who I would've been if I'd never went there. My father was supposed to give evidence too, but at the last minute they decided they didn't need him as they had all the evidence they required. He sat in for the rest of the trial and reported what was going on to me. He said he cried in court and hoped the jury saw it.

At the end of the last day, the defence barrister said to the jury in her closing argument: 'Does this woman seem like a vulnerable girl to you? You saw how she treated me.'

She was even trying to use my courage against me! Maybe I was no longer a vulnerable girl when I was in that witness box, but I was when I was raped.

The jury agreed.

Ali Sultan was found guilty of two rapes and one attempted rape and sentenced to a minimum seven years in prison, and another five years on licence, making that 11 years in total. I was in court for the sentencing with my father. When Ali was being taken back down to the cells, he turned around and saw us. He never made eye contact with me but he stared right at my father. My father stared right back at him.

Later, my STO told me that a Superintendent of West Mercia Police praised my performance and said I was 'the best witness he'd ever heard in a trial of this kind'. I guess he meant I hadn't allowed myself to be bullied by the defence counsel in the same way as they had ganged up on and bullied a lot of very young, vulnerable girls a few years earlier, during Operation Chalice.

I've mentioned a chart I made during the abuse which helped me stay sane. It showed how the men were connected through social circles and family, and this made me realise I was remembering everything the way it happened. If I'd been drunk when I was abused,

I wouldn't have remembered or noticed the connections. So, one of my strongest messages to young girls in a grooming situation is DON'T DRINK! It might seem like it makes things easier to cope with, but it only makes things worse. The chart also helped me see that, even though they considered themselves to be 'family' and not a gang, they were definitely organised. Grooming gangs operate differently to other, more recognisable gangs – they have smaller clusters that are connected to other small clusters that are part of the same extended family, and the group as a whole is massive.

In my chart, I coloured the ones I was scared of in red and marked the ones who raped me with an X. It showed a clear difference between the men in Telford and the men in Birmingham. I was traumatised by violent rape in Telford, and that trauma groomed me to accept what happened in Birmingham as being the life I deserved. Rape is rape, and I was raped in both places. But the abuse became desensitised and normalised and I became compliant with it.

I also identified relationships between different groups. They used me as a favour between one gang and another, to create alliances between different families, as well as between single individuals. When I looked at the chart, it was almost as if I was a drug being supplied and distributed, along with a lot of other girls I didn't know about at the time – from rapists in Telford, to emotional groomers in Birmingham, to friends and associates elsewhere in the country. It was an organised network. Sometimes it was just one man passing me on, like Tamjeed from Telford who passed me to Cemal Abassi from Birmingham because they met in prison.

I guess my story also highlights how the prison system spreads the grooming and abuse amongst already convicted criminals, through the use of mobile phones.

The chart helped me understand how it happened, and that helped me feel more in control of it. It was a way of processing it. To know and understand how they worked and how they operated gave me a sense of closure. Everything I could do to understand from the outside gave me a sense of control after I'd felt so out of control on the inside. Going back to Birmingham to work and learning the geographical locations I was in when I felt so lost made me feel like I wasn't lost any more. Living in Birmingham and walking around in the daytime made me less afraid of those streets and I gained a sense of ownership over them. I'd recommend this as a healing process for any survivors of abuse.

I felt a sense of satisfaction and closure after sentences were passed on Shahmeel and Ali Sultan. Details of the trials of the men who raped me were published in the newspapers and it felt weird, like it wasn't me they were talking about. They gave me pseudonyms like 'Tammy' and 'Davea' in the reports, and I felt like an outsider looking in. The reports gave me the opportunity to look at my situation objectively, for the first time. I saw how I was manipulated psychologically as well as physically, and it helped me to finally break the chains of confusion and melancholia that held me prisoner for so long.

Although some of my abusers were convicted, many others got away with it. Because I was able to articulate it in the way I did, I wasn't seen as a vulnerable human being, not by the police, social services or even people close to me. I wasn't seen as vulnerable in the way people expect vulnerability to look. I was seen as 'allowing' the violence to happen to me, as if I had the power to stop it. My vulnerability was judged by how I spoke, stood, appeared – not by what happened to me or the power dynamics I lived under.

Because I could speak clearly, I was treated as though I invited the abuse onto me. This is called betrayal trauma – you reach out for protection and, instead, you're judged and blamed. It's how a lot of abuse goes unreported.

19

After The Darkness

My job helped me with my self-hatred, as I was caring for others. I spent two years working in care homes, looking after elderly people with dementia. I gained a lot of satisfaction from caring for patients with mental illness. I cared on a one-to-one basis for people who'd taken overdoses and had no previous contact with the mental health services. I was the first mental health professional they came into contact with and it was important for me to make a good impression and not traumatise them any more than they were already. For me to do that, I had to be comfortable with myself, comfortable with who I was. I gave them all the time in the world and cared for them to the best of my abilities, in an effort to make myself feel like I was worth something.

I felt I had committed so many sins in life that I needed to dedicate what was left of it to doing good. I needed to redeem myself and my worth as a human being. I never really lost hope – even though it seemed like it sometimes – no matter how bad things got. Even when I had nothing or nobody, I never lost hope. I hoped that if I kept trying to choose the good life, then I'd eventually get there, even though I messed up again and again and made massive mistakes. I survived, whether by luck or by the grace of God. I got out alive somehow, even though I kept putting myself into situations where God had to save me – or at least that's what it seemed like to me at the time.

Back then I kept thinking it wouldn't turn out that way. One day, God was going to run out of chances to give me. But something kept me alive until I figured out how to stop myself from doing the crazy, suicidal things I was doing. I believed God was keeping me alive for a reason, that he must've wanted me alive, but I didn't know why. If there was a reason, then it's still a mystery to me.

But I suppose what we call 'God' is bigger than our human understanding. In this world, we can never understand what 'God' is or what 'his' plan is – we can never understand the meaning of our lives. Infinity and eternity are concepts we just can't comprehend; our human intellects aren't equipped for it. And maybe we're not meant to understand, maybe it'll all become clear in some future life, when we evolve into a better species.

I still believe in some realisation of 'God', but it's a personal thing. Nowadays I choose not to follow any organised religion because I feel they're too strongly influenced by human beings. And human beings can't tell me what 'God' wants or thinks or feels and they can't say what's right or wrong anymore. I have my own god now – my own 'Allah' – an entity that's given every human being the power, the instinct, to find answers within themselves. Mental illness can cloud that instinct and make our minds play tricks on us – it uses that instinct against us.

When I was going up to Birmingham, I knew what I was doing was wrong and I was putting myself in danger, in the way of abuse and degradation, but I ignored my instinct. I didn't trust it. I didn't trust myself. I continued to do the wrong thing, over and over again, driven by what I believed was a demon inside me, but what was really the trauma in my head. I had to relearn how to follow my instinct and fix it so the alarm bells went off at the right time.

I accepted a long time ago that the meaning of life was too big for me to understand. So, if 'God' does have a plan for me, I don't get it right now – and that's all right.

I include my nursing ethics in my religion – I live and work by the nurses and midwives code, to treat people as individuals and provide person-centred care. I have a duty to protect people and anyone who comes within my sphere of service, no matter who they are. I asked the god I believed in back then for help and he made me a nurse – maybe that was the plan? If it was, then the way to repay him is to use the training skills I've acquired to serve and help people.

Back in university, we were told that nurses are the real superheroes and we have power other people don't have and that with great power comes great responsibility. Every person I help makes up for a sin I committed against myself. And that helps to relieve my guilt and delusions of inferiority, which are classic associations of sexual abuse and post-traumatic stress disorder.

My father blamed my mother for what happened to me. He said it happened to me because my mother asked me to leave and that's why my father felt the way he did. I suppose something terrible like that affects everyone involved, and blame is something that's always attributed in one direction or another. We all tried to understand why it happened and found lots of reasons, as well as ways it could've been avoided. Personally, I never blamed my mother – I just felt very upset that I couldn't tell her what was going on in my life. I think that's why I cried every time I thought about her, it brought back that horrible, sickening feeling I got when I longed to tell her, but couldn't. I don't know how to explain why that was, why I couldn't tell her.

I lived with my father for two years after the last trial. In September 2015, I began therapy that helped me understand myself better, and understand my behaviour, and predict it before it happens. It helped me find better coping mechanisms to overcome my everyday stresses.

In March 2016 I passed my driving test and bought a car. It was a big moment for me; It meant more independence and a better job, and it helped me to keep moving forward. The job was in a secure forensic unit, working with offenders, and it was my first proper job in mental health nursing. I was nervous at first, when I found out that most of the patients were sex offenders. But, when I went through the induction training, I realised I already knew a lot of it. Only I had to learn the hard way how to deal with abusers and manage to stay alive.

I realised I'd developed skills other people didn't have. I'd developed an in-depth, first-hand knowledge of the thought-processes of groomers and manipulators. It's important to confront the person who's offending, even if they're offending in a very minor way. Tell them it's inappropriate, you don't want it and, now they know you don't want it, if they don't stop it's sexual harassment and they're breaking the law. I just wish I'd known these things when I was 18. Back then, I wouldn't have wished my treatment on any other human being, so why did I accept it for myself?

I believed I was worthless and deserved it. So I had to remind myself that I was a human being and, no matter how low I felt, I was still a human being. It worked sometimes – sometimes it didn't.

Once I was abused by sex offenders, now I help to rehabilitate them.

Full circle!

I have a good work ethic, always have. It's something I'm proud of. Working helped me maintain some stability in my life when everything else was falling apart around me. It was a lifebelt I could cling to. My job still helps me with my self-esteem because I believe in the Nursing and Midwifery Council code and I don't judge the people I care for, I try to understand them. I've learned that most sex offenders have been abused themselves as children. It makes me wonder how bad the lives of the men who raped me were when they were kids. Some of the Asian men I met told stories about losing their virginity at the age of 10 – even younger – but they didn't accept this as sexual abuse.

I'm good at my job. Better than most, if I do say so myself. I've had some great feedback from supervisors and managers. And I've gone from strength to strength. I'd like to do a master's one day. I haven't decided what subject yet, but there's lots of exciting courses to choose from using my mental health nursing degree.

My options are completely open. I just know my destiny is to help people, and maybe I'm better at that because I've had such first-hand experience of trauma. I can understand individuals better than others and make more accurate interpretations of their behaviour. One thing I try to believe is that no one is all bad – even the worst offender must have some small spark of humanity inside them.

I hope I'm right.

I've been in touch with other survivors and I attend meetings across the country, spending time with people who've been through abuse and who want to talk about it with someone who understands, who doesn't recoil in shock and horror at the terrible circumstances of their lives. I encourage other survivors to get therapy, even if they think they don't need it or it won't help them. It will. It helped me. Victims can get a year's free therapy on the NHS and can also claim Criminal Injury Compensation. The money won't change what happened, but it might just pay for driving lessons or a small car or a deposit on a flat – things that can help you move on and that you might otherwise be unable to afford.

I also encourage people not to drink, as you know already. My abuse could've been a lot worse if I wasn't able to think straight in dangerous situations. Alcohol is also a depressant and I was depressed enough without any more being heaped on top of it through alcohol. It's not a good way of coping – it's a maladaptive coping mechanism. Find a better way.

I used to write my feelings down in my journal – keeping them in a diary instead of inside my head. It helped show me that I was having revolving repetitive thoughts. I don't remember thinking them, but it's in the journal, so I must have. I also try to discourage 'slut-shaming' – that attitude got me raped in the first place and contributed to my continuing abuse for years. That is, I'm a slut, therefore it's okay to treat me as sub-human – I'm ruined, fallen, broken. No, I'm a human being and deserve to be treated as one.

In 1860, Florence Nightingale didn't just lay the foundation for professional nursing, she also helped abolish harsh anti-prostitution laws against women. But have people's minds changed all that much since? Society still harshly judges women who've been subjected to rape and sexual exploitation – a bit like Hester Prynne, the unmarried mother in the novel *The Scarlet Letter*, who had to wear a scarlet 'A' on her dress to shame her for refusing to name the father of her out-of-wedlock child. She had to live apart from the community with her illegitimate daughter. The themes of the book are shame and social stigma, that sins result in expulsion and suffering.

What's changed?

My mother and her new husband got divorced some years ago – I guess he wasn't right for her after all. She and I are close again now, like we used to be. She's the woman who brought me up to care for people, as she did. I didn't mean to follow in her footsteps by becoming a nurse – it just happened. But I'm glad it did.

Amanda and I are close too, closer than we were. The circumstances that made me leave home were just sheer bad luck. Everyone was stressed out and everyone was blaming everyone else. I love Amanda, and Amanda loves me. We will always have each other's backs.

I love my brother Richard too. I regret the years I missed growing up with him, but we're putting that right now.

When I needed help, my father was there and he offered me a safe haven to help me get back on my feet. I love him very much. I believe that family is like a sacred blessing, tied together by blood. Even when we fall out, we're still connected. I owe it to my family to live the best life I can because that's all they ever wanted for me.

After I moved out of my father's place, I got a two-bedroom flat of my own. I wanted the spare room so I could settle in a place where I might one day have a baby. I have a small network of friends now, *real* friends. People who are good to be with and who don't want to use me in some exploitative way. And I really love my parents. Despite being alone for a lot of the traumatic times, I don't think I could've got this far without them. They're the best parents I could ask for and, without that grounding of the decent stuff I learned from them before I was raped, things might be a lot worse today.

20

Hindsight

The psychosis of the perpetrators isn't often discussed. As children, I'm sure Shahmeel and Ali suffered trauma from witnessing rape, with adults around them teaching them it was okay, that it was normal. It was another form of child abuse. I'm sure Ali had unresolved mental health issues and was in denial about what shaped him into the abuser he was. Neither he nor Shahmeel were born that way, they learned it. I'm not excusing their behaviour, just trying to explain it.

Shahmeel's father was a known grooming gang member. He was a rapist, abusing and trafficking children for money. Shahmeel was brought up in that environment and so was Ali. In effect, they were learning the grooming process while they were still children themselves. By the time they got to me, they'd had many years of grooming experience. They were seasoned rapists who understood trauma better than most counsellors, better than the police, better than the lawyers.

When I reported my rape, I was sold a lie. They told me the information would be recorded as evidence, if it happened again. But it was just filed away and forgotten. When Operation Chalice started, I had to report it all over again, because it had been lost in the system and they knew nothing about it.

Once everything settled down, I realised I had to get back out into the world, socially I mean. I was only in my mid-20s and still had most of my life ahead of me. It was almost a year since I'd finished with the court case against Ali Sultan and I started therapy. Getting myself out into the social world was part of my personal rehabilitation. It was a form of self-imposed exposure therapy. I felt I needed some kind of practical guidelines – a kind of 'dos and don'ts' of how to behave in normal company. A blueprint of how not to give off the wrong signals, of what to say and what not to say, how to observe reactions and body language. Simple stuff that would come naturally to people who hadn't been trafficked and traumatised. I had to do it in real time, on my own, through trial and error. It was scary!

I went to parties, but never drank, always keeping my wits about me, practising normal social interaction, just chilling and chatting. It was going well for several months, until this guy called Mike asked me for my phone number. I hesitated. Should I give it to him now? How much did he know about me? Would he consider me to be easy if he knew what I'd been through? I withheld my number and we left it so. I saw him again and again at various places and he became a familiar face in my social circle. So, when he asked me out on a date, I accepted.

Mike was a charismatic man, funny and easy-going. We got to know each other well over time and, knowing I was a qualified mental health nurse, he asked me if I'd help him with a personal matter.

'Depends on what it is.'

'My brother. He's epileptic, from being beaten up badly by police when he was younger.'

His name was Ron and his seizures weren't being well managed due to his challenging behaviour. He'd been hospitalised after being found wandering naked down the middle of the road. Mike asked me if I'd come to the hospital to meet his brother and give him some advice about controlling and caring for him.

Ron had a severe cognitive disability due to hypoxia and he hadn't been taking his medication. I was happy to help as best I could, advising about safeguarding and ensuring contact and communication with family, involvement in multi-disciplinary team meetings and anything else I could do. I met with Ron's mother and, all of a sudden, found myself heavily involved with a highly emotive Jamaican family and a culture which was outside the scope of my experience. On one occasion, Mike and his mother were having a very loud exchange and I almost bolted for the door. They weren't really arguing, they were just emotional and distressed because they both loved and cared for Ron so deeply. I learned that I didn't have to be afraid of a bit of shouting.

I was grateful to Mike and his family for helping me to reintegrate myself into mainstream society. Eventually, I felt comfortable enough to explain my social rehab experiments and my reasons for doing them, trying to find a place where I belonged. It was still a case of trial and error and I needed patience from the people I was socialising with. He understood. He was supportive and made every effort to understand me. His patience and social charisma helped me a great deal and he provided guidance, reassurance and support with compassion. I can never thank him enough.

Mike wanted to be a taxi driver and, for that, he had to complete a disclosure and barring service check. I came over to his place one day after it had arrived and I'd never seen a DBS as long as that. It was all grand theft auto offences dating back to when he was as young as 14 years old. He wasn't surprised or embarrassed about it and he told me he'd been a kind of junior Robin Hood character, stealing high-performance cars to order from the super-rich, selling them to a Turkish gang, and recycling the money he made into the poor areas of London, the city where he was brought up. It was, and still is, an amazing story of racism and brutality, but with a zest for life that was truly epic. I'd never met a man so humble, so caring, so deeply understanding and thoughtful, so hardworking and principled. He's writing his own memoir now and hoping to find a publisher for it in the near future. It will be called *Speed Merchant* by Mike Guépard.

Mike and I eventually split up. I mentioned that I wanted children and that worried him. He'd had three of his own and didn't want to bring any more into a world which he considered to be growing more polarised and dangerous by the day. He told me I was ready to ride off into the sunset, now that he'd helped me to rehabilitate. He told me I should find a suitable young man who didn't have any children and it would be selfish of him to try to keep me to himself. I was angry and upset – I felt he was dumping me and sending me to find the 'perfect man' who I knew didn't exist. But he was right – and we're still the best of friends and communicate often.

Thanks Mike.

This is only a theory and I may be wrong but, looking back, I can see that I might have been drawn to autistic partners, even before I had the knowledge to understand what that meant. After grooming and sexual exploitation, my idea of a 'normal' man was distorted. When harm comes from people who present as respectable and socially skilled, those traits stop feeling safe. I didn't have a reliable internal guide for distinguishing between a good man and a man who wanted to manipulate me. At times, I was afraid of all men. The fear wasn't always logical, but it was real. Even innocent moments could trigger it. When trauma teaches you that danger hides behind social ease and confidence, your nervous system starts looking for safety elsewhere.

When I met a man who was socially different, direct in communication, clear and literal yet sometimes awkward, that difference felt safe. That kind of man wasn't polished, couldn't easily hide who he was and his intentions felt easier to read. Traits that others might describe as quirky or unconventional felt grounding to me. Straight talking. Emotional sincerity. A lack of social performance. These qualities reduced uncertainty, and uncertainty had been the most dangerous thing in my past.

In that context, it made sense that I felt safer with men who communicated differently. It wasn't about seeking a diagnosis or labelling. It was my nervous system learning to associate clarity with safety and ambiguity with threat. What once confused me now seems understandable. It made me reflect differently on my relationship with Barak. I now wonder whether part of that breakup was linked to neurodivergent differences, rather than the idea that everything was my fault because of my mental health crisis at the time. If Barak was autistic, it may have been genuinely difficult for him to understand me, particularly as I didn't divulge the full extent of my abuse.

My recent partner was diagnosed with autism, and I myself had been eventually diagnosed with attention deficit hyperactivity disorder. So what I was like when I was young, my naivety and dyslexic personality, were all symptoms of the ADHD. It wasn't an easy match for me to be with an autistic person. Some of my needs and reactions were difficult for him to understand and some of his responses and ways of processing were difficult for me to understand. We had to work, constantly, to learn each other's communication styles and adapt to each other's needs. And I guess you know that ADHD has now been linked to the gut microbiome – in other words, the bacteria living in the gut. They reckon the gut can influence mood, cognitive function and mental health. Gives a whole new meaning to the old saying, "you are what you eat". Anyway, I'm determined not to repeat the mistakes of the past. I now realise something important – if you're drawn to an autistic partner, because of the qualities you value – honesty, directness, sincerity, lack of pretence – then you have to accept that partner fully. You can't just pick and choose the bits of a person you're willing to live with and expect them to change the rest just to suit you.

Going through the diagnostic journey with my recent partner taught me a great deal about autism. So I decided to adapt my role as a Primary Care Mental Health Professional and train in autism assessment. The combination of Autism Assessor and Mental Health Nurse has been deeply enlightening, from both a neurodivergent and trauma perspective. One of the most important things I've learned is about social communication and affect. If people find you strange, misunderstand you, that's not necessarily a negative reflection on you as a person. It says as much about the misconstruer as the misunderstood.

I've learned that life's too short not to be yourself. Exist as you are and speak honestly. Some people won't like you for that, and it's their failure, not yours. Some people will understand you – and that's enough!

I shouldn't have been doing drugs and never would have, had I been in the right mental state. I was unwell in my head, in my heart and soul – really suffering and very vulnerable, being exploited daily. I blamed myself back then, but I don't now. I don't blame the young girl I was, going through what I did, not being responsible for my own actions. The demon that possessed me is gone now. I realise it was in my head rather than inside my body. Addiction is often misunderstood, it's not always about pleasure and partying. Sometimes it's about survival. Sometimes it's about a nervous system that's been pushed beyond the limits of its endurance. I don't excuse my addiction, but I understand it now.

If I could go back in time, I wonder if I would be able to do things differently? Certainly with the knowledge and experience I have now, I would. But I didn't have that clear-headedness. If I'd had more support from the police, social services and the SAU, then maybe.

There's a lot going on in the media now around grooming gangs. But it wasn't being addressed properly in the past, either by the government or the police – and it's still not being addressed properly. What I mean by 'addressed' is the sexual aspect of it, the details, like how the police convinced me to sign a form saying it was consensual. They failed to address the scope of it and the ethnicity aspect, because many of the perpetrators weren't and aren't Pakistani, even though right-wing elements in the media and far-right organisations would have you believe that. In fact, the highest percentage of perpetrator ethnicity is white. They failed to do due diligence and expose the other cultures involved. I would encourage anyone who's concerned and worried that 'Islamists' are to blame, to do their own research. And by 'research' I don't mean TikTok or Facebook or Elon Musk's controversial X. Don't be a sheep. Think for yourself, not what the racists want you to think.

As white people, we don't really consider ourselves to be a separate culture. We believe we're normal, whatever that means. Other people have a culture, not us. We don't like to admit how vulnerable we are. We prefer to believe that bad things happen to others – the weak, the careless, the irresponsible, the different. This belief makes us feel safer, but it's not true. We socially isolate ourselves within our denial. I know because I was like that myself, until the Muslim women accepted me and helped me to open up and see the reality of myself. Many times I truly believed that a god – some god, any god – had saved my life and, with that, came responsibility. I started to think, *one day I might not be saved again.* That helped me to stop putting myself in danger. It helped me to break away from the psychological pull of the gang. It helped regulate my anxiety, my mood, my sense of self-worth. I mean, if this god thought I was worth saving, then I must matter. I can't be completely worthless.

I came to understand that I could influence how people treated me by how I dressed, what I said, what I did and didn't disclose. I could choose not to admit that I was a grooming gang survivor. I could choose not to admit I spoke to God. I could choose how I presented myself, depending on the circumstances of the occasion. It wasn't manipulation – it was survival. I learned this from men who told me white girls got raped because of how they dressed. I learned it from wearing the *hijab*. I learned it from the courts. I learned it from understanding how little space there is for women who don't fit the expected image of the perfect victim.

The court process has stayed with me. I still think about it. I still remember it. Some of it was traumatic and always will be. It's not something you simply 'get over' – being questioned, watched, judged and spoken about in a way that leaves a mark. Even when time passes, the memory stays close to the surface. At the same time, it made me stronger. It made me want to help others who have to go through it. I'm no longer afraid of it, I don't want anyone to feel alone, facing that process.

I have great respect for the women speaking out in newspapers, like Fiona Goddard, who was abused by a gang in Bradford as a child, and helping with sexual exploitation research, like Joanne Phillips and Emily Vaughn, and all the survivors on the grooming gang panel who are demanding systematic change and refusing to be silenced. They're the real heroes. The survivors who stood in court, relived the trauma and helped put the perpetrators away are the reason any justice happened at all. What's missing is not survivor resilience. It's institutional respect.

The system is quick to congratulate itself, but slow to recognise the ongoing impact on those who made accountability possible. Survivors are expected to carry the long-term consequences quietly, while focus shifts elsewhere, to the politicians and pulpiteers.

Make no mistake, it was serious abuse that resulted in prolonged trauma. I was used and humiliated to the very core. The level of humiliation that eventually leads to suicide. It hurts to talk about it, even now, but I'm doing it to expose what was happening and is still happening. Many people who experienced what I did will have trouble revealing the humiliation, admitting it, even to a therapist. It's the sort of thing nobody wants to relive. I'm doing it to educate others and to counteract the trolls out there who react with cynicism and self-righteous arrogance, while having never experienced it for themselves. It's easy to judge and people are good at it, they sometimes even like to do it. It's called schadenfreude – holier than thou – the smirk syndrome. Nobody can make me feel any worse about myself than I did then. But I know who I am now.

I no longer practise Islam, but the religion holds a special place in my heart. It helped me hold onto my sanity when it was drifting further and further away from me. There's an *ayah* verse in the Qur'an that used to speak to me and it still does now, when I look back: *'After hardship will come ease.'*

Survivors of grooming and sexual exploitation often experience identity fragmentation, loss of moral coherence and chronic shame. The religious framework, if you can call it that, which I experienced offered me cognitive and emotional containment by restoring my sense of order, predictability and moral clarity. Years after the darkness, after therapy and while writing my book, I was finally able to break free of confusion. I revisited what happened with clarity rather than numbness. I even got back in touch with Barak and learned that he was safe, well and happy.

That mattered a lot to me.

21

The Now

I've worked across many areas: Neuro-rehab, forensic services, crisis lines, among other sectors. Ironically, I've even worked with sex offenders and, in that respect, I suppose you could say my life has come full circle – from being abused, to rehabilitating abusers.

Working with sex offenders was very insightful and I still use the techniques I learned to this day, both in my professional and personal roles.

Following that, I went to work for the NHS in acute wards where I was able to develop expert skills in de-escalation and communication in highly emotional situations. I moved to London and took part in a training programme in trauma-informed stabilisation therapy, where I was encouraged to think about what 'happened' to the individual, rather than what 'was wrong with them'. I learned how to lead workshops on developing self-compassion, mindfulness, crisis planning and much more.

I then moved on to the Single Point Of Access mental health urgent advice crisis and referral line, where I would answer emergency calls all through Covid lockdown. I was good at interpreting the symptoms of trauma crisis callers, like vivid flashbacks, PTSD, psychosis, and those at risk to themselves. I'd been through it all myself. While I was there, I was seconded onto the Trust's Sexual Safety Policy as a 'lived experience' consultant.

I continued to work with the Single Point Of Access for three years before making a radical change. I still considered Telford to be a town full of unconvicted rapists, but I'd reached a point in my recovery from PTSD where I felt I needed to face that fear head on. I felt I'd been run out of my home by those rapists and I needed to return to desensitise myself, to exorcise myself and continue to repair my relationship with my family. I was a senior mental health nurse by then, having been qualified for 10 years and I wondered if Telford had learned anything after the initial grooming gang scandal. An independent inquiry was happening and I wondered if things were better now.

There was a job as a Mental Health Practitioner working for a Primary Care Network, which entailed spending alternate days at a few GP practices across Telford. It sounded perfect, having face-to-face contact with patients instead of talking to them on the phone. There was one problem though, one of the surgeries was in the same area as some of my previous abusers. Would it be a bad idea to go there? I thought about it and realised that backing off would be feeding into the PTSD – I should be free to take a job wherever I wanted and still be safe. But was I wrong? I applied for and got the job and nothing bad happened. Nothing. I was right not to back away.

I loved working for the people of Telford, where I came into contact with other grooming gang survivors. I didn't disclose my own experience as that wouldn't have been appropriate but I knew how to help others, survivors of various violent crimes – child abuse, domestic abuse, stalking, harassment, workplace bullying and other traumas like bereavement, neurodivergence, anxiety and depression and terminal cancer.

I didn't hear anything from the Telford Independent Inquiry, not even at work in the GP surgeries – nothing about changes being made or recommendations being put in place. When it concluded, ITV contacted me for comment, but I had no idea what to say. Even though I'd given all my evidence to them, there were no regular updates and I didn't know what was going on. They said the inquiry had been successful, but I was a grooming gang survivor and a senior healthcare professional living and working in Telford and I just thought, '*has it?*' My evidence was randomly returned to me in the post, with no comment. No 'thank you for sharing', no 'this is what has changed', no 'we couldn't have done it without the survivors'. Nothing.

In November 2024 I received a decision in writing from the National Referral Mechanism (NRM), a UK framework for identifying and supporting victims of human trafficking and modern slavery. It involves a structured process where designated "first responders" (police, local authorities) refer potential victims to a competent authority – the Home Office or National Crime Agency – for a decision on their victim status, ensuring access to tailored support, protection, and assistance.

They accepted that I'd been a victim of modern slavery. It came as a bit of a surprise, as I'd been waiting four years. I found it quite grounding and it provided some answers I didn't know I needed. I started to research more into modern slavery and went to the Modern Slavery in the UK conference, reflecting on 10 years of the Modern Slavery Act and the work of the Bakhita Centre. I found it really inspiring and realised that my story was part of something much bigger than myself, much bigger even than grooming gangs, part of global abuse involving multiple different forms, depending on the country in which it was happening. Like grooming gangs, county lines and trafficking in the UK, forced labour in Germany, domestic servitude in France, child marriage in India, violent criminal gangs in Mexico, sweatshops in Bangladesh – the list goes on – the rich get richer. I joined some modern slavery charities after that as a 'lived experience' consultant.

I started a Postgraduate Certificate course at Masters level and passed all my exams and assignments with very high marks, then started a Foundation Certificate course in counselling skills and practise. This was something I'd wanted to do even before the darkness, but changed my mind after the abuse started as I completely lost my sense of future. There was no future at that time or, at least, I believed there wasn't.

In early February 2025 I found out that Ali Sultan was being released from prison. This wasn't just a setback. It wasn't something I could 'manage' or 'work through quietly'. It shook everything. Everything became destabilised, even my work. My role at the hospital was sort of decommissioned or terminated and I was redeployed. Although it wasn't given as the official reason, the main funder became aware that I was a survivor of Ali Sultan and I was working in the same locality that he'd previously frequented. I guess they saw me on BBC's *Newsnight* and, as they were the GP practice for Ali Sultan's family, the risk of confrontation was too great.

It came as a shock and disappointment, as it was upsetting for all my patients. One was an ex-gang member who had a lot of trauma and was just opening up. He didn't trust anyone else. I was in the middle of a counselling course and that, too, became destabilised. Studying counselling requires emotional regulation, safety and stability. Those things were taken away from me overnight. At the same time, my family relationships were affected. This kind of thing doesn't stay neatly contained within the individual it directly affects – it ripples out, spreads into workplaces, relationships, homes. His release didn't exactly reopen my trauma, but it reorganised my life around it.

What makes this harder to accept is that I was central to securing his conviction. I gave evidence. I endured the process. I paid the psychological price for helping put him in prison. Yet, when it came to his release, I was treated as irrelevant. Authorities congratulated themselves on his rehabilitation. They spoke about progress, risk management, moving forward. But they failed to protect, or even properly inform, the person whose life had already been blown up by his actions. I wasn't asking for special treatment, just basic dignity and consideration. I wasn't considered, I wasn't respected and I wasn't protected.

About two days after finding out Ali was being released, I got a call from *The Daily Mirror* asking how I felt about it. They'd found out the week before, so the newspapers knew before I did. I was then invited to speak about it on BBC's *Newsnight* while, at the same time, Elon Musk was barraging his X platform with posts about grooming gangs and referencing 'The Rape Of Britain'. I felt that Musk must also have known that Ali was getting out and timed his onslaught appropriately But how could he have known? The same way as the newspapers did.

I got in touch with Sarfraz Manzoor, a journalist and author who'd interviewed me in 2018 for a book he was writing about the misunderstandings and stereotyping of Muslims, which covered the topic of grooming gangs in a chapter. He came up to Telford and interviewed me for a piece in *The Times.*

Also around this time, I was experiencing exploitation by the far right, in particular, Stephen Yaxley-Lennon and it set me back in my recovery. It threatened everything that was important to me – my honesty, my integrity and my character, which was just beginning to emerge anew. It also threatened my safety, because I had done a lot to protect my identity from the gang. I'd stayed away from the electoral register and waived my right to vote, so that I wouldn't be easily found. If I applied for credit, like when I bought my first car on finance after passing my test, I used a letter from the police explaining why I wasn't on the electoral register – that I was a victim of gang-related crime and needed protection. So, when Yaxley-Lennon, aka Tommy Robinson, turned up uninvited at my house, I wanted to know how he got my address. He wouldn't say. I felt violated and threatened again.

Alarm bells immediately rang in my head and my awareness of danger went into high alert. I didn't know what he wanted and I didn't particularly want to revisit my abuse at that vulnerable time. I don't even want to talk about the encounter now. He tried to discuss specific memories which I have locked away to avoid thinking about them. Yaxley-Lennon retraumatised me when I was in crisis and feeling suicidal. He recorded everything I said to him and put it into his documentary, including my address, even though he promised me he wouldn't.

I just wanted to pretend it never happened. That was difficult because even Elon Musk saw what Yaxley-Lennon did to me and they both thought it was okay, that there was nothing wrong with it. How do I know he knew? Because he commented on 'The Rape Of Britain', which was the title of Yaxley-Lennon's documentary, which I was a part of. Musk posted a tweet that he'd seen it, so he knew of me and what happened.

I did report Yaxley-Lennon's visit at the time, but he hadn't committed a criminal offence so the police weren't interested. At the moment I feel powerless as far as this episode in my life is concerned. However, I don't think it should be narrated in this book.

So I'll just leave it there – for now.

After the postgrad course concluded, I decided to take a MSc in psychological trauma with the University of Birmingham, which I'm currently halfway through and consider it to be one of the best decisions I've made for myself. I also set up a website last year – www.shesaskingforit.com – and started a blog which I haven't had time to update.

Last August, my father was diagnosed with stage 4 melanoma that had spread to his liver and lungs. This was a terrible blow for all the family. He sold his house and came to live with me so I could look after him. I love my dad very much and always have. I love him being close and looking after him is no trouble. The decision came as a surprise to the rest of the family, but not to me. I've always been that person, even if I didn't know it, even if the darkness obliterated it for a while. But I'm back now and I have a love for the human condition that's part of my DNA. My dad shares his wisdom and knowledge and the good memories and we go for coffee and cake and I'm so happy that we have this time together.

I was accepted onto the NWG (Network for Womena and Girls) Grooming Gang Survivor Panel for the National Inquiry into grooming gangs in September 2025. I'm limited regarding the amount of information I'm allowed to divulge about the meetings, due to confidentiality and political reasons and I've signed a non-disclosure agreement, but I'll share what I'm allowed to. When I look back at the terms of reference, I don't remember individual arguments as clearly as the atmosphere – the tension in my body – the atmosphere in the room. The sense that something important was happening very fast, before anyone had time to catch their breath.

Survivors were brought together with very little preparation and asked to step straight into a high-stakes, emotionally charged space. We were expected to debate definitions, scope, accountability and political boundaries almost immediately. There was an assumption, I think, that one introductory meeting would be enough, that once survivors were in the room, the rest would take care of itself. It didn't.

Survivors were rushed directly into the most stressful part of the process without time to build safety, trust or shared understanding. There were no group preparation sessions, no opportunity to establish norms, to process fears, to understand roles and limits, or to feel psychologically grounded before being asked to influence the architecture of a national inquiry. The expectation seemed to be that survivors would simply rise to the occasion. But trauma doesn't work like that.

For people with histories of exploitation, coercion and institutional betrayal, safety isn't created by invitation alone. It's built slowly, through predictability, pacing, choice and containment. When those elements are missing, the nervous system responds long before the rational mind can intervene. What looks like anger, conflict or difficult behaviour is often a survival response to feeling overwhelmed, unheard or powerless. The process was driven by an external political timetable, not the needs of the people in the room. Deadlines were tight. Decisions were urgent. Everything felt very last-minute. The pressure to move quickly seemed to outweigh the responsibility to move carefully. From the outside, this might have looked efficient. From inside the room, it felt destabilising.

Asking survivors to perform under pressure replicated the very dynamics that harmed them in the first place – being rushed, overridden, expected to comply, expected to cope. We were placed in a pressurised environment where emotions were already running high, then asked to hold the weight of national accountability. For some, that was too much. I wasn't surprised when survivors later described feeling controlled, silenced or manipulated. I could understand how easily that could happen when people were overwhelmed and felt they had no room to breathe.

I don't believe the harm that followed was intentional, but when survivor wellbeing is subordinated to political timelines, the result is predictable. People reach their limit. Trust fractures. Some walk away because staying is more damaging than leaving. I stayed, but I could understand why others didn't. This is the uncomfortable truth that sits behind the resignations and the headlines. The process itself became part of the harm, not because the survivors were that fragile, but because the system didn't adapt to the reality of trauma. It expected survivors to adapt instead.

In my opinion, if this inquiry is to succeed, it must learn – not defensively or performatively, but honestly. Survivor involvement can't be rushed, it can't be treated as an add-on to the political schedule. It must be designed with the same care and precision we claim to want for justice itself. Otherwise we risk recreating the very conditions survivors have spent their lives trying to escape.

As the meetings progressed, survivors repeatedly asked what influence their involvement actually carried. Many weren't seeking reassurance or emotional validation, just honesty. Uncertainty is destabilising. When communication paused at critical moments, survivors were left to manage uncertainty alone, which eroded trust further. Eventually, the survivor panel was ended and, while they said engagement would continue in a different form, no clear information was offered about how that future group would be constituted. I felt angry at that final meeting. I still feel angry.

Over the last 10 years or so, something else has been happening alongside the institutional fallout. A divide opened up between survivors themselves. It was a painful split and watching it unfold was upsetting. I wanted to see survivors support each other and I felt confused and saddened by how quickly lines were drawn. In conversations I've had since, many people described feeling anxious and mistrustful and excluded. Some of it comes from years of being disbelieved and let down. When trust has been broken so often, it becomes difficult to know when to hope again. There's a sense that exploitation hasn't ended, just changed shape. Frustration is sometimes aimed at other survivors instead of the institutions and politicians exploiting them. Blame shifts sideways, rather than upwards.

I don't know if this kind of division exists in other survivor categories. Maybe there's something specific about grooming gang abuse that makes it worse. It sits within intense political and media debate. Survivors are often pulled into arguments about race, religion and public policy that they don't choose. The pressure is constant. Resources are limited. Opportunities to be heard feel scarce. Division grows. If this inquiry is to matter, it not only needs to recognise past failures, but the ways in which harm is still being repeated. That includes harm happening within spaces that are meant to support survivors.

Nevertheless, I'm glad I took part in the panel. I'm glad I stayed, even when the process stirred difficult emotions. From the beginning, I often felt powerless and, in many ways, that feeling never fully went away. What changed was how I responded to it. I worked through those emotions and continued to contribute, even when it was uncomfortable to do so. By the end I reached a quiet clarity. If those responsible for shaping the inquiry are wise, they'll listen. If not, it isn't a reflection of the worth of the survivor panel, but of their own limitations.

If I'm needed again in the future, I'm not difficult to find. I have a public body of work and a clear voice. But, at this point, my focus is elsewhere.

Once I qualify in my MSc, I have ambitions to start my own business as an expert in psychological trauma. I'd like to advise health-care organisations on their psychology trauma policies and develop treatment programmes. Maybe one day I could become a leading expert. I don't know – I'll have to see.

Finally, writing this book has given closure to that bad part of my life. It's been a sort of exorcism in a way, and I'd like it to be more than just a memoir. I want it to explain the mindset of the victim, what it's like to be inside the head of someone who's being horrendously abused. This is widely misunderstood: why victims would go back to the abuse; why they can't seem to break away from it. I hope that, for the first time, readers will be able to put themselves in the shoes of an abused girl and know what it's really like.

I suppose the ultimate goal of writing this book was to show other victims that there is a different life – there is willpower and strength inside themselves. I didn't always believe they were in me and I struggled to find them. But I carried on, aimed for the good and hoped for the best and eventually I got there.

I eventually discovered the me that I was meant to be – and the future me is waiting around the corner. I can't wait to meet her.

Acknowledgements

I want to start by thanking my parents for backing me, believing in me, and never trying to make me smaller than I am.

Thank you to my brother and sister, and to my two grandmothers, for your wisdom, your love, and the parts of me that come from you.

To my family, my friends, and the people who showed up for me properly, you know who you are. Thank you for the encouragement, the honesty, and for reminding me who I am when I lost sight of it. And to those who let me sit in your homes with my laptop, writing through it all so I didn't have to be alone, you probably don't realise how much that mattered, but it did.

A special thank you to Mike and Aaron and their families, for staying steady through the highs, the lows, and everything in between. You didn't just support me, you stayed.

To the people behind this book, my co-writer John McDonald, my publisher Mirror Books, editors Christine Costello and Clare Fitzsimons, and everyone who helped shape this into something real, thank you for trusting the story and not trying to soften it.

To the work that shaped me, Anglia Ruskin University and my tutors during my undergraduate degree, my time in mental health, my training, the people I've worked with and learned from, you've challenged me, grounded me, and forced me to think deeper than I ever thought I could.

To survivors, especially the ones who are still figuring it out, still untangling things, still carrying what no one sees, this is for you.

Whether your voice is loud or completely silent, it counts. So much of my strength has come from other survivors, from the courage I've witnessed in you. I wouldn't be where I am today without that.

There was a time in my life when I was surrounded by people who didn't value me, didn't protect me, and didn't deserve me.

Now, I am surrounded by people who are real, safe, and good, and that is something I will never take for granted. You've shown me that a different life isn't just possible, it's real.

And finally, to myself.

For getting through it.

For unlearning what needed to be unlearned.

For refusing to stay stuck in places that were breaking me.

And for writing this, even when it would have been easier not to.